Classic AMERICAN Cars

EXP. 3-31-50

1949 PENNA

ED637

QUENTIN WILLSON

Classic AMERICAN *Cars*

Photography by
Matthew Ward

DORLING KINDERSLEY

LONDON • NEW YORK • SYDNEY • MOSCOW

This book is dedicated to the millions of Americans who were fortunate enough to own these cars.

A DORLING KINDERSLEY BOOK

PROJECT EDITOR
PHIL HUNT

ART EDITOR
KEVIN RYAN

EDITOR
JILL FORNARY

DESIGNER
CLARE DRISCOLL

MANAGING EDITOR
FRANCIS RITTER

MANAGING ART EDITOR
DEREK COOMBES

DTP DESIGNER
SONIA CHARBONNIER

PICTURE RESEARCHER
SAM RUSTON

PRODUCTION CONTROLLERS
RUTH CHARLTON, ROSALIND PRIESTLEY

First published in Great Britain in 1997
by Dorling Kindersley Limited,
9 Henrietta Street, London WC2E 8PS

A CIP catalogue record for this book is available
from the British Library

ISBN 0-7513-0473-5

Colour reproduction by Colourscan, Singapore
Printed and bound in Belgium

NOTE ON SPECIFICATION BOXES
Every effort has been made to ensure that the information supplied in
the specification boxes is accurate. Unless otherwise indicated, all
figures pertain to the particular model in the specification box. Engine
capacity for American cars is measured in cubic inches (cid). A.F.C. is
an abbreviation for average fuel consumption.

CONTENTS

FOREWORD
J.D. Power

AMERICAN CARS HAVE TAKEN A BAD RAP over the past half century. Yet, for all the criticisms, it's fair to say that the American motor industry brought us the things we love most about the automobile.

American cars gave us electrically adjustable seats, windows, and mirrors, automatic transmission, air-conditioning, two-tone paint, and Wonder Bar radios. More recently, they've provided us with remote buttons to lock and unlock the doors, airbags, and catalytic converters. They might not be highly regarded for engine efficiency, pin-sharp handling, or stunning looks, but, when it comes to delivering what customers want in an easy and reliable package, American cars have always led the world.

Aficionados may balk at accepting the cardinal role that US iron has played in the development of today's reliable, safe, comfortable, and convenient machines, but they should read this book with an open mind. Many of the innovative automotive features we take for granted originated in American cars. A technological history that started back in 1911 with the development of the electric starter fast-forwards through this book's pages to today's symbol of convenience, the cup-holder.

Now is the perfect time, as we near the millennium, to look back at the evolution of America and her cars and reflect on her contribution to the advancement and refinement of the automobile. Quentin Willson's nostalgic look at the American classic car is for most of us a delicious and delightful trip back to a world that will never be the same again. Enjoy the ride.

J.D. Power III
CHAIRMAN OF J.D. POWER ASSOCIATES

Author's Preface

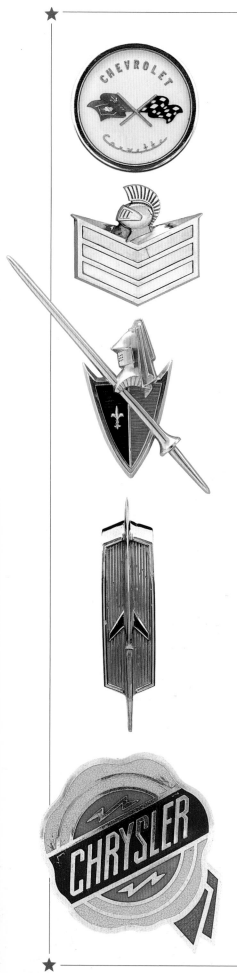

I T WAS THE LONG, HOT SUMMER of '69 that did it. I was a wide-eyed English 11-year-old at grade school in a small town 50 miles outside of Chicago. Dad was doing a sabbatical year lecturing at the local University, and I was having the time of my life driving American cars.

I'd fallen in with a kid called Nicky, whose father owned the biggest GM dealership in Illinois. Their vast clapboard house sat in 10 acres with a huge yard strewn with Pop's trade-ins. There'd be lines of cast-off 'Cudas, Firebirds, Caddys, and Continentals, and each with the keys temptingly hidden under the sun visor. Nicky was the sort of kid my parents had spent months warning me against, which is why I liked him on sight. He could tell a 260 V8 from a 289 with his back turned, and he'd spend hours explaining about hemi-heads and Positraction. I was a mightily impressed 11-year-old.

And that year was what really got me into cars. Every day after school I'd cycle up to Nicky's place and we'd borrow a Fairlane, a Mustang, or an Eldorado and practise power slides and handbrake turns. Nobody wanted old muscle cars and every week Nicky's Dad would bring home yet another load of heavy metal. Boss Mustangs, Coronet Hemis, Chevelle SSs, Pontiac GTOs: we drove them all. I owe Nicky a big debt of gratitude. He showed a shy English kid in short pants two of the wildest things in life – America and American cars.

This book is a eulogy to those formative years, a homage to all those wicked wheels. It's not meant to be the definitive list of best or worst, rather a nostalgic trawl through some of the most captivating and compelling cars ever.

THE MOST INFLUENTIAL CARS IN THE WORLD

1951 CHRYSLER IMPERIAL

FOR THE BEST PART OF THREE decades the world has sniggered up its sleeve at American cars. To listen to the torrent of ridicule, you'd think Detroit's offerings of the Forties, Fifties, and Sixties were designed by madmen on their way to the asylum. The British sneered at their unseemly girth, weight, and size, the Germans mocked Motown's build quality, and the Italians would rather have walked than commit stylistic suicide behind the wheel of a Cadillac Eldorado. Even some native Americans joined the chorus of dissenters. John Keats in *The Insolent Chariots* remarked with rancour that "American automobiles are not reliable machines for reasonable men, but illusory symbols of sex, speed, wealth, and power for daydreaming nitwits". Only the French, bless them, actually reckoned a Pontiac Parisienne was glamorous enough for posing on the Périphérique. But were American motor cars as dire as the pundits said? Were they really that ridiculous?

Perhaps jealousy is the word we're looking for. America's prosperity

IKE ARRIVES IN STYLE
In November 1952, an impressed world watched Dwight Eisenhower celebrate his election to the presidency of the most powerful nation on earth in a shining Lincoln Capri Convertible the size of a small house.

in the post-war years was all spangled exuberance and cheerful opulence. While Europe trundled about in dumpy little grey-and-black boxes with all the charisma of church pews, Americans squealed around in glittering, pastel-coloured rocketships. Europe was winding her windows down by hand, while Americans were operating not just their windows but their seats, boot releases, and transmissions at the touch of a chromium-plated button. The nearest we Europeans got to American cars was on the flickering screen. We envied all those lantern-jawed heroes who could one-hand huge Chevrolets round corners while smoking a cigarette and still manage to feign an expression of complete and utter boredom.

1949 CADILLAC SERIES 62
While Europe was filling in the bullet holes and struggling to rebuild her devastated cities with money borrowed from America, Americans were tooling around in dreamboats like the '49 Cadillac.

Power-sliding never looked so easy or so much fun. The cars we watched in the movies seemed to be built on the same grand scale as the stars who drove them and, if we'd been honest, we would have cut off bits of our anatomy just to sit in the passenger seat. Americans were living the good life through their cars, and Europe's resentment was nothing more than old-fashioned envy.

Keeping the Customer Satisfied

In retrospect, the cars that Detroit rolled out in the three decades after World War II were shining stars of the world's automotive firmament. This was the most imaginative and fertile period of car design ever, when every stylistic sleight-of-hand, and then some, was used in the deepest and most inventive examination of the consumer psyche by any industry in the history of the world. Simply put, American automobiles defined the vernacular of the modern motor car. They not only gave us panoramic windscreens, two-tone paint, and whitewalls, but also those little touches that mean so much, like cruise controls, air-conditioning, AM/FM radios, power windows and seats, not to mention automatic transmission and power steering.

In 1959, the buyer of a Chevrolet Impala was faced with an *embarras de richesses* of factory and dealer-installed optional equipment.

HARLEY J. EARL
1893–1969

HARLEY EARL, GM's chief stylist, was the man who shaped millions of American cars. "You design a car so that every time you get in it's a relief – you have a little vacation for a while." The first motor mandarin to really understand that consumers don't buy cars with their heads but their trousers, Harley Earl invented automotive attitude.

In 1956, Earl headed GM's state-of-the-art $125 million Tech Centre and led a styling team of 1,200 people. Every year they took automotive design over the edge and back again.

In the chain of command, Earl was somewhere between God and President, without the latter's limitations. GM's corporate culture elevated stylists over engineers, who were relegated to the role of rude mechanics employed to turn Earl's whims of steel into production realities. In his tenure at GM, Harley Earl took the solemnity out of the American car and replaced it with a chromium smile.

HARLEY J. EARL

EARL'S PROTOTYPE LE SABRE SHOW CAR BOASTED A CONVERTIBLE TOP THAT CLOSED AUTOMATICALLY WHEN IT SENSED RAIN

1954 CHEVROLET CORVETTE
The '54 drastic plastic Corvette is a perfect example of Earl's stylistic audacity. He knew there was a whole hinterland of buyers out there bursting for some automotive bravado, so he layered on the charisma with a trowel.

The order form listed a furlong of 78 different accessory choices ranging from a Super Turbo-Thrust V8, Positraction rear axle, and Turboglide automatic transmission, through power steering, brakes, windows, and seats, to electric rear-tailgate glass on station wagons. The roster of comfort and vanity options on offer was even longer. Consumers could enrich their lives with de luxe steering wheels, shaded rear windows, air-foam seat cushions, tri-volume horns, simulated wire-wheel covers, tissue dispensers, Magic-Aire heaters, tinted Soft Ray glass, and Strato-Rest headrests. The culture of convenience was running riot.

By the time the Mustang appeared in mid-'64, Ford had turned the option list into an arcane art form. Not only could you choose from a whole hill of engines, transmissions, and axles, there were now specially named generic option groups to consider.

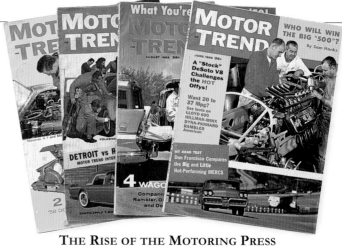

THE RISE OF THE MOTORING PRESS
By the mid-Fifties, the public was obsessed with automobile styling, and the shape of cars to come was a national talking-point. The news-stands groaned with auto magazines and GM were spending $162 million a year on advertising to persuade consumers to debauch themselves with tail fins.

The GT Equipment Group, the Handling Package, the Rally Pack, the Visibility Group, and the Interior Decor Group were all part of the pony car building-block philosophy: give buyers a sexy-looking car as a platform and allow them to customize it to their own individual specifications. Not for nothing did the Ford ads trumpet "Mustang – Designed To Be Designed By You". With so many options available, the San Jose factory could literally churn out an entire year's Mustang production without any two cars ever being exactly the same.

Power to the People

But transatlantic metal gave the world much more than just chrome and creature comforts. American cars also gave us fun in the form of the ever-higher numbers at the tips of their speedometer needles. Detroit's horsepower gallop began in '51 when Chrysler let loose its 180 bhp Fire-Dome V8.

—RAYMOND LOEWY—
1893–1987

RAYMOND LOEWY DESIGNS REPRESENT the articulation of plenty that hallmarks post-war America. He shaped everything from pencil sharpeners, Studebakers, the interior of Skylab, and Coca-Cola dispensing-machines to the inside of JFK's official jet, Air Force One.

Many of Loewy's creations have become foundation stones of modern design; the Studebaker Avanti of '63, the Coldspot refrigerator, the Greyhound Scenicruiser bus, and the Hallicrafter radio all illustrate his key contribution to American design. His motoring credits include the Studebaker Commander, Starliner, Golden Hawk, and Champion. A maverick to the last, he reckoned design was "far too important to be left in the careless hands of company men in suits". He will be remembered as one of the prime architects of the American Dream.

DESIGNER OF THE COCA-COLA DISPENSER

LOEWY AND HIS FAMILY POSE BY THE SENSATIONAL AVANTI

THE '57 STUDEBAKER GOLDEN HAWK

MOTORAMA
GM's Motoramas were the wildest car shows ever conceived. Regularly pulling up to two million visitors, there were dancers, actors, musical stage shows, and amazing displays of post-war technical prowess. From 1949 to 1961, they showcased new products and were GM's most powerful weapon in the marketing war.

FUTURISTIC CHASSIS
The begadgeted '57 Mercury Turnpike Cruiser was hailed as "space age design for earth travel". Apart from a chassis like the Brooklyn Bridge, it had Air Cushion suspension and push-button automatic transmission.

This was followed by Chevy's small-block V8 of '55. Five years later, the Chrysler 300F was stampeding out 400 bhp, and by '63 a Hi-Po T-Bird was displacing 427 cubes and red-lining the dynamometer at a jaw-dropping 425 bhp. Then in '66 Chrysler went ballistic with their 426 Hemi, firing the first serious salvo of the performance war that was to send horsepower ratings spiralling through the stratosphere. The heat had been turned up to maximum, and by the late Sixties a super-warm Chevy Chevelle SS was pumping out a thundering 450 bhp.

Those were the days when anyone with enough bucks could saunter into their local showroom, tick all the right boxes on the options list, and find themselves master of absolutely apocalyptic horsepower. They were mass-produced cars that, in a straight line, could run bumper-to-bumper with hand-fettled Ferraris, Jaguars, and Aston Martins. Today those performance figures are impressive enough, but back then they were heart-stoppingly quick. Even the monickers were enough to hurry the hormones. Eliminator, Marauder, Cougar, Cyclone, Thunderbolt, and Charger were machines that could accelerate to 60 in the time it took to say

their names. The world's greatest democracy really did offer power to the people, and it came in the wrapping of the muscle car. Never had so much heave been available to so many for so little.

Behind a Painted Smile

Automotive historians may claim that Europe was more technically audacious with its unitary bodies, radial-ply tyres, and four-wheel drive. Certainly the British pioneered disc brakes and fuel injection, the Germans perfected millimetrically precise build quality, and the Italians made V12 engines almost reliable. But Detroit could come up with plenty of wizardry too. Look at some of the show cars, particularly from GM's Motoramas, and you'll see that innovation was not only being actively pursued, it was in rude health. These cars were plugged up like the Pentagon, with transistorized electrical systems, magnesium bodies, automatic transaxles, special tiny engines to drive accessories, TVs instead of rear-view mirrors, and even gas turbine engines. Harley Earl's 1951 Le Sabre, named after the F-86 jet fighter, stood no higher than a mailbox, had built-in automatic jacks for changing wheels, and a power-operated convertible top that automatically raised when it sensed rain on the console.

1957 CADILLAC COUPE DE VILLE
The '57 Coupe de Ville came with air-conditioning as standard. In Britain, the amount of buildings with air-con could be counted on the fingers of one hand.

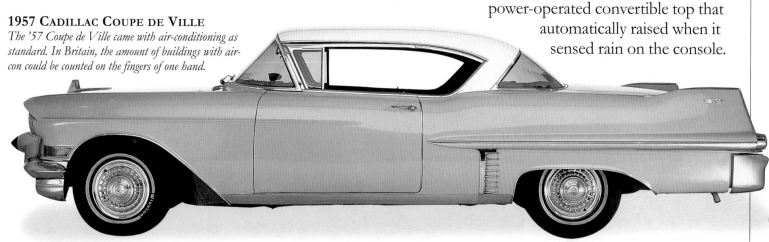

POWER BRAKES
Stopping a Detroit dinosaur took some effort, and by the mid-Fifties most cars had power drum brakes as an option. As the picture shows, power-assisted brakes were meant to help "the lady".

POWER WINDOWS
Electric windows appeared in the late Forties and, by 1955, were de rigueur. This was an age when almost every minor control was designed to be activated by a dainty finger.

BILL MITCHELL
b.1912

MITCHELL'S CLASSIC BUICK RIVIERA

BILL MITCHELL TOOK OVER as Vice-President of GM's styling division after Harley Earl retired in 1959. He claimed that to be a real car designer you had to have "gasoline in your veins". Under Earl he designed the 1938 Cadillac 60 Special, but went on to oversee the Chevrolet Corvair of 1960, the Buick Riviera of '63, the split-window Corvette Sting Ray of '63, the Oldsmobile Toronado of '66, and the Chevrolet Camaro of '67. He admired clean, sculptured lines and rejected the bosomy, rounded shapes favoured by Earl.

In the 1970s he bemoaned the blandness of Detroit's offerings. "They all look alike. I have to read the goddam badges to know what they are." After his retirement, Mitchell still rode a Yamaha 1000 motorbike and enjoyed a much modified Pontiac Trans Am powered by a Ferrari Daytona engine.

MITCHELL WITH HIS MAKO SHARK SHOW CAR, WHICH WAS SAID TO BE HIS ALL-TIME FAVOURITE DESIGN

Mercedes, 47 years later, have just got round to using rain sensors to actuate the windscreen wipers on their E-Class range.

In 1959, GM touted its Firebird III at the New York and Boston Motorama shows. Billed as "Imagination In Motion", it had an ultrasonic key that you aimed at the door, a cockpit pre-heater, a formed plastic interior, and the steering wheel, transmission lever, brake, and throttle were all worked from a single joystick control. The Whirlfire GT 305 regenerative gas turbine unit developed 220 bhp through a differential-mounted gearbox and De Dion transaxle. Braking was courtesy of an aluminium drum anti-lock system with a grade retarder on the differential. This was wildly futuristic gadgetry that in 1959 must have seemed like it came straight out of the pages of *Buck Rogers and the Forgotten Planet*. Behind the revolving stage shows and the pageantry, Motoramas showed America and the rest of the world that the white-coated eggheads in GM's technical labs were slipstreaming a vapour-trail into the future. Against Detroit's backdrop of prodigious innovation, the European motor industry's efforts looked almost tame.

Sultans of Style

But the Big Three auto manufacturers – GM, Chrysler, and Ford – knew that technical features alone wouldn't move metal. What buyers wanted was street-strutting style, and nobody supplied dash and flash like Uncle Sam. The post-war American Dream was founded on the concept of "populuxe", or luxury for all. By the late '50s, the average Chevrolet or Buick was groaning under the weight of 20 kg (44 lb) of twinkling chrome and luxury add-ons. In 1949, Harley Earl's finny Cadillac was considered the last word. By '55, its styling motifs had percolated to even the humblest Chevy. Fins, sweepspears, and the two front-end protuberances known as Dagmars gave customers an extra receipt for their money and sales of new cars in '55 totalled $65 billion, or 25 per cent of the Gross National Product. Americans were willing, grateful even, to spend vast amounts of money on two-and-a-half tons of candy-pink space rocket simply because it transported them into another world.

DRIVE-IN MOVIES
In 1955, Detroit rolled out eight million new cars, and teenagers with after-school jobs were a perfect target market. The automobile allowed youth to escape the middle-aged morality of Main Street America and savour the romance and passion of the drive-in.

GLIMPSE OF THE FUTURE
The Firebird II, III, and XP-21 were all GM show cars exhibited at the Motorama exhibitions of the Fifties. Incredibly futuristic, they boasted technical wizardry like automatic steering sensors and even gas turbine engines.

SPACE CULTURE
Space-age styling metaphors were plastered over the Fifties American car. Speed, rocket ships, and outer space became the national narcotic.

And despite what the sceptics would have us believe, behind all that gratuitous glitz were some of the world's most significant cars. You simply can't deny the huge influence of creations like the Mustang, Corvette, Jeep, GTO, and Thunderbird. They were pioneering designs that changed the shape and styling of cars forever. And every last one of them was conceived and built in America. Europeans may have been envious, but they were quick enough to mimic what they saw. By the Sixties, the British had two-tone Vauxhall Crestas, finned Zephyrs and Zodiacs, sweepspears on Sunbeam Rapiers, and quad headlights on Rolls-Royces. The French pasted Detroit's styling cues onto the Simca Aronde, Vedette, and Facel Vega, and even the Germans can't claim they weren't occasionally inspired. In 1961, Mercedes launched their four-door 190 saloon. Teutonic perfection incarnate maybe, but what were those two weird little flourishes on the rear? Dainty little tail fins. The world's oldest car maker had publicly admitted that when it came to

style, Detroit had taught all there was to know. The influence of America's auto stylists was incredibly far-reaching, and there wasn't a car company in the world that didn't cull something from Motown's awesome aesthetic arsenal.

Britain might have been first with the sports car and Italy the coupe, but America came up with machines that could literally be all things to all men. Reacting exactly to what the market wanted, Detroit fielded the personality car. Thunderbirds, Rivieras, Cougars, Barracudas, Camaros, and Firebirds were brilliant niche products that offered consumers cars that were distinctive and separate. One ad for the Dodge Challenger promised "a car you buy when you don't want to be like everyone else". And by offering a raft of options longer than the Gettysburg Address, Dodge were telling the truth.

1957 DODGE CUSTOM ROYAL
Dodge's '57 model range had a lowered silhouette, "Swept Wing" styling, and tail-lights that looked like jet-engine afterburners. The F15 jet fighter in the background was meant to reinforce the tenuous relationship between car and plane.

Bucket seats, mag wheels, centre consoles, and various instrument packs all gave buyers more choice than there were atoms in the universe. The Ford Mustang was the world's fastest-selling car not because it was dynamically special, but because its appeal was wider than that of any other car before or since. And Motown's trick of piling on the personality undeniably influenced everything from the Ford Cortina to the BMW 3-Series. The modern cult of auto individuality began in the USA.

Gurus of Glitz

One reason why American cars of the period were so remarkably influential was the quality of their designers. Men like Harley Earl, Raymond Loewy, Lee Iacocca, Bill Mitchell, and Virgil Exner were sculptors in steel and visionaries driven from within. One contemporary said of Earl: "He was like a Roman Emperor in Constantinople. Nobody in the history of industry ever had such an incredible effect over man-made objects like Earl." Raymond Loewy, creator of the Studebaker Avanti, also designed streamlined trains and the Lucky Strike cigarette pack. Loewy once said, "Pride, social consciousness, and the desire to serve mankind better are the only inspirations a designer needs". History will rank luminaries like these as the grand masters of design who between them changed the face of 20th-century consumer culture irreversibly. They gave the American car its dazzle and swagger, they lowered, lengthened, and widened it, gave it half a hundred stylistic metaphors, more glass than a greenhouse, and pushed the envelope of design to its absolute limit. They gave the automobile optimism and hope. They made it a machine that promised unlimited possibilities.

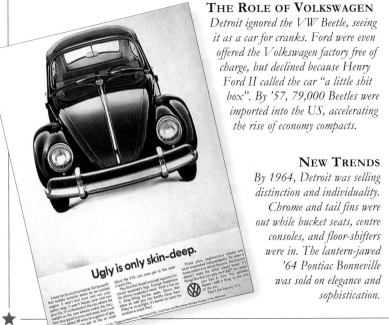

GLAMOUR AT THE TOP
The baby boomers of the Sixties bought US iron in vast numbers. JFK and Jackie Kennedy personified the new-age Camelot dynasty and swept around in glamorous Lincoln Continental Convertibles. With a matinee idol as President, life took on the excitement of a Hollywood movie.

LEE A. IACOCCA
b.1925

IACOCCA'S ORIGINAL PONY LOGO

LEE IACOCCA IS WIDELY regarded as the father of the greatest automotive success in post-war history, the Ford Mustang. As Ford's precocious General Manager in 1961, the 36-year-old Iacocca came up with the idea of a sporty compact to woo the burgeoning youth market. He reasoned that if the performance of a car like the Corvette could be stuffed into an affordable car for the masses, it would sell like hotcakes. And it did.

The Mustang remains the world's fastest-selling car; by its first birthday, it had racked up nearly half a million sales. It was the first of the pony cars, a breed of two-door personal coupes that went on to wow America for the best part of 20 years. Without Iacocca's vision, determination, and tenacity, one of the world's most memorable cars might well have remained just a doodle on the back of an envelope.

IACOCCA IS SEEN AS THE "FATHER" OF THE MUSTANG

And America's preoccupation with how things looked wasn't just self-obsessed narcissism, it helped keep the machinery of mass consumption turning. Good design was the American Way and a million miles from Europe's puritanical austerity of line. This was the great liberal phase of American styling and it flourished because it was essential to the nation's economic health. Yearly model changes, or what Harley Earl chose to call "dynamic obsolescence", guaranteed not only an annual orgy of buying but also that the less affluent could purchase last year's cast-offs at used-car prices. The designer anticipated the public's desires and kept his creations just an arm's length away, so the buyer always had next year's model to look forward to, yet another dream to pursue.

Dreaming Out Loud

For three decades, Detroit fuelled a massive metallic fantasy that Americans believed in and the rest of the world desired. And it was a fantasy engineered by a deliberate corporate policy of encouraging dreams. Detroit invented the "dream car" at a moment in American history when the future looked bright, exciting, and almost close enough to touch. American cars looked the way they did because that was the way America looked. Scholars who trawl through the social history of the United States could do worse than study her cars, because American automobiles tell us more about America's past than a whole library of history books ever could.

ORIGINAL MUSCLE
John DeLorean, Pontiac's Chief Engineer, shoe-horned the division's biggest V8 into the timid little Tempest, creating one of the first muscle cars, the Pontiac GTO. It was an instant hit with speed-thirsty youngsters.

After World War II, America didn't have a single bomb crater anywhere and the '49 Roadmaster mirrors a population looking forward to a brave new world of plenty. The happy and handsome '55 Chevrolet Bel Air epitomizes the confident consumption of the Fifties boom years, while the baroque '59 Cadillac reveals a nation so near to satiety that it had forgotten the itch of desire. By 1960, America was losing her arrogance, and the austere and anxious 1962 Chevy Corvair reflects a society in the grip of paranoia. While Vietnam and race riots raged, the belligerent Dodge Charger R/T of 1968 betrays a country at war with itself. After the fat and glittery Fifties and Sixties dreamboats came the lean and hungry Chevrolet Vegas and Ford Pintos. And by the time the abstemious and severe Cadillac Seville debuted in 1975, the dream had evaporated completely. And that's maybe the most fascinating and compelling thing about watching American cars. They've always precisely mirrored the highs and lows of the American Way.

Uniquely American

The cynics should remember that while it's easy to snigger at machines that turned dreams into dollars, it's even easier to lose sight of the purity of vision, the genius, and the humanity that made Detroit's tremendous achievements possible. American cars may have been continually satirized for the vice of flamboyance, but it was exactly that florid styling that gave them their greatest virtue. It blessed them with a genuinely

GLAMOROUS AND FUN
This Chrysler 300X research car is being tried out by the 1966 Miss World. Even though the extreme experimentation of the Fifties had gone, research projects still offered publicity for manufacturers in the Sixties.

hopeful, twinkling innocence. And it doesn't matter that all those strident Oldsmobiles, DeSotos, and Plymouths didn't obey European strictures of order and elegance. They had an infectious optimism and cheer that actually made Americans feel better about themselves and the nation they lived in; Detroit was selling a welcome distraction from heartbreak. As Virgil Exner once said, "A well-styled car will make a man feel better at the end of his journey than when he started". For 30 years the American automobile hasn't only entertained millions of Americans, it's given the rest of the world a unique glimpse behind the curtain of the American Dream. Motown's glory years may have gone, but they'll never be forgotten.

1966 FORD MUSTANG
This milestone car was born halfway through 1964 and continues to this day. If any car sums up the spirit of American auto manufacturing, it must be the Mustang. In automotive history no other car has flown from the showrooms faster than Ford's pony prodigy.

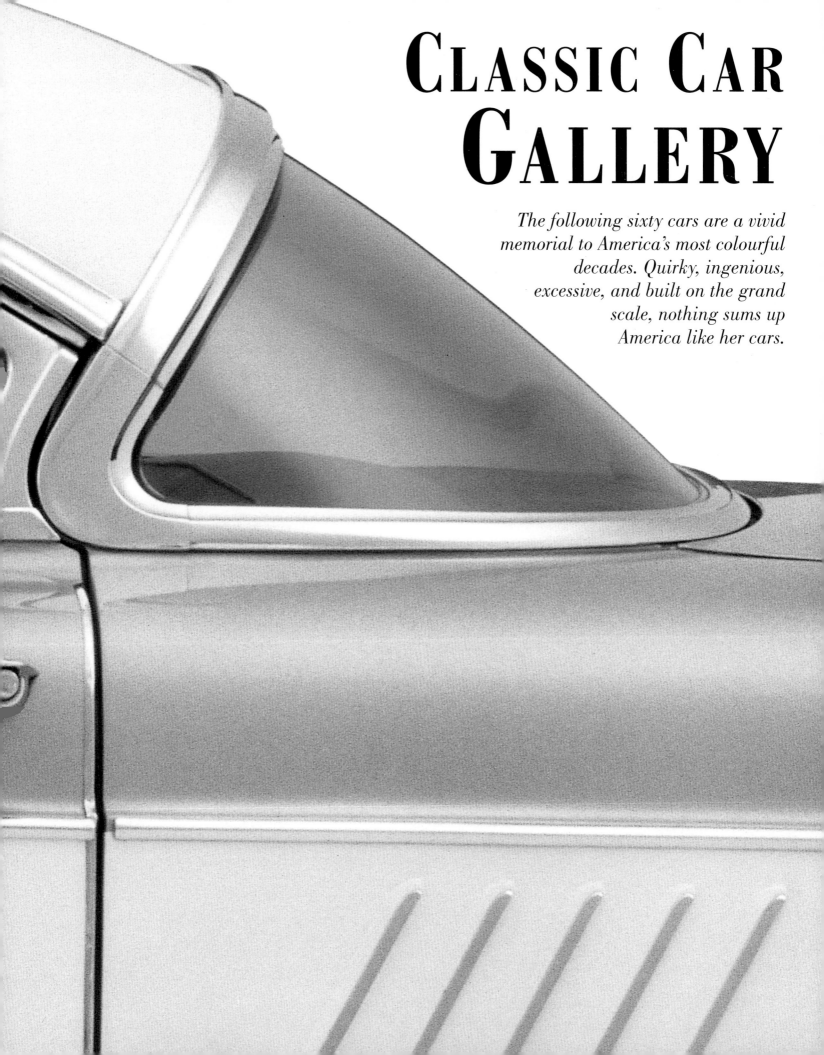

CLASSIC CAR GALLERY

*The following sixty cars are a vivid
memorial to America's most colourful
decades. Quirky, ingenious,
excessive, and built on the grand
scale, nothing sums up
America like her cars.*

The Forties

America's intervention in World War II filled the nation with a self-confidence that would fertilize phenomenal post-war industrial growth. The automobile industry never had it so good.

CHRYSLER'S 25TH ANNIVERSARY MODEL WAS THE FIRST ALL-NEW POST-WAR STYLING CHANGE

MODERN AMERICA began in 1945. Post-war austerity didn't last long, and by the late Forties American workers produced 57 per cent of the world's steel, 60 per cent of the oil, and 80 per cent of all the cars on the planet. In the five short years after the end of the war, Americans were able to buy electric clothes-driers, long-playing records, Polaroid cameras, frozen foods, and automatic garbage-disposal units. It was a brave new world of miracle materials like plastics, nylon, Styrofoam, vinyl, and chrome. What had once seemed science fiction was suddenly everyday life.

The GI Bill of Rights in 1945 invigorated the economy and stimulated education, industry, and business, kick-starting the biggest consumer boom the world has ever seen. Houses for heroes became a national priority and, between 1945 and 1950,

15 million shot up all over America. The Levitts of Levittown fame could build one in just 16 minutes, charging $7,990 for a four-and-a-half room, two-storey with central heating, refrigerator, washing machine, and an eight-inch Bendix television set. Marriage rates soared and American newly-weds

1941 LINCOLN ZEPHYR V12
Lincoln's '41 Zephyr V12 carried over many pre-war styling elements. Tall, long, and boxy, it wasn't until 1942 that it got a mild facelift. The last pre-war Lincoln rolled out of the factory on 10 February the same year.

	1940–1945	1946	1947	1948	1949
AUTOMOTIVE	• Streamlining percolates down even to lowly **Chevrolet**s • Harley Earl and design team view P-38 Lightning pursuit plane • Supercharged **Graham** is fastest car powered by side-valve six • **DeSoto** build fuselage sections for the Martin B-26 • **Chrysler** resume car production in 1945	• 50th Anniversary of US car industry • **Ford** are biggest manufacturer, producing 468,022 cars • Steel strike and shortage of materials affect car industry • **Lincoln** Continental is pace car at Indianapolis 500 • **Mercury** launch Sportsman Convertible with wood body panels • **Pontiac** dust off pre-war Silver Streak styling	• **Chevrolet** now America's No. 1 car maker with 671,546 cars • **Frazer** and **Kaiser** are first US cars to exhibit new post-war styling with unbroken lines • Virgil Exner designs new enclosed-body **Studebaker** Champion • **Pontiac** build a rear-mounted straight-eight engine • Woody look is all the rage • Whitewall tyres now available • Henry Ford dies	• **Cadillac** bring out dramatic new 62 Series with dorsal fins • **Hudson** launch famous "Step-Down" body • **Pontiac** introduce Hydra-Matic automatic transmission • Rare and radical **Tucker** Torpedo unveiled • Charles Nash dies • **Willys** launch the Jeepster, America's last true touring car	• **Ford** return to the top spot, making an extraordinary 1,118,308 cars • **Buick** debut new Roadmaster • **Chevrolet** make first major restyle since the war  1949 HUDSON SUPER SIX
HISTORICAL	• Japanese bomb Pearl Harbor (1941) • First US troops land in Europe (1942) • US miners' strike (1943) • Eisenhower masterminds D-Day (6 June 1943) • Glenn Miller disappears over English Channel (1944) • A-bomb on Hiroshima (1945) GENERAL DWIGHT D. EISENHOWER	• United Nations holds first session • IBM introduce electronic calculator • First sub-surface atomic explosion at Bikini Atoll • Ten Nazi war criminals executed at Nuremburg • *Road to Utopia* opens with Bob Hope and Bing Crosby	• Marshall Plan offers massive aid for post-war Europe • US crusade against Communism begins • Soviets test A-bomb • Plutonium is discovered • John Cobb sets land speed record of 634 km/h (394 mph) • Bell XI plane breaks the sound barrier at over 965 km/h (600 mph) • Rita Hayworth divorces Orson Welles	• Soviets blockade Berlin and their envoy to the UN walks out • Truman wins Presidency • Transistor is invented • Kinsey Report on American sexual mores is published • Kansas ends prohibition • Tennessee Williams wins Pulitzer Prize for *A Streetcar Named Desire* • George Orwell publishes *1984* • Norman Mailer publishes *The Naked and the Dead*	• Berlin blockade ends • Truman says he won't hesitate to use the A-bomb again, but publicly tries to calm "red hysteria" • Einstein publishes *Theory of Gravitation* • Actor Robert Mitchum jailed for smoking marijuana • RCA launch new system for broadcasting colour TV pictures • 7" vinyl records first available

1948 LINCOLN CONTINENTAL COUPE
Although largely unchanged from 1946 models, the $4,662 '48 Continental was considered one of the most glamorous cars you could buy at the time. The Metropolitan Museum of Modern Art selected it as one of the eight automotive "works of art". Time magazine also ranked it in their top 10 of 100 best-designed products.

RITA HAYWORTH'S CONTINENTAL
Movie star Rita Hayworth had the necessary $2,812 to buy one of only 850 '41 Lincoln Continentals, as did architect Frank Lloyd Wright, who described it as "the last classic car built in the United States". This was one of the final cars produced before the US entered the war.

flocked to the suburbs. Precisely nine months after VJ-Day, the cry of the baby rang out across the land; by the end of '46, 3.4 million had been born. Radio and TV shows like *The Adventures of Ozzie and Harriet* portrayed a cosy domestic idyll of plenty and normality. In 1948, 172,000 American households each paid $200 to buy a television set. By 1950, 7½ million families were glued to the tube. And, looking through that new window on the world, American expectations grew grander and grander.

The Rebirth of the Industry

Clearly, the nation now needed a different kind of mobilization. In steel-starved 1945, new car sales totalled just 69,500. By 1949, this had risen to a staggering 5.1 million. Buyers were so desperate to own new Chevys and Fords that they not only paid full list price but slipped the dealer a fan of dollars to jump the queue. An ad for the 1945 model Buick featured a shimmering car emerging from a gloomy scene of war. The copy read, "Buicks are for the lively, exciting, forward-looking world so many have fought for". In a *Saturday Evening Post* article entitled "Your Car After the War", a man called Harley Earl prophetically predicted low, futuristic machines with curved windscreens and slipstream bodies.

Although the metal in showrooms after 1945 was mainly a pre-war lunch warmed over, aerodynamic styling and technical advancement gradually seeped into the brochures. Two significant engineering developments dominated the decade: the V8 engine and the automatic gearbox. It was General Motors who pioneered a generation of V8s, along with the seminal Hydra-Matic and Dynaflow self-shifters. Innovation was everywhere, not least in Preston Tucker's spectacular helicopter-engined Tucker Torpedo of 1948.

But it was that man Harley Earl who came up with probably the greatest automotive innovation of the late Forties – the infant fin. His '48 Cadillac wore two strange little bumps on its rear, and from that point the vernacular of the post-war American automobile was defined. Cars would never be mere transport again.

1947 CHRYSLER TOWN AND COUNTRY
Chrysler's Town and Country series of 1947 was a new departure from pre-war designs. Wood had previously been used only on station wagons, but the T & C Sedan had unique wood-bodied sides.

1943 WILLYS
Jeep MB

WILLYS LOGO ON THE ENGINE BLOCK

AS ONE WAR CORRESPONDENT said, "It's as faithful as a dog, as strong as a mule, and as agile as a mountain goat". The flat-winged Willys Jeep is one of the most instantly recognizable vehicles ever made. Any American TV or movie action hero who wasn't on a horse was in a Jeep. Even General Eisenhower was impressed, saying "the three tools that won us the war in Europe were the Dakota and the landing craft and the Jeep".

In 1940, the American Defense Department sent out a tough spec for a military workhorse. Many companies took one look at the seemingly impossible specification and 49-day deadline and turned it down flat. The design that won the tender and made it into production and the history books was a mixture of the ideas and abilities of Ford, Bantam, and Willys-Overland. A stunning triumph of function over form, the Jeep not only won the war, but went on to become a cult off-roader that's still with us now. The Willys Jeep is surely the most original 4x4 by far.

PRESIDENT-ELECT EISENHOWER VISITING TROOPS IN KOREA IN 1952

ENGINE
Power was from a Ford straight four, which took the Jeep to around 96 km/h (60 mph), actually exceeding US Army driving regulations. The hardy L-head motor developed 60 bhp, and the Warner three-speed manual box was supplemented by controls allowing the driver to select two- or four-wheel drive in high or low ratios.

QUICK-RELEASE CLUTCH DISENGAGES ENGINE FAN FOR FORDING STREAMS AND RIVERS

DUAL-PURPOSE HEADLIGHT
The headlight could be rotated back to illuminate the engine bay.

FRONT VIEW
Earlier Jeeps had a slatted radiator grille instead of the later pressed steel bars, as here. The silhouette was low, but ground clearance high to allow driving in streams as deep as 53 cm (21 in). Weather protection was vestigial.

DORCAS

LEFT-HAND SUSPENSION SPRINGS HAD A STIFFER RATING TO COPE WITH THE WEIGHT OF THE ENGINE

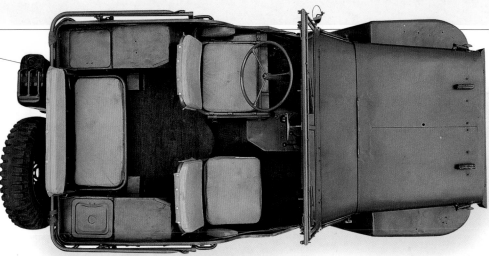

READY FOR
ANYTHING,
JEEPS CAME
WITH
PETROL CAN,
SHOVEL,
LONG-
HANDLED
AXE, AND
GRAB BARS

EXTENDED LIFESPAN
The Jeep was a brilliantly
simple engineering solution
to the problem of rugged
mobility at war, but the life
expectancy of an average
vehicle was expected to be less
than a week! In practice, many
have survived to this day.

SPECIFICATIONS
MODEL 1943 Willys Jeep MB
PRODUCTION 586,000 (during
World War II)
BODY STYLE Open utility vehicle.
CONSTRUCTION Steel body and
chassis.
ENGINE 134cid straight four.
POWER OUTPUT 60 bhp.
TRANSMISSION Three-speed
manual, four-wheel drive.
SUSPENSION Leaf springs front
and rear.
BRAKES Front and rear drums.
MAXIMUM SPEED 105 km/h
(65 mph)
0–60 MPH (0–96 KM/H) 22 sec
A.F.C. 5.7 km/l (16 mpg)

EXPOSED COLUMN
Driver safety wasn't a Jeep strong point. Many GIs
ended up impaled on the steering column even after
low-speed impacts. Only the generals fought the war
in comfort, and Jeep accommodation was strictly no
frills. Very early Jeeps have no glove compartment.

WHAT'S IN A NAME?
Jeeps were first called General Purpose
cars, then MA, and finally standardized as
MB, but to this day nobody's sure from
where the unofficial Jeep name originated.
Some say it is a phonetic corruption of
GP, or General Purpose, others that it
was named after a curious
little creature called Eugene
the Jeep who appeared in
a 1936 Popeye cartoon.

HAND-
OPERATED
WINDSCREEN
WIPERS

DOORS WOULD HAVE
ADDED WEIGHT, SO SIDE
STRAPS WERE A TOKEN
GESTURE TOWARDS
DRIVER SAFETY

FIRST PRODUCTION
JEEP MODEL, THE MA,
HAD A COLUMN CHANGE

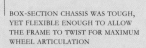

BOX-SECTION CHASSIS WAS TOUGH,
YET FLEXIBLE ENOUGH TO ALLOW
THE FRAME TO TWIST FOR MAXIMUM
WHEEL ARTICULATION

HIGH CLUTCH, NARROW
FOOTWELL, AND UNMOVABLE
SEAT FORCED A DRIVING
POSITION WITH KNEES SPLAYED

1943 WILLYS JEEP MB

EVOLUTION OF THE JEEP

THAT THE LEGENDARY quarter-tonne Jeep was in fact a mish-mash of available components virtually thrown together at record speed is amazing enough. But no-one could have predicted that it would eventually create a whole new market for lifestyle leisure vehicles. Willys were to survive into the Fifties and Sixties, but investment was lacking until Chrysler acquired Jeep in the Eighties. Now the brand is in the ascendancy and giving rival Land Rover some stiff opposition.

1942

WILLYS AND FORD JEEPS saw service in every theatre of war, and the two versions were almost identical. By August 1945, when wartime production of the Jeep ended, the two companies together had manufactured over 600,000 Jeeps. The US Army still carried on using Jeeps well into the Sixties, and some European armies still use them now.

KEY FEATURES
- Wartime Jeeps used the L-head straight four from production cars of the early '40s
- Willys bid lowest for the Jeep contract, but the Defense Department included Ford
- Tiny Bantam company produced 3,000 Jeeps

1950

WILLYS WERE QUICK to identify a burgeoning domestic market, so they cleaned up their warhorse and marketed it in a more civilized guise. One of the first civilian Jeeps, the Jeepster Phaeton, was introduced in 1948–49 and sold well in its opening years. This 1950 model sported a revised grille and improved engine, but sales fell by over 60 per cent.

KEY DEVELOPMENTS
- High-compression 7.0:1 cylinder head option available
- Split windscreen rigid with chrome surround
- Mechanically-operated soft-top
- Rear wheels gain modesty wings

WILLYS TRIED TO broaden the Jeep's appeal by bringing out a small Jeep-based station wagon. It was a longer car, built on the same wheelbase, and sold from 1946 to 1951. All were painted maroon with wood trim and had dual wipers, front bumper guards, and rails. Six-cylinders boasted wheel trim rings, cigar lighter, and whitewalls.

KEY DEVELOPMENTS
- Restyled grille is divided by five horizontal bars
- New centre gauge dash design and wrap-around rear bumper
- The first Jeep with a single-piece windscreen

1943 WILLYS Jeep MB

WAR HERO
World War II made the Jeep's reputation – it was used on battlegrounds the world over, and appears in this poster recruiting soldiers to fight in China.

JOINT EFFORT
Of the 135 manufacturers contacted by the Defense Department, only Willys and Bantam rose to the challenge. Ford presented their version some time later.

THE JEEP MAY HAVE HAD COMPETENCE AND CHARISMA, BUT IT ALSO HAD A PRODIGIOUS THIRST FOR FUEL

DAMPING IS BY LEAF SPRINGS AND HYDRAULIC SHOCKS WHICH GIVE A SURPRISINGLY GOOD RIDE

1962

JEEP PRE-DATED Range Rover by a decade with its oversized, go-anywhere four-wheel drive station wagon. With ample accommodation for at least five and a massive luggage deck, it became a favourite of intrepid outdoor types. Trim levels could be specified, marking the Jeep's most significant departure from its utilitarian military image.

KEY DEVELOPMENTS
• Called the Wagoneer, this new Jeep was all-new in a market all on its own
• Gladiator pick-up available
• Willys name was dropped in 1963 and changed to Kaiser-Jeep Corporation

1971

BY THE MID-SIXTIES, manufacturers were seeing a new all-terrain leisure market emerge. International Harvester launched the Scout, and Ford joined in with the Bronco. Lacking real investment, Jeep based a new car, the Jeepster Commando, on the Wagoneer's wheelbase. A roadster, station wagon, and convertible were offered.

KEY DEVELOPMENTS
• Five engines offered, from a 134cid four to a 304cid V8
• Press acclaim new Jeeps, saying "passenger comfort is way above average"
• Jeepster had a 257 cm (101 in) wheelbase

1976

BASED ON JEEP'S hefty Cherokee station wagon, the Honcho was the company's big pick-up for the Seventies. The most popular engine was the V8. Jeep got the luxury sport utility vehicle ball rolling with the full-size Cherokee, but it wasn't until the compact four-door models were introduced that sales really took off.

KEY DEVELOPMENTS
• AMC acquire Kaiser-Jeep Corporation and become largest 4x4 manufacturer in US
• Range Rover's success in the UK expands the off-roader market

1994

AFTER YEARS OF SUCCESS with the smaller Cherokee, Jeep came up with the larger and more luxurious Grand Cherokee in the mid-Eighties. With every possible luxury, it was strong competition for the big Japanese 4x4s and now-legendary Range Rover. Priced competitively, it was espoused as a very practical suburban trinket.

KEY DEVELOPMENTS
• Jeep now a division of the Chrysler Corp.
• Grand Cherokee with V8 now has 201 km/h (125 mph) performance
• Improvements include ABS, air-conditioning, and low-emission engine

EASY ACCESS
The Jeep's bonnet was secured using quick-release sprung catches. The upper catch held the fold-down windscreen.

TRENDSETTER
Those stark wings and large all-terrain tyres may look humble and functional, but the Jeep's claim to fame is that it spawned utility vehicles from Nissans and Isuzus to Discoverys and Range Rovers.

JEEP FIREPOWER
The Jeep remains very popular with fans of military memorabilia, especially in its various specialist guises. This archive shot – taken in Germany – shows a Jeep fitted with a potent anti-tank cannon.

LONG-STROKE SIDE-VALVE FLAT-TOP FOUR DEVELOPED PLENTY OF STUMP-PULLING TORQUE

AXLES ARE FULLY FLOATING WITH BENDIX-WEISS, RZEPPA, OR SPICER CONSTANT VELOCITY JOINTS

1948 TUCKER
Torpedo

EXTRAVAGANT ORNAMENTATION

THERE'S NO OTHER POST-WAR CAR that's as dramatic or advanced as Preston Tucker's futuristic '48 Torpedo. With four-wheel independent suspension, rear-mounted Bell helicopter engine, pop-out safety windscreen, and uncrushable passenger compartment, it was 20 years ahead of its time.

"You'll step into a new automotive age when you drive your Tucker '48", bragged the ads. It was a promise that convinced an astonishing 300,000 people to place orders, but their dreams were never to be realized. Problems with the engine and Tuckermatic transmission, plus a serious cash-flow crisis, meant that only 51 Torpedos left the Chicago plant. Worse still, Tucker and five of his associates were indicted for fraud by the Securities Exchange Commission. Their acquittal came too late to save America's most eccentric car from an undignified end.

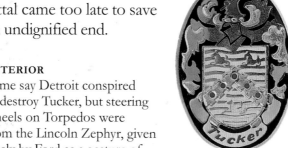

HOLLYWOOD PORTRAYAL
The 1988 film *Tucker: The Man and His Dream* starred Jeff Bridges and told a none-too-accurate story of an impassioned genius thwarted by Detroit's Big Three. In reality, Tucker failed because the project was underfunded.

FAMILY BADGE
The horn on the steering wheel lay flush for safety, and was adorned with the Tucker family crest in injection-moulded acrylic, suggesting a Cadillac-type bloodline.

INTERIOR
Some say Detroit conspired to destroy Tucker, but steering wheels on Torpedos were from the Lincoln Zephyr, given freely by Ford as a gesture of help. Although the interior was groaning with safety features, the Tucker sales team reckoned it was too austere.

REAR LIGHT, LIKE MUCH OF THE TUCKER, WAS BOUGHT IN, AND IS A PRE-WAR DODGE DESIGN

REAR ENGINE WAS PLACED CROSSWISE ON THE OVERHANG BETWEEN THE TWO INDEPENDENTLY SPRUNG REAR WHEELS

VENTS WERE TO
REDUCE THE
CONSIDERABLE
ENGINE
HEAT

SPECIFICATIONS

MODEL 1948 Tucker Torpedo
PRODUCTION 51
BODY STYLE Four-door sedan.
CONSTRUCTION Steel body
  and chassis.
ENGINE 335cid flat six.
POWER OUTPUT 166 bhp.
TRANSMISSION Three-speed
  Tuckermatic automatic, four-speed
  manual.
SUSPENSION Four-wheel
  independent.
BRAKES Front and rear drums.
MAXIMUM SPEED 193 km/h
  (120 mph)
0–60 MPH (0–96 KM/H) 10.1 sec
A.F.C. 10.6 km/l (30 mpg)

LOW PROFILE

One of the fastest cars on
American roads, the Tucker
had a low floor that gave it a
huge aerodynamic advantage.
The roof tapered in two directions to
reduce lift forces, and the drag coefficient
was as low as 0.30. The Torpedo's top speed
was 193 km/h (120 mph), and an astonishing
10.6 km/l (30 mpg) was possible.

AN INSTANT HIT

The public loved the Tucker not only
for its comfort, power, and safety, but
also because the styling was completely
free from the usual pre-war clichés. The
prototype was ready in 60 days and more
than 5,000 people attended the launch.

WHEN THE
TUCKER WAS
PREVIEWED
TO THE PRESS,
THE FRONT
BUMPER WAS
MADE OF
WOOD

DARING CYCLOPS
HEADLIGHT
SWIVELLED WITH
THE FRONT WHEELS

STEERHORN
BUMPER
GAVE THE
CAR A
DRAMATIC
FRONTAL
ASPECT

WITH NO
ENGINE UPFRONT,
LUGGAGE SPACE
WAS COMMODIOUS

ENGINE

The first Tucker engine was
a monster 589cid aluminium
flat six that proved difficult
to start and ran too hot. It
was replaced by a 6ALV 335cid
flat six, developed by Air-Cooled Motors of
Syracuse. Perversely, Tucker later converted
this unit to a water-cooled system.

SLIPPERY FRONT WAS DESIGNED
TO CLEAVE THE AIR

THE CAR OF THE FUTURE HELD BACK IN THE PAST

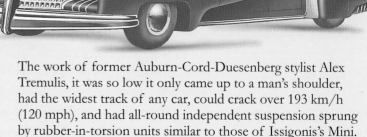

ARTWORK OF A
PROTOTYPE
1947 TUCKER
TORPEDO

PRESTON TUCKER WAS AN EXTRAORDINARY automotive maverick. An unlettered engineer whose favourite phrase was "our boss is bigger than all of us, and it's the automobile", he was a well-connected wheeler-dealer who'd made a fortune from the design of a gun-turret mounting for World War II bombers. Obsessed by a dream of building the most advanced passenger car in the world, he secured the lease on a vast plant in Chicago previously used to build engines for Boeing Superfortresses. A born deal-maker, he'd shrewdly raised $8 million franchising 1,800 Tucker dealerships before his automotive vision of the future was even in running prototype form.

The Torpedo was so different from anything else on four wheels that it was a complete sensation.

PRESTON TUCKER

The work of former Auburn-Cord-Duesenberg stylist Alex Tremulis, it was so low it only came up to a man's shoulder, had the widest track of any car, could crack over 193 km/h (120 mph), and had all-round independent suspension sprung by rubber-in-torsion units similar to those of Issigonis's Mini.

But the much-vaunted 589cid helicopter power plant was a nightmare, as was the troublesome Tuckermatic transmission, which was later replaced by a modified Cord gearbox. Tucker's tribulations soon leaked out to the press, who'd heard that prototypes sent to dealerships were plagued with glitches.

1948 TUCKER
Torpedo

INTERIOR WAS DESIGNED BY
AUDREY MOORE, WHO HAD
WORKED WITH RAYMOND
LOEWY ON STUDEBAKERS

NOVEL ENGINE WAS
POSITIONED LOWER
THAN THE REAR
PASSENGER SEAT TO
DIMINISH NOISE,
HEAT, AND FUMES

REAR DEFROSTER WAS
ONE OF ONLY FOUR
OPTIONS AVAILABLE

PRESTON TUCKER
DEMANDED A
"SASSY" REAR
END FROM HIS
DESIGN TEAM

HELICOPTER HELL
The early 589cid modified helicopter engines were a bit of a disaster. One test driver, Gene Haustein, described them as "slow as the moon coming up, making a noise like a barrel full of monkeys with the lid propped open".

Tucker

MANUFACTURER
1 5
ILLINOIS 48

The situation got worse. Tucker had raised capital by a conventional stock market issue, but he fell foul of the Securities Exchange Commission because the production cars didn't include all the audacious technical features he'd listed in his prospectus: direct fluid drive, disc brakes, sealed cooling system, electronic ignition, and fuel injection. The suits from Wall Street claimed that the cars being offered to the public did not fulfil Tucker's grandiose promises. The Tucker Corporation was therefore guilty of fraud.

PRESTON IN HIS DREAM CAR

After an essential $30 million loan was refused, Tucker was forced into voluntary liquidation. The tragedy was that Tucker could have sold every car he made, and he even had

TUCKERS WAIT OUTSIDE COURT DURING THE TRIAL

a float of several million dollars in the bank. The Chicago plant closed in the summer of 1948, by which time 37 Torpedos had been produced. In the end, volunteer workers assembled another 14 cars from remaining parts.

Fifty-odd years later, the Torpedo remains one of America's most charismatic classics, and mint specimens can sell for up to $300,000. Many are proudly exhibited in museums, and some have even racked up a quarter of a million miles without incident. The Torpedo was meant to herald the brave new world of post-war America but failed because it was too complicated, too daring, and too under-resourced. A perfect exemplar of American automotive genius, Tucker's precocious prodigy was guilty of just one sin – it bloomed too soon. Five years later the story might have been very different.

UNIQUE AND EXCITING

The front was like no other American car, with a fixed circular headlight lens that pivoted with the steering and a front panel that blended artfully into the bumper and grille.

FRONT AND REAR SEAT CUSHIONS COULD BE INTERCHANGED TO SPREAD WEAR AND TEAR

SEAT BELTS WERE NEVER FITTED BECAUSE THEY WERE THOUGHT TO SUGGEST THAT THE CAR WAS UNSAFE

RADIO WAS AN OPTIONAL EXTRA

THE TORPEDO WAS ONE OF THE FIRST WIDE-TRACK CARS AND HAD EXCEPTIONAL CORNERING ABILITY

THE TORPEDO COULD BRAKE TO A STOP IN HALF THE DISTANCE OF AN AVERAGE CAR

1949 BUICK
Roadmaster

THE '49 ROADMASTER TOOK the market's breath away. With a low silhouette, straight bonnet, and fastback styling, it was a poem in steel. The first Buick with a truly new post-war look, the '49 was designed by Ned Nickles using GM's new C-body. It also boasted two bold new styling motifs: Ventiports and an aggressive 25-tooth "Dollar Grin" grille. Harley Earl's aesthetic of aeronautical entertainment worked a treat and Buick notched up nearly 400,000 sales that year. Never mind that the windscreen was still two-piece, that there was no power steering, and the engine was a straight eight – it looked gorgeous and came with the new Dynaflow automatic transmission. The Roadmaster, like the '49 Cadillac, was a seminal car and the first flowering of the most flamboyant decade of car design ever seen.

GUN-SIGHT
BONNET
DECORATION

DASHBOARD
The instrument panel was new for '49 and described as "pilot centred" because the speedo was positioned straight ahead of the driver through the steering wheel. The design was taken straight from Harley Earl's Buick Y-Job.

REAR LIGHT CLUSTER
The Art Deco tail-lights looked upmarket and blended smoothly into the rear wings. Nobody could have guessed that they were emergent fins which, in 10 years, would mushroom to almost comical proportions.

VENTIPORTS
Open Ventiports were sealed mid-year because a high-school principal complained that male students used those on his Roadmaster to relieve themselves.

SPOTLIGHT WITH
MIRROR WAS A
$25 OPTION

VENTIPORTS GAVE THE
IMPRESSION OF A FIRE-
BREATHING JET ENGINE

CHEAPER
BUICKS HAD
ONLY THREE
VENTIPORTS,
BUT THE
LAVISH
ROADMASTER
SPORTED
FOUR

ELEGANT FLOURISH
COMPLETES THE SWOOPING
TEARDROP REAR

SPECIFICATIONS

MODEL 1949 Buick Roadmaster
Series 70 Sedanette
PRODUCTION 18,415
BODY STYLE Two-door
fastback coupe.
CONSTRUCTION Steel body
and chassis.
ENGINE 320cid straight eight.
POWER OUTPUT 150 bhp.
TRANSMISSION Two-speed
Dynaflow automatic.
SUSPENSION Front and rear
coil springs.
BRAKES Front and rear drums.
MAXIMUM SPEED 161 km/h
(100 mph)
0–60 MPH (0–96 KM/H) 17 sec
A.F.C. 7 km/1 (20 mpg)

RAISED PROFILE

The Roadmaster may have
shared its body with the
Oldsmobile 98 and the Cadillac
Series 62, but it gave Buick a
distinction never seen before.

NEW AUTOMATIC

Dynaflow automatic
transmission was
introduced in 1948 as
an option on the Roadmaster.
By '49 it had become standard
equipment on the Series 70 Roadie
and an immensely popular option on
Series 50 and, later, Series 40 models.

ALTHOUGH DIVIDED BY A
CENTRE PILLAR, WINDSCREEN
GLASS WAS CURVED

ENGINE WAS
FITTED WITH
HYDRAULIC
"LASH-ADJUSTER"
THAT KEPT EACH
OF THE 16 VALVES
CORRECTLY SET
AND SILENCED

THE ROADMASTER BEGAN
THE TREND FOR LOWER,
SLEEKER STYLING

THE GM C-BODY HAD
CLOSED QUARTERS
AND SEDANETTE
STYLING

ENGINE

The Roadie had a Fireball straight-eight cast-iron 320cid engine
that always started with a roar because the starter switch
was connected to the accelerator and engaged
by depressing the pedal all the way to
the floor. The Fireball pushed out 150
ponies and breathed through
Stromberg or Carter carbs.

DYNAFLOW WAS SUCH
A NEW IDEA THAT
BUICK PROUDLY
SCRIPTED
IT ONTO
THE REAR
WING

TYRES WERE
820 x 15
WHITEWALLS

EVOLUTION OF THE BUICK ROADMASTER

FOR YEARS GM'S COPYWRITERS crowed that "when better cars are built, Buick will build them", and in a sense that hyperbole was true. In its day, the gloriously voluptuous Roadmaster was a serious set of wheels, only one step down from a Cadillac, and to own one meant you really had arrived. Big, bold, and brash, the '49 was perfect for its time. Optimistic, opulent, and glitzy, it carried strident styling cues that told people a block away that this was no ordinary car, this was a Buick – even better, the very best Buick money could buy.

ADVERT FOR THE 1956 ROADMASTER STRESSED THAT IT WAS THE "BUICK OF BUICKS"

1945–46

THE FIRST POST-WAR Buicks were practically unchanged from 1942, with engines that dated back to 1936 and chassis frames that originated in 1933. But they did have all-coil suspension and Harley Earl styling, and the Roadmaster Convertible was Buick's fastest and most glamorous car. Buick did well in '46, producing more than 156,000 cars.

KEY FEATURES
• Permi-Firm steering on all models
• Two-tone instrument panel with wood grains
• Only three-speed manual transmission available
• Standard vacuum-operated windscreen wipers

1953

IN '53 THE ROADMASTER gained the first Buick V8, nicknamed the "Nail-Head" because of the small diameter of its valve heads. The nose was shortened to accommodate the smaller lump, and power steering, power brakes, and Dynaflow drive became standard. This was Buick's 50th anniversary, celebrated by the seven millionth Buick built.

KEY DEVELOPMENTS
• New V8 engine goes into 50 per cent of all Buicks
• Calendar year production total tops 485,000
• Dynaflow gets twin turbines, which increases torque by 10 per cent
• 80 per cent of Buicks have Dynaflow

1949 BUICK
Roadmaster

A CAR TO ASPIRE TO
Roadmaster was a brilliant name for the top-of-the-line Buick and soon became the preferred transport of professionals who couldn't quite make it to Cadillac territory.

PRISMATIC REAR-VIEW MIRROR WAS AN OPTIONAL EXTRA

THE '49 ROADIE WAS THE PUREST AND MOST BEAUTIFUL BUICK EVER MADE

1955	1957	1991	1994
	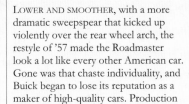		

1955

A MAJOR FACELIFT for '55 didn't do much for the Roadmaster. The vertical grille bars were replaced by a tight mesh, and the body styling was distinctly slab-sided. The Ventiports and bonnet ornaments stayed, but the result was a much blander machine. The public cared not, buying nearly 800,000 Buicks to put them in industry third place.

KEY DEVELOPMENTS
- Gold-coloured Roadmaster script and bonnet ornament
- Convertible gets standard leather
- 10 choices of interior trim
- Eight millionth Buick rolls off the line

1957

LOWER AND SMOOTHER, with a more dramatic sweepspear that kicked up violently over the rear wheel arch, the restyle of '57 made the Roadmaster look a lot like every other American car. Gone was that chaste individuality, and Buick began to lose its reputation as a maker of high-quality cars. Production was down 24 per cent.

KEY DEVELOPMENTS
- Revised front suspension with ball-joint mounting
- Grille reverts to vertical bars
- New two-piece torque tube
- New engine mountings
- Nine millionth Buick hits the showroom

1991

BUICK RESURRECTED the Roadmaster name for 1991 after a foolish and inexplicable 33-year hiatus. Riding on a body-on-chassis design dating back to '77, the '91 Roadmaster was a shadow of its former self. Long, heavy, and ungainly, it bore too obvious a resemblance to other GM products and had completely lost all character.

KEY DEVELOPMENTS
- Roadmaster name first appears on aero-look eight-passenger station wagon
- Fuel-injected 5.0 V8
- Driver's-side airbag and ABS standard
- Improved suspension gives better stability
- Same chassis and mechanicals as Chevrolet Caprice

1994

THERE WERE ONLY minor changes to the Roadmaster in '94, the main one being the optional Corvette-based 260 bhp V8. The rear-drive sedan and station wagons continued, and stock power was from the 5.7 V8. This year's models returned only 5.7 km/l (16 mpg) in urban driving. Alas, the once great name had been sacrificed on the altar of badge engineering.

KEY DEVELOPMENTS
- Station wagons get rear-facing two-place third seat and vista roof
- Solar-Ray tinted windscreen
- Improved sound deadening
- Lock-out switch for power windows
- Sedan roof pillars hinder visibility

LOUD AND PROUD

The centre of the steering wheel was one of five places where Dynaflow was written on the car. The steering itself was unassisted and required a hefty five turns lock-to-lock.

INTERIOR FABRICS WERE PLUSH, WITH A CUSTOM TRIM OPTION

FULL-WIDTH BENCH SEATS WERE STANDARD ON THE '49 ROADIE

BUICK STYLING

Gun-sight bonnet ornament, bucktooth grille, and Ventiports were flashy styling metaphors that would become famous Buick trademarks.

BUICK EIGHT

ROAD MASTER

18 363
52   WYOMING

1949 CADILLAC
Series 62

THE CADILLAC SCRIPT IS FAMOUS THE WORLD OVER

WE OWE A LOT TO the '49 Cadillac. It brought us tail fins and a high-compression V8. Harley Earl came up with those trendsetting rear rudders, and John F. Gordon the performance motor. Between them they created the basic grammar of the post-war American car.

In 1949 the one millionth Cad rolled off the production line, and the stunning Series 62 Fastback or Sedanette was born. Handsome and quick, with Hydra-Matic transmission, curved windscreen, and hydraulically operated front seats and windows, it was a complete revelation. Everybody, including the haughty British and Italians, nodded sagely in admiration and, at a whisker under $3,000, it knocked the competition dead in their tracks. As Cadillac adverts boasted: "The new Cadillac is not only the world's most beautiful and distinguished motor car, but its performance is a challenge to the imagination". The American Dream and the finest era in American cars began with the '49 Cadillac.

— BENTLEY CONNECTION —

THE CLASSIC 1952 BENTLEY R-TYPE Continental certainly bears a startling similarity to the '49 Cadillac. Motoring academics have frequently hinted at plagiarism, suggesting that the Bentley's comely teardrop shape was inspired by Harley Earl's design. Naturally, the boys at Bentley declined to comment, but nonetheless the two cars do display an uncanny kinship of line. However, far from waving writs about, Earl, Cadillac, and GM took a philosophical approach and simply smiled quietly to themselves. For after all, we all know that imitation is the most sincere form of flattery.

1952 BENTLEY R-TYPE CONTINENTAL

GLORIOUS TAPERING ROOF LINE MADE DUMPY EUROPEAN CARS LOOK LIKE DELIVERY VANS FOR CHURCH PEWS

CADILLAC CREST
The "V" emblem below the crest denoted V8 power, and the basic badge design remained unaltered until 1952.

BODY STYLE
Hugely influential body design was penned by Harley Earl and Julio Andrade at GM's styling studios. Many of the '49 features soon found themselves on other GM products such as Oldsmobile and Buick.

TYRES RAN AT ONLY 24 PSI, MAKING UNASSISTED STEERING HEAVY

MASCOT

The famous streamlined Art Deco goddess bonnet ornament first appeared after the war and continued unchanged until 1956. America's most prestigious car wore its mascot with pride.

INTERIOR

The cabin was heavily chromed, and oozed quality. Colours were grey-blue or brown with wool carpets to match, and leather or cloth seats. Steering was Saginaw, with standard four-speed auto transmission.

ACCOLADES

British motoring journalist S.C.H. Davis rated the '49 one of the six outstanding cars of the two post-war decades. *Motor Trend* magazine named it "Car of the Year".

WHILE STYLING WAS SIMILAR TO THAT OF THE '48 MODEL, THE NEW OHV V8 IN THE '49 WAS AN INNOVATION

CHROME SLASHES WERE INSPIRED BY AIRCRAFT AIR INTAKES

FUEL FILLER-CAP WAS HIDDEN UNDER TAIL-LIGHT, A CADILLAC TRAIT SINCE 1941

FIN STYLING

The rear fins, inspired by the Lockheed P-38 aircraft, became a Caddy trademark and would reach a titanic height on '59 models.

SPECIFICATIONS

MODEL 1949 Cadillac Series 62

PRODUCTION 92,554 (all body styles)

BODY STYLE Two-door, five-seater fastback.

CONSTRUCTION Steel body and chassis.

ENGINE 331cid V8.

POWER OUTPUT 162 bhp.

TRANSMISSION Four-speed Hydra-Matic automatic.

SUSPENSION *Front*: coil springs; *Rear*: leaf springs.

BRAKES Front and rear drums.

MAXIMUM SPEED 161 km/h (100 mph)

0–60 MPH (0–96 KM/H) 13.4 sec

A.F.C. 6 km/l (17 mpg)

EVOLUTION OF THE CADILLAC SERIES 62

'48 WAS THE YEAR of the fin and the year of the crème des Cads. Cadillac designers Bill Mitchell, Harley Earl, Frank Hershey, and Art Ross had been smitten by a secret P-38 Lockheed Lightning fighter plane. Mitchell admitted that the P-38's fins "handed us a trademark nobody else had". Cadillac also had Ed Cole's OHV V8, some 10 years in the making. With a brief to reduce weight and increase compression, the end result was an engine with more torque and better mileage than any other at the time.

1955 ADVERTISING BROCHURE

1941

THE '41 CADILLACS had a powerful, sweeping glamour that was the envy of custom coachbuilders the world over. Hopes of returning to the wheel of a romantic '41 Series 62 Convertible kept many a GI sane. With egg-crate grille, swooping wings, concealed fuel filler, and Hydra-Matic shifting, it was the last word in modernity.

KEY FEATURES
• Horsepower up from 135 to 150 bhp
• New coffin-nose hood
• Optional Hydra-Matic transmission
• Record 59,572 models sold
• Genuine top speed of 161 km/h (100 mph)

1947

AFTER A FOUR-YEAR consumer drought, Cadillac found themselves with 200,000 orders and only 104,000 cars. Although a warmed-over pre-war design, the '46 and '47 Cads had a sleek, wind-cheating smoothness full of rapid purpose. They were classically correct and aesthetically stunning – not bad for a car with two tonnes of bulk.

KEY DEVELOPMENTS
• First true "jellybean" body shape
• Smoothest car engine of its day
• Sombrero deep-dish wheel covers
• Modified Cadillac "V" crest
• Grille bars reduced from six to five

1949 CADILLAC
Series 62

BELIEVE THE HYPE
Cadillac advertisements trumpeted that the '49 was "the world's most beautiful car", and the simple yet elegant styling caught the public's imagination.

AMONG MINOR DESIGN CHANGES FROM 1948 WAS THE MORE SQUARED-OFF REAR

LG·136
NY EMPIRE STATE 57

1949 CADILLAC SERIES 62

1948

THE '48 CADILLAC was the first to define the shape of the typical post-war American family sedan. A magnificent design package, it was clean, curvaceous, and beautiful, and that '49 engine was a honey. With the best styling and the finest engine in the business, Cadillac became the zenith of good taste.

KEY DEVELOPMENTS
• First of the fins
• First-generation modern GM OHV V8
• Class-leading economy and performance
• Distinctive fastback styling
• First luxury hardtop
• Front wing line within bodywork

1955

'55 WAS A BANNER year for the motor industry as well as Cadillac's most successful to date, with 141,000 units built. Horsepower was up to 250 (270 in the Eldorado), and the Florentine roof was extended to sedans. Even the Dagmars were bigger, causing many complaints from other drivers savaged in parking lots.

KEY DEVELOPMENTS
• Eldorado has all accessories as standard except air-conditioning
• Compression ratio improved
• Redesigned egg-crate grille
• New rectangular side lights below headlights
• Extended side moulding

1959

OUTRAGEOUS AND ebullient, the '59 Cadillac had ridiculously extravagant tail fins. The ultimate iron dinosaur, it was soon pilloried as proof that late Fifties America was out to lunch. But because of its flamboyance, the '59 is now a fiercely prized collector's car, with Biarritz Convertibles fetching as much as Ferraris.

KEY DEVELOPMENTS
• New 390cid engine
• Improved power steering
• Revised suspension
• World's highest tail fins
• 14 models in four series available

1961

ALL '61 MODELS CAME with the 390cid, 325 bhp V8, and the new, crisp styling was inspired by GM's Bill Mitchell, who had begun to clean up the Caddy look in 1960. Family resemblance was strong, with the Series 62 hardtop coupe looking very much like the upmarket de Ville, and the Eldorado Biarritz almost identical to the Series 62 Convertible.

KEY DEVELOPMENTS
• Rubberized front and rear coil springs replace problematic air suspension system
• Wheelbases shorter on most models
• Self-adjusting brakes from 1960, plus an automatic vacuum parking-brake release
• All Cads offer lifetime chassis lubrication
• Dual exhausts no longer available

NEW POWER UNIT
The trendsetting new OHV 331cid V8 developed 160 bhp and weighed 85 kg (188 lb) less than the reliable but bulky L-head design. It made the '49 one of the fastest cars on the road.

CURVED WINDSCREEN WAS A NOVELTY FOR A 1949 CAR

PROTOTYPE ENGINE WAS RUN FOR 541 HOURS AND FOUND TO BE IN PERFECT CONDITION

GRILLE WAS HEAVIER ON THE '49 THAN ON THE '48, AFTER FRANK HERSHEY TOLD HARLEY EARL THAT HE WAS NOT KEEN ON THE ORIGINAL DESIGN

LG·136
NY EMPIRE STATE 57

1949 PONTIAC
Chieftain

STYLISH CHIEFTAIN LOGO

UP TO '49, PONTIACS looked and felt like pre-war leftovers. Sure, they were reliable and solid, but they had a reputation as middle-of-the-road cars for middle-aged, middle-class buyers. Pontiac were out of kilter with the glamour boom of post-war America. 1949 was a watershed for Pontiac – the first post-war restyles were unveiled, with the new Harley Earl-designed envelope bodies trumpeted as "the smartest of all new cars". In reality, their Silver Streak styling was old hat, tracing its origins back to the Thirties. But although mechanically tame – with aged flathead sixes and eights – the '49 Chieftain Convertibles mark the transition from upright pre-war designs to post-war glitz. These were the days when the modern convertible really came into its own.

INTERIOR
A three-speed manual gearbox was standard, but Hydra-Matic automatic was available as a $159 option. There was no power steering or power brakes.

CHIEFTAIN ORNAMENT
The Indian chief bonnet mascot never smiled but the head was illuminated at night by a 2 watt bulb that gave a warm, yellow glow.

WINDSCREEN
This was called the Safe-T-View and was one of a series of gimmicky Pontiac names that also included Carry-More boot, Tru-Arc Safety Steering, and Easy-Access doors.

REAR AXLE
Optional rear axle ratios were Standard, Economy, and Mountain.

DECORATION
The five parallel chrome bars were a Silver Streak hallmark and were aped by the British Austin Atlantic.

ENGINE
Six-pot engines were cast iron with four main bearings, solid valve lifters, and a puny Carter one-barrel carb. Choosing the straight eight gave you a measly extra 13 bhp but only cost $23 more. Pontiac did not offer a V8 unit in any of their models until 1955.

SPOTLIGHTS
Dual side-mounted spotlights were trigger-operated.

1949 PONTIAC CHIEFTAIN CONVERTIBLE DE LUXE
Adverts promised that "Dollar for Dollar, You Can't Beat a Pontiac", and the Chieftain was proof that Pontiac weren't bluffing. Convertibles cost just $2,183 for the six and $2,206 for the eight and were remarkable value for money. The engine was set well forward in a very rigid cantilever box girder frame, and the rear seat was positioned ahead of the rear axle and wing to give what Pontiac dubbed a "cradle ride".

CHROME PANEL
Extravagant gravel guards only appeared on the De Luxe and added a classy flourish.

REAR BUMPER
Intricate bumper was designed to prevent young women in hooped skirts from getting them caught in the bumper when opening the boot.

SPECIFICATIONS
MODEL 1949 Pontiac Chieftain Convertible
PRODUCTION Not available
BODY STYLE Two-door convertible.
CONSTRUCTION Steel body and chassis.
ENGINE 239cid straight six, 249cid straight eight.
POWER OUTPUT 90–103 bhp.
TRANSMISSION Three-speed manual, optional four-speed Hydra-Matic automatic.
SUSPENSION *Front:* coil springs; *Rear:* leaf springs.
BRAKES Front and rear drums.
MAXIMUM SPEED 80–95 mph (129–153 km/h)
0–60 MPH (0–96 KM/H) 13–15 sec
A.F.C. 15 mpg (5.3 km/l)

The Fifties

The post-war feel-good factor made the Fifties a decade of unprecedented leisure and prosperity. In this heady new world of television, rock 'n' roll, nuclear power, and the space race, Americans reached for the Moon.

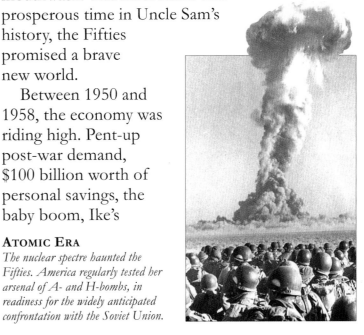

FAIRLANE, "THE TOUCH OF TOMORROW" IN '57

NEVER AN ERA remembered for highbrow culture, life in Fifties America did imitate art – but it was art viewed through a flickering screen. Shows like Walt Disney's weekly *Disneyland*, the *I Love Lucy* sitcom, and the *Ed Sullivan Show* changed the country's mindset. Television became a national narcotic and the tube of plenty. With seven million sets sold every year, the old order had no choice but to quietly evaporate. Television changed America's consciousness forever.

Although McCarthyism, the shadow of nuclear terror, and the Korean War dominated headlines, most Americans were busy having a good time with their bobby socks, Tupperware parties, barbecued steaks, and Billy Graham's way to God without sacrifice. These were the years of rampant consumerism, when the country binged on a

decade-long spending spree. In 1952, Americans spent $255 million on chewing gum, $235 million on greeting cards, and a staggering $23 million on mouthwash. The most stable and prosperous time in Uncle Sam's history, the Fifties promised a brave new world.

Between 1950 and 1958, the economy was riding high. Pent-up post-war demand, $100 billion worth of personal savings, the baby boom, Ike's

ATOMIC ERA
The nuclear spectre haunted the Fifties. America regularly tested her arsenal of A- and H-bombs, in readiness for the widely anticipated confrontation with the Soviet Union.

	1950	1951	1952	1953	1954
AUTOMOTIVE	• **Chevrolet** are America's No. 1 car maker with 1,498,590 cars • First proper Motorama show opens at New York Waldorf • Only 333 **Volkswagen** Beetles sold in entire US • First modern compact introduced, the **Nash** Rambler • **Ford** win coveted Fashion Academy award for styling • **Chevrolet** offer new fully automatic Powerglide transmission	• Ford-O-Matic is **Ford**'s first fully automatic transmission • **Chrysler** announce all-new 331cid hemi-head V8 for the New Yorker, plus power steering for first time • *Hop Up* magazine launched, for hot-rodders and customizers • Office of Price Stabilization allows some car manufacturers to raise prices • One in three cars is automatic	• National steel strike and Korean War slow auto production • **Buick** are third largest maker of convertibles and largest hardtop builder • **Ford**'s first totally new body since 1949 features one-piece curved windscreen • 95 per cent of all **Ford**s have V8s • Office of Price Stabilization drops pegging of new car prices • War cuts make whitewalls scarce	• **GM** lose $10 million • **Dodge** launch famed Hemi V8 and new option, air-conditioning • More chrome as war eases • **Chrysler** introduce PowerFlite automatic 1953 CADILLAC ELDORADO	• **Ford** overtake **Chevrolet** as top maker, with 1,165,942 cars • Spinner hubcap becomes most popular accessory in America • Harley Earl previews first Firebird experimental car at Motorama
HISTORICAL	• President Truman sanctions building of US's first H-bomb • Mao Tse Tung and Stalin sign Mutual Defence Treaty • Joseph McCarthy launches crusade against Communism • First major US battle in Korea • First kidney transplant • Drive-in cinemas being built at rate of 2,200 a year • Nuclear test in Nevada desert • *The Third Man* wins Oscar for black-and-white photography	• Average salary is $1,456 p.a. • *A Streetcar Named Desire* voted best film of 1951 • US Atomic Energy Commission says it can produce electric power from nuclear reactors • *Betty Crocker's Picture Cookbook*, first out in '50, sells its millionth copy	DWIGHT EISENHOWER CELEBRATES ELECTION VICTORY IN 1952  • Eisenhower elected President with largest-yet popular vote • Contraceptive pill introduced • Gene Kelly stars in *Singin' in the Rain* • TWA launch tourist class air travel • Nationally televised detonation of atomic bomb in Nevada desert	• Marilyn Monroe is America's favourite pin-up and appears on the cover of *Playboy* • Khrushchev new Communist Party leader after Stalin's death • Levis are America's No. 1 jeans • A young Elvis Presley walks into Sun Studios, Memphis • *From Here to Eternity* premieres • Soviets admit they have H-bomb • Cinemascope launched • New "stiletto" heels panned as dangerous	• First McDonald's is born • Eisenhower proposes new Interstate highway system • IBM launch first computer • Boeing unveil prototype 707 • Second H-bomb exploded at Bikini Atoll • Elvis sings *That's All Right* • Racial segregation outlawed in US schools • Premiere of *Seven Brides for Seven Brothers* • First nuclear sub launched

DOMESTIC UTOPIA
Set pieces such as this illustrated the Fifties suburban dream, with well-appointed house, Mom with her "New Look" clothes, and Dad and Junior admiring the family's shiny new 1951 Ford Custom.

were buffed to a high sheen or swathed in chrome so a narcissistic nation could admire its reflection.

The middle-class suburbanite looked out of his window and coveted his neighbour's possessions. Success was measured in material terms – a gas barbecue, a swimming pool, a white Corvette. This credo of instant gratification changed everything, including the nation's eating habits. In 1954, Ray Kroc of San Bernadino, a high-school drop-out, came up with a newfangled stand for selling French fries, soda, and 15¢ hamburgers. Today it's a fast-food empire known as McDonald's.

Interstates, and new technology meant that by the end of the decade more than 80 per cent of Americans had not only electric lighting but also refrigerators, telephones, and televisions. Suburbia became a paradise of comfort and convenience, with ranch-style homes, double garages, expansive front lawns, and kitchens with a new state-of-the-art Colorama Frigidaire.

Bright New World

Consumer durables were curvy, bosomy, and brightly coloured. Buyers had had enough of the austere penury of khaki and navy blue, and wanted up-to-the-minute modish pastels to show that their purchases were brand-new. Pink became the colour, as worn by Elvis, Mamie Eisenhower, Cadillacs, steam irons, and even Dad's button-downs. Surfaces

LUSHLY-UPHOLSTERED LOOKS
The mildly rounded 1950 Nash Rambler shows the first flowerings of curvilinear, volumetric design. By the end of the decade, an obsession with full contours would change the American car into a four-wheeled bordello.

1955	1956	1957	1958	1959
• Highest **Ford** output since 1923, but **Chevrolet** are back on top, producing 1,704,667 cars • Big Three auto manufacturers dominate 97 per cent of market • US production at post-war high • Auto makers agree to ban advertisements promoting performance and horsepower • **Cadillac** sales peak at 141,000 • Chic new **Ford** Fairlane launched • 60,000 foreign cars imported into US, including 25,000 **VW** Beetles	• **GM** spend $125 million on new technical centre in Michigan • Federal Highway Act passed • Raymond Loewy blasts "jukeboxes on wheels" *LIMITED EDITION 1956 DeSoto Adventurer*	• **Ford**, with all-new styling, outsell **Chevrolet** 1.67 million to 1.5 • New **Ford** Skyliner is world's first hardtop convertible • **Chevrolet** offer fuel injection and first 1 hp/cu in engine • Thunderbird sales up by half • Edsel launched • New magazine *Custom Cars*	• **Chevrolet** regain lead in car manufacture, with 1,142,460 built • Industry-wide recession; sales worst since World War II • **Chevrolet** introduce highly unpopular seat belts • Thunderbirds get four seats • **Ford** offer Level-Air ride for one year only • 50th birthday for **Chevrolet** • **GM** employ four women in their design department • **Studebaker** offer compact Lark	• Virgil Exner admits that with fins he'd "given birth to a Frankenstein" • Highest fins ever on 1959 Cadillac, although **Ford**, **Lincoln**, and **Mercury** fins almost disappear • **Chevrolet** show their controversial "batwing" fins • **Chrysler** offer Golden Lion V8 • Compact **Ford** Falcon introduced • Flat-six **Chevrolet** Corvair launched • **Chrysler** 300D gets fuel injection • Britain launches the Mini • **Plymouth** Sport Fury introduced
• Disneyland opens in California • James Dean dies in car crash • New phrase "Rock 'n' Roll" coined by DJ Alan Freed • 3-D movies launched • *Billboard* introduces Top 100 record chart; Bill Haley's *Rock Around the Clock* is No.1 for 25 weeks • Marlon Brando wins Best Actor for *On the Waterfront* • Soviets test H-bomb	• Martin Luther King Jr. fights for black rights using peace • JFK goes for Vice-President nomination • To celebrate 11 hit records, Elvis buys his first pink Cadillac • First video tape shown • *My Fair Lady* opens • 60 per cent in US own homes *JAMES DEAN*	• USSR first in space with Sputnik • Eisenhower and Nixon sworn in for second term • Jack Kerouac's novel *On the Road* published • Breathalyzer tested to measure alcohol on drivers' breath • "Cat", "dig", "cool", "square", and "hip" enter the language • Elvis in first film, *Jailhouse Rock* • Bogart dies of throat cancer • Jerry Lee Lewis sings *Great Balls of Fire*	• First US satellite launched • Pan American World Airways begin first transatlantic flights • NASA created • Elvis drafted • First stereo record on sale • Hope Diamond donated to Smithsonian Institution • *West Side Story* opens • Danny and the Juniors have smash hit with *At the Hop* • Last Communist newspaper, *The Daily Worker*, folds	• Fidel Castro becomes Cuban premier • Nixon and Khrushchev hold "kitchen debate" • First Russian rocket to reach moon • UK's first motorway, the M1, opens • Buddy Holly dies • Bobby Darin wows with *Mack the Knife* *HULA-HOOP*

PATRIOTIC PURCHASING
The auto industry was the biggest player in the nation's economy, and consumers obsessed with keeping up to date were persuaded that buying a new car every year would help to build a stronger America.

With less time spent on cooking and eating, Americans had more time for shopping. Parents raised in the Depression had no problem swallowing the mantra that more was most definitely better. Teenagers and adults alike gorged on everything from Bill Haley records and hula-hoops to cashmere sweaters, trips to Hawaii, and hot-rods. Madison Avenue spent $10 billion a year to persuade consumers that improving their lives with material possessions wasn't just alright, it was the American Way. This illusion of fulfilment was made possible by a small rectangle of plastic dubbed the credit card. Diners' Club appeared in 1950, followed by the American Express card, and by the end of the decade Sears Roebuck alone had over 10 million credit accounts.

Prosperity brought leisure, and American consumers spent $30 billion a year killing time. Sales of power tools, model kits, stamp albums, and painting sets soared. In two years Craftmaster sold Paint By Numbers sets to the value of

MAGIC KINGDOM
Disneyland, opened in 1955, was like a living TV, where visitors could change channels from medieval castles to rocket ships, with souvenir shops serving as "commercials".

NEW ROCK 'N' ROLL AGE
The name of Bill Haley's group, the Comets, echoed America's fascination with rockets and the space age. Between 1955 and 1957 their hit Rock Around the Clock *was in the US charts for 37 weeks.*

$10 million and even Eisenhower was a regular dauber. For Americans wanting somewhere to go to spend time and money, the $17 million Disneyland was opened by Walt Disney on 13 July 1955, watched by 24 live ABC cameras and hosted by none other than Ronald Reagan. Two years later Disney's dream world had welcomed 10 million visitors, most of whom arrived by car.

Freedom on Wheels

The massive American automobiles of the Fifties, although they looked like rocket-launchers with 38D cups, were built as family cars, perfect for weekend outings and holidays. As one Ford ad of the period put it, the car promised "freedom to come and go as we please in this big country of ours". A freedom from the sameness of the suburbs and the ennui of prosperity, the car became a symbol of blissful escapism.

LOW-SLUNG PROFILE
By mid-decade, American cars had become so long and low that many reached only to shoulder height. The motor manufacturers followed a dramatic "squashing" policy all through the Fifties, and this 1957 Mercury Turnpike Cruiser is as squat as they come. The Turnpike Cruiser boasted gadgets such as a retractable Breezaway rear window and a 49-position driver's seat.

HARD-SELL WITH CLASS
Cars were sold hard on television, and Lincoln used the Ed Sullivan Show *to highlight their 1955 line-up. Their elegant spokeswoman, Julia Meade, wearing an evening dress and running her gloved hands over the upholstery, was the first TV personality to be wholly identified with a single product.*

BIZARRE CREATIONS
By the end of the Fifties, automotive styling had become so extravagant that panning the American car became a pastime that threatened to replace baseball as a national sport. Within a few short years of its launch, this outlandish 1959 Cadillac Series 62 would be lampooned as a figure of fun.

By 1956 America owned three-quarters of all the cars in the world. Freeways, multi-level parking lots, shopping malls, drive-in restaurants, and cinemas sprouted like dandelions after rain. Americans got high on an orgy of Naugahyde and power steering.

Buying into the American Dream

Suddenly stylists replaced designers, and the car shed its machine-like properties to become an instrument of fantasy. Not everyone was enthralled; Woodrow Wilson called the American car "a picture of the arrogance of wealth", and John Keats in his *Insolent Chariots* said "there is little wrong with the American car that is not wrong with the American public".

But Americans were willing, indeed eager, to spend vast amounts each year on a machine that symbolized their desires, reflected themselves, and expressed their fantasies. Detroit made them believe that ever-increasing consumption would genuinely help to build a brighter and richer America.

PUTTING ON THE RITZ
The 1953 Packard Caribbean Convertible was one of the most spectacular and lavish cars of the decade. A design that evolved from Packard's recent Pan American show cars, it outsold its arch-rival, the glamorous Cadillac Eldorado.

And buy they did. In 1955 Detroit shipped eight million new cars to showrooms, accounting for $65 billion or 20 per cent of the Gross National Product. GM became the first corporation to earn $1 billion in a single year, and their touring Motorama exhibitions drew two million visitors at every stop. The affluent society rolled effortlessly on, cushioned by fat Goodyear whitewalls. The American car of the Fifties may have been all jets and Jane Russell, but it fanned the flames of the new industrial prosperity, created those rows of neat clapboard houses and those miles of arrow-straight freeways, and gave America an upward mobility that was the envy of the world.

1950 CHRYSLER
Imperial

THE IMPERIAL FOUR-DOOR SEDAN COST $3,055 BEFORE
OPTIONAL EXTRAS WERE ADDED

IN 1950 CHRYSLER WERE celebrating their silver jubilee, an anniversary year with a sting in its tail. The Office of Price Stabilization had frozen car prices, there was a four-month strike, and serious coal and steel shortages were affecting the industry.

The '50 Imperial was a Chrysler New Yorker with a special roof and interior trim from the Derham Body Company. The jewels in Chrysler's crown, the Imperials were meant to lock horns with the best of Cadillac, Packard, and Lincoln. With Ausco-Lambert disc brakes, Prestomatic transmission, and a MoPar compass, they used the finest technology Chrysler could muster. The trouble was, only 10,650 Imperials drove out of the door in 1950, the hemi-head V8 wouldn't arrive until the next year, buyers were calling it a Chrysler rather than an Imperial, and that frumpy styling looked exactly like what it was – yesterday's lunch warmed up again.

ENGINE
The inline L-head eight developed 135 bhp and had a cast-iron block with five main bearings. The carburettor was a Carter single-barrel, and Prestomatic automatic transmission with fluid drive came as standard.

CHRYSLER LOGO
The celebrated designer Virgil Exner joined Chrysler in 1949 but arrived too late to improve the looks of the moribund Imperial.

INTERIOR
Chryslers' interiors were as restrained and conservative as the people who drove them. Turn-key ignition replaced push-button in 1950, which was also the first year of electric windows.

WINDSCREEN
The front screen was still old-fashioned two-piece flat glass, which made the Imperial look rather antiquated.

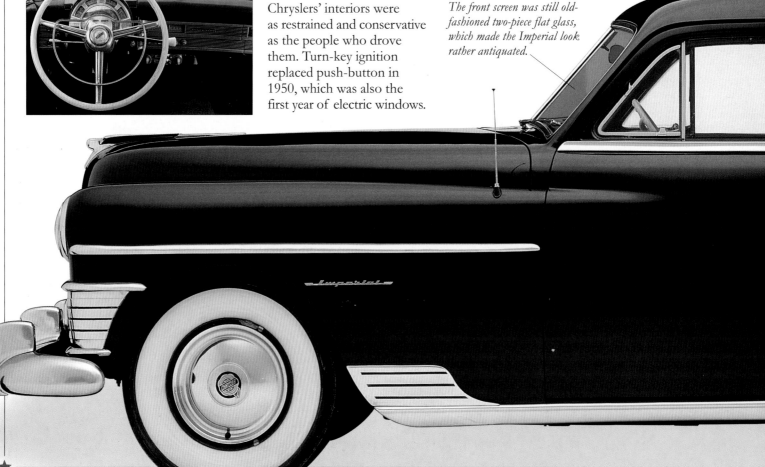

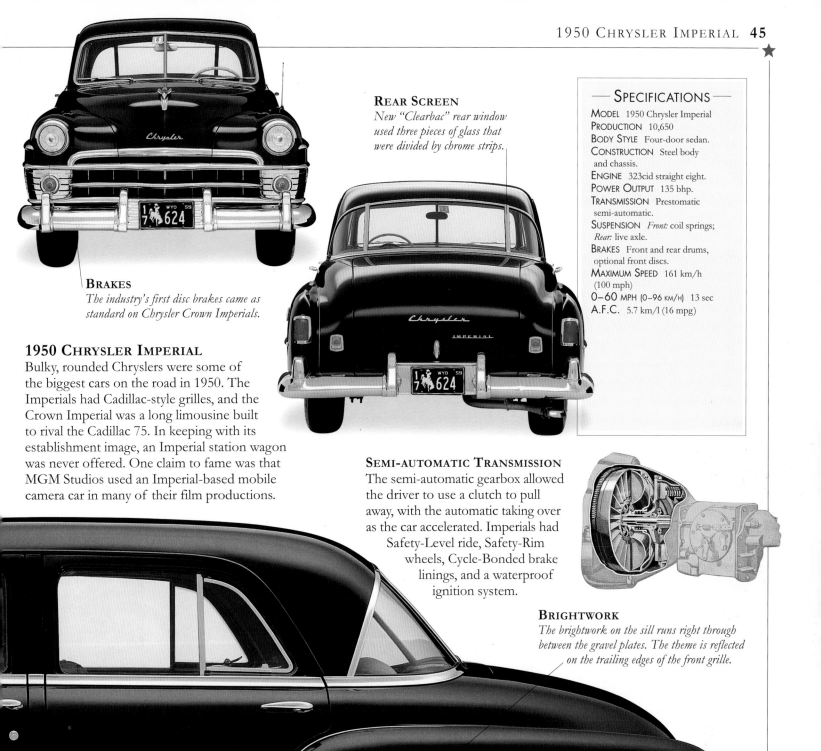

REAR SCREEN
New "Clearbac" rear window used three pieces of glass that were divided by chrome strips.

SPECIFICATIONS
MODEL 1950 Chrysler Imperial
PRODUCTION 10,650
BODY STYLE Four-door sedan.
CONSTRUCTION Steel body and chassis.
ENGINE 323cid straight eight.
POWER OUTPUT 135 bhp.
TRANSMISSION Prestomatic semi-automatic.
SUSPENSION *Front:* coil springs; *Rear:* live axle.
BRAKES Front and rear drums, optional front discs.
MAXIMUM SPEED 161 km/h (100 mph)
0–60 MPH (0–96 KM/H) 13 sec
A.F.C. 5.7 km/l (16 mpg)

BRAKES
The industry's first disc brakes came as standard on Chrysler Crown Imperials.

1950 CHRYSLER IMPERIAL

Bulky, rounded Chryslers were some of the biggest cars on the road in 1950. The Imperials had Cadillac-style grilles, and the Crown Imperial was a long limousine built to rival the Cadillac 75. In keeping with its establishment image, an Imperial station wagon was never offered. One claim to fame was that MGM Studios used an Imperial-based mobile camera car in many of their film productions.

SEMI-AUTOMATIC TRANSMISSION
The semi-automatic gearbox allowed the driver to use a clutch to pull away, with the automatic taking over as the car accelerated. Imperials had Safety-Level ride, Safety-Rim wheels, Cycle-Bonded brake linings, and a waterproof ignition system.

BRIGHTWORK
The brightwork on the sill runs right through between the gravel plates. The theme is reflected on the trailing edges of the front grille.

1950 DeSoto
Custom

HERNANDO ADORNS
THE DESOTO LOGO

THE DESOTO OF 1950 had a glittery glamour that cheered up post-war America. Hailed as "cars built for owner satisfaction", they were practical, boxy, and tough. DeSoto was a long-time taxi builder that, in the steel-starved years of 1946–48, managed to turn out 11,600 cabs, most of which plied the streets of New York.

Despite more chrome upfront than any other Chrysler product, DeSotos still laboured on with an L-head six-pot 250cid mill. The legendary Firedome V8 wouldn't arrive until 1952. But body shapes for 1950 were the prettiest ever, and the American public reacted with delight, buying up 133,854 units in the calendar year, ranking DeSoto 14th in the industry. Top-line Custom Convertibles had a very reasonable sticker price of $2,578 and came with Tip-Toe hydraulic shift with Gyrol fluid drive as standard. The austere post-war years were a sales Disneyland for the makers of these sparkling cars, but DeSoto's roll couldn't last. By 1961 they'd disappeared forever.

ADVERTISEMENT
During the 1950s, car advertising copy became extravagant, relying more on hyperbole than fact. This DeSoto promotion was no exception.

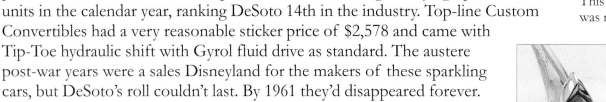

DESOTO MASCOT
Optional bonnet mascot was one Hernando DeSoto, a 17th-century Spanish conquistador. The mascot glowed in the dark.

REAR WING
The DeSoto body shape still carried hints of the separate wings of pre-war cars.

GRILLE
The mammoth-tooth grille would be scaled down for 1951. '50 models are easily spotted by their body-colour vertical grille divider, unique to this year.

INTERIOR
'50 DeSotos came in two levels of trim. De Luxe, the poverty package, was outsold three to one by the plusher Custom, at $200 more. Direction signals and back-up lights were offered as standard on the Custom, while options included heater, electric clock, and two-tone paint. Convertibles came with whitewalls and wheel covers.

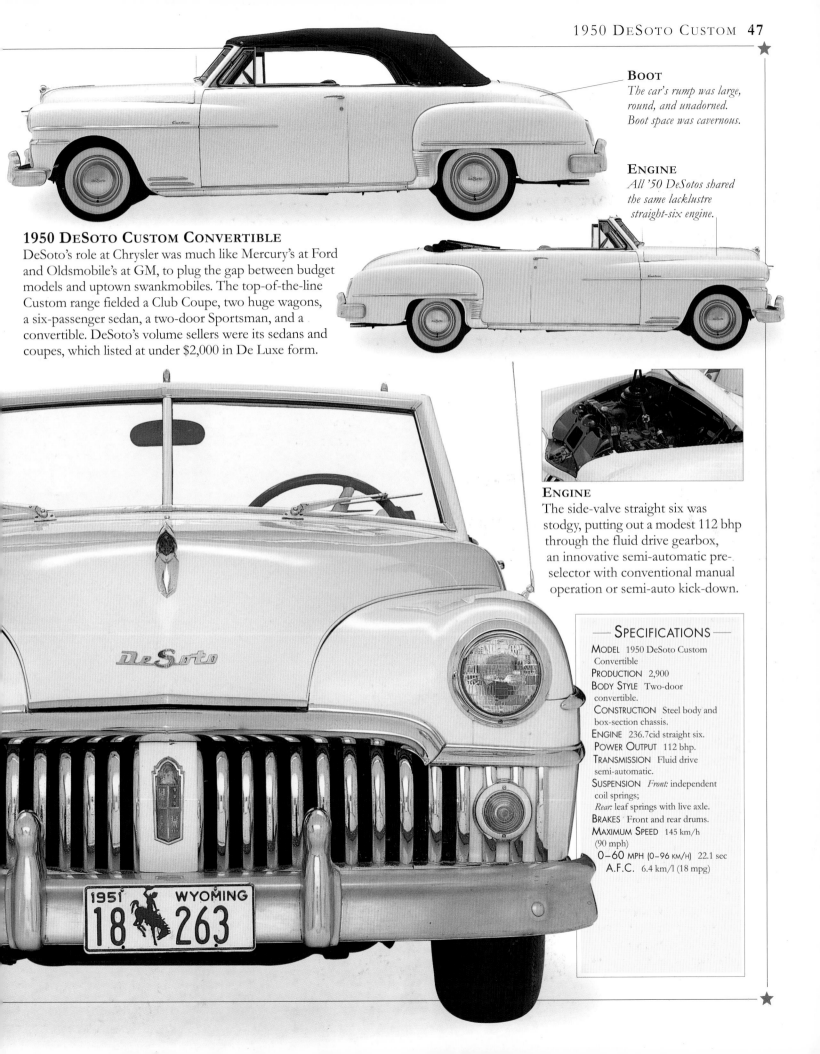

BOOT
The car's rump was large, round, and unadorned. Boot space was cavernous.

ENGINE
All '50 DeSotos shared the same lacklustre straight-six engine.

1950 DeSoto Custom Convertible

DeSoto's role at Chrysler was much like Mercury's at Ford and Oldsmobile's at GM, to plug the gap between budget models and uptown swankmobiles. The top-of-the-line Custom range fielded a Club Coupe, two huge wagons, a six-passenger sedan, a two-door Sportsman, and a convertible. DeSoto's volume sellers were its sedans and coupes, which listed at under $2,000 in De Luxe form.

ENGINE
The side-valve straight six was stodgy, putting out a modest 112 bhp through the fluid drive gearbox, an innovative semi-automatic pre-selector with conventional manual operation or semi-auto kick-down.

SPECIFICATIONS

MODEL 1950 DeSoto Custom Convertible

PRODUCTION 2,900

BODY STYLE Two-door convertible.

CONSTRUCTION Steel body and box-section chassis.

ENGINE 236.7cid straight six.

POWER OUTPUT 112 bhp.

TRANSMISSION Fluid drive semi-automatic.

SUSPENSION *Front:* independent coil springs; *Rear:* leaf springs with live axle.

BRAKES Front and rear drums.

MAXIMUM SPEED 145 km/h (90 mph)

0–60 MPH (0–96 KM/H) 22.1 sec

A.F.C. 6.4 km/l (18 mpg)

1952 KAISER
Henry J. Corsair

KAISER LOGO ON THE
STEERING WHEEL

IN THE EARLY 1950s, the major motor manufacturers reckoned that small cars meant small profits, so low-priced transportation was left to independent companies like Nash, Willys, and Kaiser-Frazer. In 1951, a streamlined, Frazer-less Kaiser launched "America's Most Important New Car", the Henry J.

An 80 bhp six-cylinder "Supersonic" engine gave the Corsair frugal fuel consumption, with Kaiser claiming that every third mile in a Henry J. was free. The market, however, was unconvinced. At $1,561, the Corsair cost more than the cheapest big Chevy, wasn't built as well, and depreciated rapidly. Small wonder then that only 107,000 were made. Had America's first serious economy car been launched seven years later during the '58 recession, the Henry J. may well have been a best-seller.

PRODUCTION
The Henry J. was built at the Willow Run factory in Michigan. Despite the caption under the main image that reads "Final inspection. Everything must be perfect", quality was poor, and the car quickly earned itself a second-rate reputation.

RACING HENRY J.
In 1952, a Henry J. entered the Monte Carlo Rally and, to everybody's surprise, finished in a creditable 20th position.

CHASSIS
The double-channel box chassis was orthodox and sturdy. The 2.54 m (100 in) wheelbase was short but the interior space generous. America's new family car was "long, low, and handsome... The Henry J. is a joy to drive and comfortable to ride in – the Smart Car for Smart People".

INTERIOR
The interior was seriously austere and gimmick-free. Apart from overdrive and automatic transmission, very few factory options were available. The few controls included starter, ignition, light, and choke switches.

REPLACEMENT WING
Bolt-on front and rear wings were part of the Henry J.'s money-saving philosophy.

COLOUR SCHEME
*Blue Satin was one of nine
colour options available.*

ROOF LINE
*High roof line owed its existence
to the fact that Kaiser's
chairman always wore a hat.*

1952 KAISER HENRY J. CORSAIR DELUXE

The stubborn head of Kaiser industries
insisted that the Henry J., originally designed
as a full-size car by designer Howard "Dutch"
Darrin, be scaled down. American Metal
Products of Detroit created the prototype,
which Darrin then tweaked, not altogether
successfully. Luggage space was among the
largest of any passenger sedan; with the rear
seat folded there was 50 cu ft of boot area.

FIN FASHION
*Modest dorsal fin was quite
fashionable for 1952.*

SPECIFICATIONS

MODEL 1952 Kaiser Henry J.
Corsair Deluxe
PRODUCTION 12,900
BODY STYLE Two-door,
five-seater sedan.
CONSTRUCTION Steel body
and chassis.
ENGINE 134cid four, 161cid six.
POWER OUTPUT 68–80 bhp.
TRANSMISSION Three-speed
manual with optional overdrive,
optional three-speed Hydra-Matic
automatic.
SUSPENSION *Front:* coil springs;
Rear: leaf springs with live axle.
BRAKES Front and rear drums.
MAXIMUM SPEED 140 km/h
(87 mph)
0–60 MPH (0–96 KM/H) 17 sec
A.F.C. 12 km/l (34 mpg)

BOSS BADGING
The Henry J. nameplate
came from Henry J. Kaiser,
chairman of the Kaiser-
Frazer Corporation.

TYRES
*Corsairs were shod with
skinny 5.9x15 tube tyres.*

1954 CHEVROLET
Corvette

CORVETTE FLAGS FOUND
ON THE CAR'S BONNET

A CARICATURE OF A EUROPEAN roadster, the first Corvette of 1953 was more show than go. With typical arrogance, Harley Earl was more interested in the way it looked than the way it went. But he did identify that car consumers were growing restless and saw a huge market for a new type of auto opium. With everybody's dreams looking exactly the same, the plastic 'Vette brought a badly needed shot of designed-in diversity. Early models may have been cramped and slow, but they looked like they'd been lifted straight off a Motorama turntable, which they had. Building them was a nightmare though, and for a while GM lost money on each one. Still, nobody minded because Chevrolet now had a new image — as the company that came up with the first American sports car.

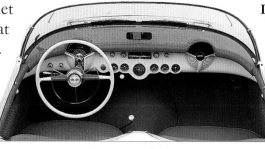

INTERNAL HANDLES
Like the British sports cars it aped, the '54 'Vette's door handles lived on the inside. Windows were apologetic side curtains that leaked and flapped; it would take two years for glass windows to come into the equation.

INTERIOR
An aeronautical fantasy, the Corvette's dashboard had a futuristic, space-age feel. Not until 1958 was the row of dials repositioned to a more practical, front of the driver, location.

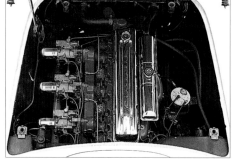

ENGINE
Souped-up Blue Flame Six may have had triple carbs, higher compression, and a high-lift cam, but it was still old and wheezy. 'Vettes had to wait until 1955 for the V8 they deserved.

ENGINE WAS MOUNTED
WELL BACK IN FRAME TO
IMPROVE HANDLING

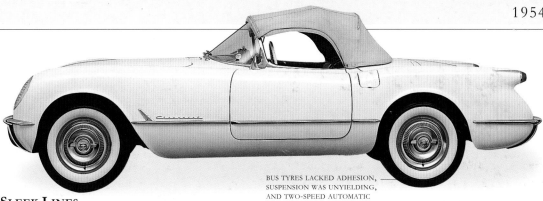

SLEEK LINES

The cute little body with minimal glitz was one of Earl's best efforts. But, being smitten with jet styling, he couldn't resist adding the "jet pod" tail-lights, which spoil the car's symmetry.

ODDLY ENOUGH, 80 PER CENT OF ALL '54 CORVETTES WERE PAINTED WHITE

BUS TYRES LACKED ADHESION, SUSPENSION WAS UNYIELDING, AND TWO-SPEED AUTOMATIC JERKED ALL OVER THE PLACE

OVERVIEW

The cleverly packaged fibreglass body was rather tricky to make, with no less than 46 different sections. The soft-top folded out of sight below a neat lift-up panel.

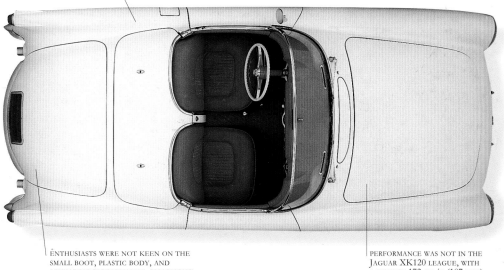

ENTHUSIASTS WERE NOT KEEN ON THE SMALL BOOT, PLASTIC BODY, AND LETHARGIC PERFORMANCE, BUT BETTER THINGS WERE AROUND THE CORNER

PERFORMANCE WAS NOT IN THE JAGUAR XK120 LEAGUE, WITH A MODEST 172 KM/H (107 MPH) TOP SPEED

SPECIFICATIONS

MODEL 1954 Chevrolet Corvette
PRODUCTION 3,640
BODY STYLE Two-door, two-seater sports.
CONSTRUCTION Fibreglass body, steel chassis.
ENGINE 235.5cid straight six.
POWER OUTPUT 150 bhp.
TRANSMISSION Two-speed Powerglide automatic.
SUSPENSION *Front:* coil springs; *Rear:* leaf springs with live axle.
BRAKES Front and rear drums.
MAXIMUM SPEED 172 km/h (107 mph)
0–60 MPH (0–96 KM/H) 8–12 sec
A.F.C. 7 km/l (20 mpg)

EXHIBITION SUCCESS

The 'Vette's shape was based on the 1952 EX-122 show car, and this was one of the few Motorama dream cars to go into production virtually unchanged. The original plan to produce the 'Vette in steel was shelved after widespread acclaim for the fibreglass body from visitors to Motorama.

OUTBOARD-MOUNTED REAR LEAF SPRINGS HELPED CORNERING STABILITY

1954 CHEVROLET CORVETTE

EVOLUTION OF THE CHEVROLET CORVETTE

HOWLING ALONG the freeways of America, the 'Vette has always been special. In fact, a whole mystique has grown up around Chevy's wild child. Perhaps it's because of its personification of rebellion, no-compromise attitude, or the people that drive them, but the 'Vette has endured as America's alter ego – proof positive that not everybody wants to pilot slushy barges half-a-block long. When the motoring day of reckoning comes, the Corvette will be up there with the best of them.

1953

THAT THE 'VETTE EXISTS at all is due to the genius of one man – Harley Earl. It started life as no more than a half-formed thought, spinning gently on a Motorama turntable. Within months, the Corvette was a reality and proved the perfect product for a generation of suburban good-timers whose beloved Levis were now feeling the strain.

KEY FEATURES
• Polo White EX-122 show car wows the crowds at 1952 Motorama
• Production cars have no exterior door handles or side windows
• Base engine is 150 bhp 235.5cid straight six
• Calendar year sales of 300 cars

1956

THE V8 LUMP & FUEL injection helped, but that swooping, coved body of '56 did more than anything to guarantee the Corvette's future. Macho, horny, and much more refined, the second-generation 'Vette ('56–'62) could now lock horns with Uncle Henry's T-Bird – and it had wind-up windows. Today, it is one of the icons of Fifties car design.

KEY DEVELOPMENTS
• New 210 bhp 265cid V8 base engine
• New curved body and tail-lights
• Outside door handles and wind-up windows instead of clumsy side curtains
• Exhausts exit through rear bumper guards
• Transistorized self-seeking radio option

1963

THE STING RAY wowed the world like the Jaguar E-Type. For the first time in the Corvette's history it was a sell-out. Demand was up by 50 per cent and the factory couldn't cope. Waiting lists stretched to infinity, and nobody got a discount. These were the most desirable Corvettes of all, and that magical '63 split-window Coupe was a car to die for.

KEY DEVELOPMENTS
• New body and Sting Ray name
• 327cid V8 option
• Improved interior with dual cockpits
• Unique split rear window
• New chassis frame
• Independent rear suspension
• Bigger drum brakes

1954 CHEVROLET
Corvette

REAR PLATE PROBLEMS
Early cars had licence plates in a plastic niche that misted up. Chevrolet inserted two bags of desiccant material to absorb the moisture.

TWIN-COWL DASH WAS PURE BUCK ROGERS

QUALITY STYLING
Rear-wing detailing is glorious, and shows Earl's genius at its very best.

IMPACT PROTECTION MAY HAVE BEEN VESTIGIAL, BUT FIBREGLASS BODY TOOK KNOCKS WELL

1968	**1978**	**1984**	**1992**

CURVY, CHARISMATIC, but compromised, the late '60s 'Vette was hardly a quantum leap forward. Emasculated by Federal interference and economic, social, and energy neuroses, Chevy were forced to tame their bad boy. Suddenly the 'Vette changed from a tyre-shredding banshee to a blow-dried boulevardier. Ironically, its popularity actually increased.

KEY DEVELOPMENTS
- New "Mako Shark" styling
- Redesigned interior
- New T-Top Sport Coupe model with removable roof panels
- Massive 427cid V8 available
- Wipers now behind vacuum-operated panel

THE CORVETTE celebrated its silver anniversary in '78, marking the moment with a new fastback roof line and wide rear window that tucked round the car's sides. The interior felt more spacious, and rear vision was vastly improved. A 'Vette was the official Indy pace car in '78 and Chevy produced a run of 6,200 limited edition look-alikes.

KEY DEVELOPMENTS
- Base engine is 350cid V8
- Larger luggage area
- Crossed flags insignia returns to nose and sides
- 500,000th 'Vette made in 1977
- Optional $995 five-speed gearbox

THE ARRIVAL OF the likes of RX-7s, Datsun Zs, and Porsche 928s meant that America's sports car had to grow up fast. The sixth-generation 'Vette of '83 was the fastest, best-handling, and most radical ever. Engineered from the ground up and truly sophisticated, it was built to take on the world's elite, while still retaining the Corvette's uniquely American personality.

KEY DEVELOPMENTS
- Hugely improved roadholding
- Steel backbone chassis with unitized body structure
- New Girlock ventilated disc brakes
- New 4+3 gearbox
- Now one of the half-dozen fastest production cars in the world

IN THE WORLD OF THE motor car, 44 years is an eternity for a model name. Yet the 'Vette has not just survived, it has prospered and become a truly great car. The one millionth Corvette rolled off the production line in 1992 and, as this book is being written, there's a new 'Vette poised to steal America's heart all over again.

KEY DEVELOPMENTS
- New 300 bhp V8
- ZR-1 option has twin-cam 32-valve with 405 bhp
- LT1 option has six-speed manual or four-speed automatic gearbox
- ABS and driver's-side airbag standard
- GM's first "passive keyless" entry system

STONE-GUARDS ON LIGHTS WERE CULLED FROM EUROPEAN RACING CARS, BUT CRITICIZED FOR BEING TOO FEMININE

EARLY PRODUCTION
The first cars were literally hand-built at the Flint, Michigan, factory. Plans to turn out 1,000 cars a month in 1954 were hit by poor early sales.

GUIDING WORDS
Earl's advice to stylists working on the Corvette was to "go all the way and then back off". They didn't back off much!

EARL ADMITTED THAT SHARK-TOOTH GRILLE WAS ROBBED FROM CONTEMPORARY FERRARIS

MN·1744
NY EMPIRE STATE 57

1954 HUDSON
Hornet

BADGE SHOWS TWO
TOWERS AND TWO
GALLEONS

HUDSON DID THEIR BEST IN '54 to clean up their aged 1948 body. Smoother flanks and a lower, wider frontal aspect helped, along with a new dash and brighter fabrics and vinyls. And at long last the windscreen was one-piece. Mechanically it wasn't bad either. In fact, some say the last Step-Down was the best ever. With the straight six came a Twin-H power option, a hot camshaft, and an alloy head that could crank out 170 bhp; it was promptly dubbed "The Fabulous Hornet".

The problem was that everybody had V8s, and by mid-'54 Hudson had haemorrhaged over $6 million. In April that year, Hudson, who'd been around since 1909, were swallowed up by the Nash-Kelvinator Corporation. Yet the Hornet has been rightly recognized as a milestone car and one of the quickest sixes of the era. If Hudson are to be remembered for anything, it should be for their innovative engineers, who could wring the best from ancient designs and tiny budgets.

INTERIOR
The dash was quite modern and glossy but still used Hudson's distinctive single-digit speedo. The Hornet's cabin was liberally laced with chrome, and trim was nylon worsted Bedford cloth and Plastihide in brown, blue, or green. Power steering was offered on Hudsons for the first time in '54.

COLOUR CHOICE
Hornets came in Roman Bronze, Pasture Green, Algerian Blue, St. Clair Grey, Lipstick Red, or Coronation Cream as here.

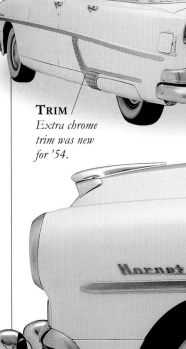

TRIM
Extra chrome trim was new for '54.

ENGINE
Amazingly, Hudson never offered V8 power, which was to hasten their downfall.

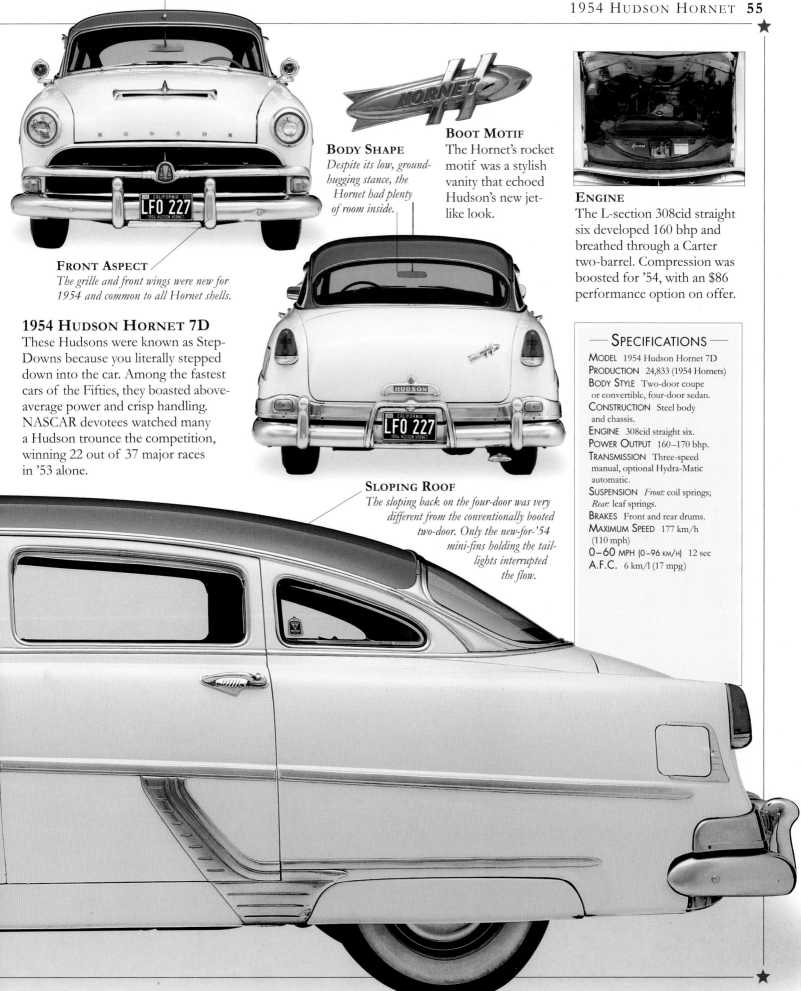

BODY SHAPE
Despite its low, ground-hugging stance, the Hornet had plenty of room inside.

BOOT MOTIF
The Hornet's rocket motif was a stylish vanity that echoed Hudson's new jet-like look.

ENGINE
The L-section 308cid straight six developed 160 bhp and breathed through a Carter two-barrel. Compression was boosted for '54, with an $86 performance option on offer.

FRONT ASPECT
The grille and front wings were new for 1954 and common to all Hornet shells.

1954 HUDSON HORNET 7D

These Hudsons were known as Step-Downs because you literally stepped down into the car. Among the fastest cars of the Fifties, they boasted above-average power and crisp handling. NASCAR devotees watched many a Hudson trounce the competition, winning 22 out of 37 major races in '53 alone.

SLOPING ROOF
The sloping back on the four-door was very different from the conventionally booted two-door. Only the new-for-'54 mini-fins holding the tail-lights interrupted the flow.

SPECIFICATIONS

MODEL 1954 Hudson Hornet 7D
PRODUCTION 24,833 (1954 Hornets)
BODY STYLE Two-door coupe or convertible, four-door sedan.
CONSTRUCTION Steel body and chassis.
ENGINE 308cid straight six.
POWER OUTPUT 160–170 bhp.
TRANSMISSION Three-speed manual, optional Hydra-Matic automatic.
SUSPENSION *Front:* coil springs; *Rear:* leaf springs.
BRAKES Front and rear drums.
MAXIMUM SPEED 177 km/h (110 mph)
0–60 MPH (0–96 KM/H) 12 sec
A.F.C. 6 km/l (17 mpg)

1954 KAISER
Darrin

"THE SPORTS CAR the world has been awaiting" was a monster flop. Designed by Howard "Dutch" Darrin, Kaiser's odd hybrid came about in 1953 as an accident. Henry J. Kaiser, the ill-mannered chairman of the Kaiser Corporation, had so riled Darrin that he disappeared to his California studio, spent his own money, and created a purse-lipped two-seater that looked like it wanted to give you a kiss.

ADVERTS CALLED IT "THE OUTSTANDING PLEASURE CAR OF OUR DAY"

Its futuristic fibreglass body rode on a Henry J. chassis and was powered by a Willys six-pot mill. Alas, the body rippled and cracked, the sliding doors wouldn't slide, and the weedy 90 bhp flathead was no match for Chevy's glam Corvette. At a costly $3,668, the Darrin was in Cadillac territory, and only 435 found buyers. Late in '54, Kaiser-Willys went under, taking the Darrin with them. Few mourned either's demise.

INTERIOR
Standard equipment included electric wipers, tachometer, and a European-style dashboard, with leather trim an optional extra. Whitewall tyres, a one-piece windscreen, and a three-position convertible bonnet were also standard.

1953 DARRIN SPORTSTER
In keeping with Kaiser's reputation for wacky, off-the-wall designs, the Darrin Sportster featured sliding doors that disappeared into the front wings. The trouble was that they rattled, jammed, and didn't open all the way.

AN UNHAPPY ALLIANCE
Henry J. Kaiser was livid that Howard Darrin had worked on the car without his permission. In the end, the Darrin was actually saved by Henry J.'s wife, who reckoned it was "the most beautiful thing" she'd ever seen.

DARRIN BODIES WERE MADE BY BOAT-BUILDERS, GLASSPAR

HOWARD DARRIN FIRST CONCEIVED HIS CONTENTIOUS SLIDING DOORS BACK IN 1922

REAR WING AND TAIL-LIGHT TREATMENT IS RESTRAINED FOR THE YEAR AND REDOLENT OF AN XK JAGUAR

REAR WING TAPERS UPWARDS TO CREATE A FINE TORPEDO-LIKE SHAPE

THE DARRIN'S FRONT WING SLOPES DOWN THROUGH THE DOOR AND MEETS A DRAMATIC KICK-UP OVER THE REAR WHEEL ARCH

SPECIFICATIONS

MODEL 1954 Kaiser Darrin 161
PRODUCTION 435 (total)
BODY STYLE Two-seater sports.
CONSTRUCTION Fibreglass body, steel frame.
ENGINE 161cid six.
POWER OUTPUT 90 bhp.
TRANSMISSION Three-speed manual with optional overdrive.
SUSPENSION *Front:* coil springs; *Rear:* leaf springs.
BRAKES Front and rear drums.
MAXIMUM SPEED 161 km/h (100 mph)
0–60 MPH (0–96 KM/H) 15.1 sec
A.F.C. 9.6 km/l (27 mpg)

BELT UP

The Darrin was remarkable for being only the third US production car to feature seat belts as standard. The other two cars were a Muntz and a Nash.

ENGINE

Kaiser opted for an F-head Willys version of the Henry J. six-pot motor, but with just one carb, it boasted only 10 more horses than standard. After the company folded, Darrin dropped 300 bhp supercharged Caddy V8s into the remaining cars, which went like hell.

STUNNING STYLING

The Darrin was beautifully styled and, unlike most visions of the future, has hardly dated at all. The Landau top could be removed and a hardtop fitted, and, with its three-speed floor shift and overdrive, it could return up to a remarkable 10.6 km/l (30 mpg).

STAR APPROVAL

The French singer Suzanne Bernard shows off the Darrin's dubious doors at the third annual International Motor Sports Show in 1954. Modern restorations have since cured the door problem, but contemporary owners found them to be gimmicky, unreliable, and plain annoying.

KAISER-FRAZER – A TALE OF MINNOWS AND SHARKS

HENRY J. KAISER

KAISER MAY HAVE BEEN an imperial name for a motor car, but it wasn't enough to crack the giant American car maker cartel. Kaiser began auto production in 1946 at Ford's vast Willow Run factory, which had produced Liberator bombers in the war. After the cessation of hostilities, the Government leased the Michigan plant to Henry J. Kaiser and Joe Frazer. Frazer was the president of the Graham Car Company, and Kaiser had earned millions mass-producing ships and houses; he was a "Midas touch" entrepreneur who was seen as serious competition for the market muscle of Ford, GM, and Chrysler.

Initially fielding a two-model programme, the Kaiser was the economy car and the Frazer the luxury job. By 1949, the company had scooped 5 per cent of the market plus a generous $44 million loan from the Government Reconstruction Finance Corporation. K-F's products were full of technical wizardry such as independent torsion-bar suspension, front-wheel drive, and two-piece tailgates on station wagons. But by 1950 the dream had peaked, and sales started to evaporate.

The Willow Run monolith turned out to be more efficient as an aircraft plant than a car factory, and costs hit the roof; Ford had wisely turned it down for that very reason. In 1950, sales were 144,000 cars, but K-F posted a $13 million loss.

THE '48 KAISER SPECIAL WAS MEDIOCRE IN DESIGN AND ENGINEERING

1954 KAISER *Darrin*

THE 90 BHP DARRIN COST $145 MORE THAN THE 150 BHP CHEVY CORVETTE

REAR ASPECT IS SURPRISINGLY BRITISH-LOOKING FOR A CALIFORNIAN DESIGN

LATE DELIVERIES
The Darrin took its time coming. It was first announced on 26 September 1952, with 60 initial prototypes eventually displayed to the public on 11 February 1953. Final production cars reached owners as late as 6 January 1954.

THE MANHATTAN OF '53 WAS SERIOUSLY HANDICAPPED BY THE ABSENCE OF A V8

A hasty restyle in '51 didn't help, and the Henry J., first of the economy compacts, was ugly, overpriced, and slow. The Frazer nameplate was dropped, and the Kaiser empire crumbled fast. Some 3,000 workers were laid off in May 1952 and, despite the addition of a "Penny-Minder" carburettor to the Henry J., it continued to bomb. Kaiser merged with Willys-Overland in 1953, and the Henry J. was finally dropped in favour of the Willys Aero. The merger gave finances a momentary fillip, and Kaisers became sleeker and more luxurious, culminating in the audacious Darrin, which turned out to be another money-loser. Willow Run was bought by GM, and in '55 Kaiser moved to Buenos Aires, where they produced the Carabela model well into the Sixties. Despite burning up $100 million, K-F couldn't break the Big Three's market domination. Apart from being unable to establish a dealer network, deeply conservative US car buyers resisted their avant-garde models. Had the parsimonious Henry J. appeared in recession-wracked 1958, when the motor market was howling for economy compacts, fortune might have smiled on Kaiser-Frazer.

HOWARD DARRIN, WHO HAD A STORMY RELATIONSHIP WITH HENRY J. KAISER

OFFENDING LEGISLATION
The prototype headlight height was too low for state lighting laws, so Kaiser stylists hiked up the front wing line for the real thing. This offended Darrin, who said it gave the car "an uphill look".

FRONT ASPECT LOOKS VERY MUCH LIKE AN EARLY VW KARMANN GHIA

HARDTOP MADE THE CABIN MUCH LESS CLAUSTROPHOBIC AND CRAMPED THAN THAT OF THE SOFT-TOP

SWIVELLING PERSPEX SIDE SCREENS REDUCED COCKPIT BUFFETING

1954 MERCURY
Monterey

MERCURY TRADE-IN
VALUES WERE THE HIGHEST
IN THEIR CLASS

FORD'S UPMARKET MERCURY nameplate was on a roll in 1954. Out went their ancient flathead V8, and in came a new 161 bhp Y-block mill. *Motor Trend* magazine said: "That power will slam you back into the seat when you stomp the throttle." Buyers loved the idea of so much heave and drove away Montereys in their thousands, sending Mercury to an impressive seventh slot in the sales league.

Chic, suave, and still glowing from the James Dean association, Montereys were perfect cruisers for these confident, fat years. Unemployment was low, wage packets were big, and the economy was thumping. Everyone wanted a Merc – "The car that makes any driving easy" – and output for 1954 was a stonking 259,300 units. The following year would be the automobile industry's best ever as punters thronged to showrooms, packing them tighter than Jane Russell's famous brassiere.

HOLLYWOOD GLAMOUR
Film star Gary Cooper poses with his 1951 Monterey. Mere mortals vied to win their dream car in 1956 when TV host Ed Sullivan gave away 80 Mercury Phaetons.

CONVERTIBLE AND CLEAR-TOP OPTIONS
This 1954 ad shows the comely Convertible, priced at $2,554. For another $28, you could own America's first transparent-roofed car, the $2,582 Monterey Sun Valley, painted in either pale yellow or mint green. The front half of the roof contained a tinted Plexiglass section that unfortunately raised the cabin temperature by about 10 degrees.

INTERIOR
Montereys had optional $140 Bendix power steering, which the industry had only just refined. Road testers of the day reckoned it to be the best set-up around. Bendix also supplied the Monterey's power brakes. Interiors came in a wide variety of solid and two-tone cloth, vinyl, and leather trim combinations.

MERCURY DASHBOARDS
RETAINED THE
INTERCEPTOR-TYPE
AIRPLANE PANEL WITH
JOYSTICK CONTROLS.

CUSTOM CHROME
Montereys were the fanciest Mercs and said as much on their front wings, which sported a medallion along with the distinctive chrome side trim. All body types in this series, except the station wagons, were called Monterey Customs and had special wide chrome on the windscreen and side windows.

HIGH PERFORMANCE
The new V8 was road-tested over four million miles, and proved highly competitive on the stock-car circuit, where Mercurys were ranked fifth in the sport.

1954 MERCURY MONTEREY
The Monterey enjoyed enviable success; the four-door sedan was the second most popular model of 1954, with 64,995 made. Customers could choose from 35 different colour schemes – 14 solid shades and 21 two-tones. The car's uptown image was reflected in colour names such as Park Lane Green, Yosemite Yellow, and Country Club Tan.

PILLARLESS COUPE
Two-door models without the central strut had a classic pillarless look with the windows down.

OPTIONAL AUTOMATIC
Options included Merc-O-Matic auto transmission along with power steering, brakes, and four-way seat. The new V161 engine had twin Tornado combustion chambers, alloy pistons, and a four-barrel Holley.

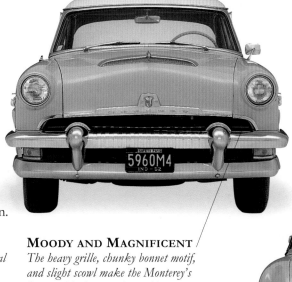

MOODY AND MAGNIFICENT
The heavy grille, chunky bonnet motif, and slight scowl make the Monterey's front end look more than a bit mean.

HOT-ROD NOSTALGIA
This rear view evokes earlier Mercurys, as loved by roof-chopping hot-rodders and famously driven over the edge by James Dean in Rebel Without a Cause.

SPECIFICATIONS

MODEL 1954 Mercury Monterey
PRODUCTION 174,238
BODY STYLE Two- or four-door hardtop, station wagon, and convertible.
CONSTRUCTION Steel body and chassis.
ENGINE 256cid V8.
POWER OUTPUT 161 bhp.
TRANSMISSION Three-speed manual with optional overdrive, optional Merc-O-Matic Drive automatic.
SUSPENSION *Front:* independent coil springs; *Rear:* leaf springs.
BRAKES Front and rear drums.
MAXIMUM SPEED 161 km/h (100 mph)
0–60 MPH (0–96 KM/H) 14 sec
A.F.C. 7 km/l (20 mpg)

1955 FORD
Thunderbird

CHEVY'S 1954 CORVETTE may have been a peach, but anything GM could do, Ford could do better. The '55 T-Bird had none of the 'Vette's fibreglass nonsense, but a steel body and grunty V8 motor. Plus it was drop-dead gorgeous and offered scores of options, with the luxury of wind-up windows. Nobody was surprised when it outsold the creaky Corvette 24 to one. But Ford wanted volume and two-seaters weren't everybody's cup of tea, which is why by 1958 the Little Bird became the Big Bird, swollen by four fat armchairs. Nevertheless, as the first of America's top-selling two-seaters, the Thunderbird fired the public's imagination. For the next decade American buyers looking for lively power in a stylish package would greedily devour every Thunderbird going.

THE POPULAR THUNDERBIRD GAINED ENOUGH EXPOSURE TO BE INCLUDED ON THIS STAMP

ENGINE
The T-Bird's motor was the new cast-iron OHV 292cid V8 with dual exhausts and four-barrel Holley carb. Compared to the 'Vette's ancient six, the T-Bird's mill offered serious shove and played a major role in the car's success.

BADGE
The Thunderbird name was chosen after a south-west Native American god who brought rain and prosperity.

POWER BULGE
The bonnet needed a bulge to clear the large air cleaners. It was stylish too.

INTERIOR
Luxury options made the Thunderbird an easy-going companion. On the list were power steering, windows, and brakes, automatic transmission, and even electric seats and a power-assisted top. At $100, the push-button radio was more expensive than power steering.

ENGINE
Power output ranged from 212 to 300 horses. Buyers could beautify their motors with a $25 chrome dress-up kit.

WINDSCREEN
The aeronautical windscreen profile is beautifully simple.

COCKPIT
When the top was up, heat from the transmission made for a hot cockpit; as a result, ventilation flaps were introduced on '56 and '57 models.

CAR AND THE STAR
The movie actress Debbie Reynolds loved her Ford Thunderbird. Today, the T-Bird is a fiercely prized symbol of American Fifties utopia. The '55–'57 Thunderbirds are the most coveted – the model turned into a four-seater in 1958.

1955 FORD THUNDERBIRD CONVERTIBLE

The styling was very Ford, penned by Bill Boyer and supervised by Frank Hershey. The simple, smooth, and youthful outer wrapping was a huge hit. A rakish long bonnet and short rear deck recalled the 1940s Lincoln Continental. Apart from the rather too prominent exhausts, the rear end is remarkably uncluttered, and the top shot shows that the T-Bird had a bright and spirited personality.

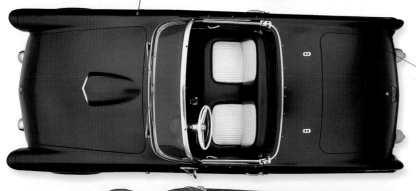

SMOOTH LINES
For 1955, this was an uncharacteristically clean design and attracted 16,155 buyers in its first year of production.

SPECIFICATIONS

MODEL 1955 Ford Thunderbird
PRODUCTION 16,155
BODY STYLE Two-door, two-seater convertible.
CONSTRUCTION Steel body and chassis.
ENGINE 292cid V8.
POWER OUTPUT 193 bhp.
TRANSMISSION Three-speed manual with optional overdrive, optional three-speed Ford-O-Matic automatic.
SUSPENSION *Front:* independent coil springs; *Rear:* leaf springs with live axle.
BRAKES Front and rear drums.
MAXIMUM SPEED 169–201 km/h (105–125 mph)
0–60 MPH (0–96 KM/H) 7–11 sec
A.F.C. 6 km/l (17 mpg)

Thunderbird

1956 CONTINENTAL
Mark II

STYLISH
MARK II LOGO

THAT THE FIFTIES MOTOR industry couldn't make a beautiful car is robustly disproved by the '56 Continental. As pretty as anything from Italy, the Mark II was intended to be a work of art and a symbol of affluence. William Ford was fanatical about his personal project, fighting for a chrome rather than plastic bonnet ornament costing $150, or the price of an entire Ford grille.

But it was that tenacious attention to detail that killed the car. Even with the Mark II's huge $10,000 price tag, the Continental Division still haemorrhaged money. Poor sales, internal company struggles, and the fact that it was only a two-door meant that by '58 the Continental was no more. Ironically, one of the most beautiful cars Ford ever made was sacrificed to save one of the ugliest in the upcoming E-Car project – the Edsel.

A CLASSY ACT
The most expensive automobile in America, the $9,695 Continental really was the car for the stars. Elvis tried one as a change from his usual Cadillacs, and Jayne Mansfield owned a pearl-coloured '57 with mink trim. The Continental epitomized the concept of "personal luxury".

ENGINE
Engines were Lincoln 368cid V8s, specially picked from the assembly line, stripped down, and hand-balanced for extra smoothness and refinement. With the exception of Packard's 374cid unit, this was the largest engine available in a 1956 production car.

INTERIOR
The classically simple cockpit could have come straight out of a British car. The interior boasted richly grained leathers and lavish fabrics. Self-tuning radio, four-way power seat, dual heater, and map lights were among an impressive array of standard features.

CABIN TEMPERATURE
Air-conditioning was the only extra-cost option.

TINTED GLASS

This was one of the no-cost extras offered. Other options included two-tone paint, an engraved nameplate, and all-leather trim. The high-quality leather was specially imported from Bridge of Weir in Scotland.

BODY HEIGHT

"Cow belly" frame was specifically designed to allow high seating with a low roof line.

1956 CONTINENTAL MARK II

With a sleek, clean front and simple die-cast grille, the only concession to contemporary Detroit ornamentation was how the direction indicators faired into the front bumper. At the rear of the car, trim fins, elegant bumpers, and neat inset tail-lights meant that the Continental was admired on both sides of the Atlantic. Unlike later models, the stamped-in spare tyre cover did actually house the spare.

SCRIPT

Continental tag revived the famous 1930s Lincolns of Edsel Ford.

STYLISH REAR

Handsome three-quarter profile echoes some Ferrari 250 models. Note how the petrol tank-cap lives behind the tail-light.

1957 CHEVROLET
Bel Air

CHEVROLET'S FLEUR-DE-LIS, A
REMINDER OF THEIR FRENCH ROOTS

CHEVROLET CALLED their '57 line "sweet, smooth, and sassy", and the Bel Air was exactly what America wanted – a junior Cadillac. Finny, trim, and handsome, and with Ed Cole's Super Turbo-Fire V8, it boasted one of the first production engines to pump out one horsepower per cubic inch, and was the first mass-market "fuelie" sedan with Ramjet injection.

Chevy copywriters screamed "the Hot One's even hotter", and Bel Airs became kings of the street. Production that year broke the 1½ million barrier and gave Ford the fright of their life. The trouble was that the "Hot One" was forced to cool it when the Automobile Manufacturers' Association urged car makers to put an end to their performance hysteria. Today, the Bel Air is one of the most widely coveted US collector's cars and the perfect embodiment of young mid-Fifties America. In the words of the Billie Jo Spears song, "Wish we still had her today; the good love we're living, we owe it to that '57 Chevrolet".

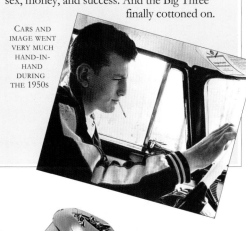

CARS AND IMAGE WENT VERY MUCH HAND-IN-HAND DURING THE 1950s

— ROCK 'N' ROLL CARS —

IN EARLY FIFTIES SITCOMS, teenagers were always seen trying to boost the keys to the Plymouth Fury from Dad's pocket. Advertisers ignored them because it was thought that they neither bought new cars or determined the family's buying decision. But Chevrolet knew better. Their V8 of '55 was the first domestic model aimed as a hot car for kids with hot dates, and college boys with after-school jobs proved to be a huge growth market. In *Rebel Without a Cause*, James Dean drove a customized '49 Merc, while Elvis Presley drove Continentals and Caddys. To Fifties youth, the American car was a duotone fashion bauble with whitewalls – a harbinger of love, sex, money, and success. And the Big Three finally cottoned on.

IF BUICK COULD ADD VENTIPORTS TO ITS WINGS, SO COULD CHEVROLET, THOUGH THE BEL AIR'S WOULD LAST ONLY A COUPLE OF YEARS

ENGINE OPTIONS
The small-block Turbo-Fire V8 packed 185 horsepower punch in base two-barrel trim. With the optional Rochester four-barrel it could muster 270 bhp. Ramjet injection added a hefty $500 to the sticker price; no surprise then that only 1,503 fuel-injected Bel Airs were sold.

THE '57 BEL AIR WAS 6.3 CM (2.5 IN) LONGER THAN THE '56 MODEL

STYLISH MOTORING

At $2,511, the Bel Air Convertible was the epitome of budget-priced good taste, finding 47,562 eager buyers. Low, sleek, and flashy, it could almost out-glam the contemporary Caddy rag-top. But the Bel Air was substance as well as style; seat belts and shoulder harnesses were available on the lengthy options list.

BEL AIR HARDTOP

The two-door hardtop model was another of the six body styles available in total.

SPECIFICATIONS

MODEL 1957 Chevrolet Bel Air Convertible
PRODUCTION 47,562
BODY STYLE Two-door convertible.
CONSTRUCTION Steel body and box-section chassis.
ENGINE 265cid, 283cid V8s.
POWER OUTPUT 162–283 bhp (283cid V8 fuel injected).
TRANSMISSION Three-speed manual with optional overdrive, optional two-speed Powerglide automatic, and Turboglide.
SUSPENSION *Front:* independent coil springs; *Rear:* leaf springs with live axle.
BRAKES Front and rear drums.
MAXIMUM SPEED 145–193 km/h (90–120 mph)
0–60 MPH (0–96 KM/H) 8–12 sec
A.F.C. 5 km/l (14 mpg)

INTERIOR

The distinctive two-tone interiors were a delight. Buyers could opt for a custom colour interior, power convertible top, tinted glass, vanity mirror, ventilated seat pads, power windows, and even a tissue dispenser.

HIDDEN FUEL CAP

In common with Lincoln and Cadillac, Chevrolet incorporated the fuel filler-cap into the chrome moulding at the rear edge of the left tail fin.

ANODIZED RIBBED PANEL SERVED TO COMPLEMENT REAR WING TREATMENT AND GAVE THE BEL AIR A TOUCH OF CLASS

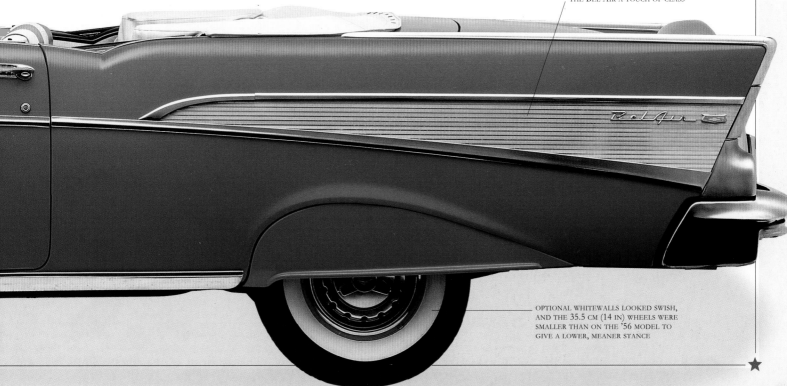

OPTIONAL WHITEWALLS LOOKED SWISH, AND THE 35.5 CM (14 IN) WHEELS WERE SMALLER THAN ON THE '56 MODEL TO GIVE A LOWER, MEANER STANCE

EVOLUTION OF THE CHEVROLET BEL AIR

THE '57 BEL AIR SUMS UP AMERICA'S most prosperous decade better than any other car. Along with hula-hoops, drive-in movies, and rock 'n' roll, it has become a Fifties icon. It was loved then because it was stylish, solid, sporty, and affordable, and it's loved now for more or less the same reasons; plus it simply drips with nostalgia. Immediately it was introduced, it was rightly hailed as a design classic. Elegant, sophisticated, and perfectly proportioned, the '57 Bel Air is one of the finest post-war American autos of all. But like so many other drop-dead gorgeous designs, Motown wouldn't and couldn't leave a good thing alone.

CHEVROLET, LIKE EVERYBODY ELSE, WERE KEEN TO CASH IN ON THE JET AGE, BUT IN REALITY THIS '55 BEL AIR LOOKS POSITIVELY DUMPY NEXT TO THE FIGHTER PLANE

Motoramic Chevrolet, stealing the thunder from the high-priced cars!

1953

IN '53, BEL AIRS came in a four-car line-up, and the name now identified the level of trim rather than the body style. At over half a million units, sales were massive, hardly surprising when you could even have the sumptuous two-door rag-top for a smudge over two thousand dollars.

KEY FEATURES
• Available as a two- or four-door sedan, two-door sport coupe, or convertible
• All-new bodies with wrap-around back light on sedans
• Power from 235cid six
• Chevy model year total is 1,356,413

1954

THE '54 LOOKED wider and more modern, the interior was even plusher with wall-to-wall carpets, it had new wheel discs, and the convertible had two-tone, all-vinyl trim. The Bel Air soldiered on with its ancient cast-iron six, but the V8 was just around the corner. Total calendar year sales were slightly up at 1,414,352.

KEY DEVELOPMENTS
• Sport Coupe had special fashion Fiesta upholstery
• An eight-passenger Townsman station wagon joined the line-up
• Four-door Bel Air is Chevrolet's most popular car for 1954

1957 CHEVROLET
Bel Air

STYLISH RESTYLE
'57 Chevys really originated in '55 with a "road-to-roof" redesign of the old line; it's a credit to Chevrolet that the car didn't lose any of its original elegance.

CONTINENTAL SPARE WHEEL CARRIER WAS A DE LUXE OPTION AND MADE THE CONVERTIBLE LOOK LIKE A DREAM COME TRUE

SUBTLE REAR FINS ARE ALMOST DEMURE COMPARED WITH OTHER CONTEMPORARY EFFORTS

THE '57 LOOKS MUCH LEANER THAN THE STOCKIER BEL AIR OF '56

1957 CHEVROLET BEL AIR

1955

A DRAMATIC AND VERY fetching restyle made the '55 Bel Air Chevy's top series again. Things got plusher and plusher, with richer upholstery and more chrome. New for '55 was Chevy's brilliant 265cid V8, which amazed both public and industry alike. Bel Air production this year topped a staggering 770,955.

KEY DEVELOPMENTS
• First year of Chevy's new V8
• Beautiful Nomad wagon joins the line-up
• V8 has optional power pack with four-barrel carb and twin exhausts
• Bel Air four-door alone sells a whopping 354,372

1956

IN '56 THE BEL AIR became a real honey of a car, taking the nameplate way upmarket. Superbly appointed inside and out, it was fast, glamorous, and ultra-desirable. And with prices remaining under $3,000, it was still a very affordable car. Chevy's model year production total hit 1,621,004, keeping it America's number one car maker.

KEY DEVELOPMENTS
• Left-hand tail-light now functions as a fuel-filler door
• Rear wheel arches are now gently scalloped
• Fuel injection available
• V8 Bel Airs now have V-shaped badges
• Nomad wagon sales decline

1958

THIS WAS THE YEAR when the Bel Air lost its lithe simplicity and looked like just another big US barge. The all-new safety girder chassis and body that looked lower, wider, and longer were hailed as the new "Dream Car" look. The Bel Air had shed its youthful exuberance, passing quietly into corpulent middle-age.

KEY DEVELOPMENTS
• First year of quad headlights
• New gullwing rear wing and deck sculpturing
• Impala (right) joins the Bel Air line

1962

IN COMMON WITH the rest of the industry, Chevrolet squared off the Bel Air's lines and chopped off its fins. Now a mid-priced product, the Bel Air was again one of Chevy's most popular confections. It was still opulent, with high-grade cloth interiors and plenty of stainless steel, chrome, and aluminium, but it had lost its uniqueness.

KEY DEVELOPMENTS
• Range is now five models, including two station wagons
• Chevrolet calendar year output peaks at 2,161,398 units

ORNAMENTATION

The rather clumsy bomb-sight bonnet ornament could be fairly described as the '57 Bel Air's only minor stylistic blemish. The public liked it, though.

THE BEL AIR CONVERTIBLE COULD BE FITTED WITH AN OPTIONAL POWER-OPERATED TOP

WHEN FITTED WITH THE SOLID-LIFTER FUEL-INJECTED V8, THE BEL AIR WAS A DEVASTATINGLY QUICK CAR

CALIFORNIA
GUG 562

1957 CHEVROLET
Bel Air Nomad

THE NOMAD'S SLANTING
TAILGATE AND STRIPES
WERE A HALLMARK

IF YOU THOUGHT BMW and Mercedes were first with the sporting uptown carry-all, think again. Chevrolet kicked off the genre as far back as 1955. The Bel Air Nomad was a development of Harley Earl's dream-car wagon based on the Chevrolet Corvette, which he fielded at the four-city Motorama of 1954.

Although it looked like other '55 Bel Airs, the V8 Nomad was the most expensive Chevy ever at $2,571, a whole $265 more than the to-die-for Bel Air rag-top. But despite the fact that *Motor Trend* described the '57 Nomad as "one of the year's most beautiful cars", with only two doors its appeal was limited, its large glass area made the cabin too hot, and the twinkly tailgate let in water. No surprise then that it was one of Chevy's least popular models. Sales never broke the magic 10,000 barrier and, by 1958, the world's first sportwagon, and now a milestone car, had been dropped.

1957 CHEVROLET BEL AIR NOMAD

Although claimed as a Harley Earl design, the Nomad was created by Chevy studio head Claire MacKichen and stylist Carl Renner. Unveiled in January 1954, the Motorama Nomad was such a hit that a production version made it into the '55 brochures. It was essentially a revival of the original Town and Country theme, and a reaction against the utilitarian functionalism of the boxy wooden wagons that had become ubiquitous in suburban America.

STATION WAGONS

FIFTIES CAR ADVERTISERS visualized the dream and wrote the script. The young American family marvelled at images of sleek station wagons outside Ivy League country clubs, or the kids and family dog piled into a vast nine-passenger woody. The wagon wasn't a compromise but an entrée into the world of private schools, old money, and wholesome domesticity. And Mom made that buying decision. She'd seen beautifully groomed suburban matrons ferrying nine Little League players to the ballpark in a Country Squire or a Ranchwagon. She cherished her wagon like her hairdresser and rumbled round the shopping mall with pride.

1958
DESOTO FIRESWEEP
4-DOOR EXPLORER

1960 FORD COUNTRY SQUIRE

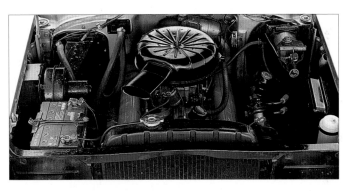

ENGINE

The base engine was a 235cid six, but many Nomads were fitted with the Bel Air's grunty 265cid V8, which had a choice of Carter or Rochester two-barrel carb. For an extra $484 you could even specify fuel injection.

ROOF INNOVATION

The Nomad was the first car to use non-structural corrugations on a roof.

CARGO FLOOR WAS COVERED WITH LINOLEUM

SPECIFICATIONS

MODEL 1957 Chevrolet Bel Air Nomad

PRODUCTION 6,103

BODY STYLE Two-door station wagon.

CONSTRUCTION Steel body and chassis.

ENGINE 235cid six, 265cid V8.

POWER OUTPUT 123–283 bhp.

TRANSMISSION Three-speed manual with overdrive, two-speed Powerglide automatic, and optional Turboglide.

SUSPENSION *Front:* coil springs; *Rear:* leaf springs.

BRAKES Front and rear drums.

MAXIMUM SPEED 145–193 km/h (90–120 mph)

 0–60 MPH (0–96 KM/H) 8–11 sec

 A.F.C. 5.3–6.7 km/l (15–19 mpg)

REAR STYLING

The embellished tailgate was lifted straight from the Motorama 'Vette and was widely praised. Even the roof line had seven transverse fluted pressings, as Harley Earl couldn't bear to see a piece of flat metal unadorned.

'VETTE LINES

Motorama 'Vette roof line was adapted for production Nomads in just two days.

FRONT ASPECT

Chevy tried to lower the Nomad's high price by using exterior trim that was identical to the other Bel Air models.

INTERIOR

Inside, the Nomad was very similar to the Bel Air, with distinctive two-tone trim and optional power seat, tinted glass, tissue dispenser, and, for the first time this season, seat belts and shoulder harnesses.

1957 CHEVROLET
3100 Stepside

SIMPLE 3100 DESIGNATION DENOTES MODEL NUMBER

CHEVY WERE ON A HIGH in the mid-Fifties. With the 'Vette, the Bel Air, and their new V8, they were America's undisputed top car manufacturer. A boundless optimism percolated through all divisions, even touching such prosaic offerings as trucks. And the definitive Chevy carry-all has to be the '57 pick-up.

It had not only that four-stroke overhead-valve V8 mill, but also various options and a smart new restyle. Small wonder it was nicknamed "a Cadillac in drag". Among the most enduring of all American design statements, the '57 had clean, well-proportioned lines, a minimum of chrome, and integrated wings. Chevrolet turned the pick-up from a beast of burden into a personalized workhorse complete with all the appurtenances of gracious living usually seen in a boulevard cruiser.

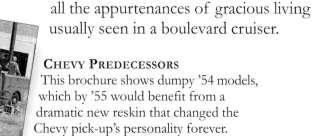

INTERIOR
The car was as stylized inside as out, with a glovebox, heavy chrome switches, swing-out driver and passenger ashtrays, plus a V-shaped speedometer. De Luxe models had two-tone seats, door trims, and steering wheel.

CHEVY PREDECESSORS
This brochure shows dumpy '54 models, which by '55 would benefit from a dramatic new reskin that changed the Chevy pick-up's personality forever.

LIGHTS
These cowled single headlights would be replaced by quad lights in '58

FLOORING
Wooden-bed floors helped to protect the load area and added a quality feel.

ENGINE
The small-block V8 produced 150 bhp and could cruise at 113 km/h (70 mph).

REAR WINDOW
De Luxe models had a larger, wrap-around windscreen.

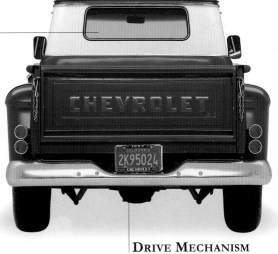

1957 CHEVROLET 3100 STEPSIDE

Chevy's '57 pick-ups can be identified by the new trapezoid grille and a flatter bonnet than '56 models. Buyers had a choice of short or long pick-up, De Luxe or standard trim, and 11 exterior colours. Engines were the 235cid Thriftmaster six or the 265cid Trademaster V8.

STEP
This neat rear step allows access to the load area and gives the pick-up its Stepside name.

DRIVE MECHANISM
From '55, all Chevys used open-drive instead of an enclosed torque-tube driveline.

SPECIFICATIONS

MODEL 1957 Chevrolet 3100 Stepside
PRODUCTION Not available
BODY STYLE Two-seater, short-bed pick-up.
CONSTRUCTION Steel body and chassis.
ENGINE 235cid six, 265cid V8.
POWER OUTPUT 130–145 bhp.
TRANSMISSION Three-speed manual with optional overdrive, optional three-speed automatic.
SUSPENSION *Front:* coil springs; *Rear:* leaf springs.
BRAKES Front and rear drums.
MAXIMUM SPEED 129 km/h (80 mph)
0–60 MPH (0–96 KM/H) 17.3 sec
A.F.C. 6 km/l (17 mpg)

1957 CHRYSLER
New Yorker

WHY CAN'T THEY MAKE CARS that look this good anymore? The '57 New Yorker was the first and finest example of Chrysler's "Forward Look" policy. With the average American production worker earning $82.32 a week, the $4,259 four-door hardtop was both sensationally good-looking and sensationally expensive.

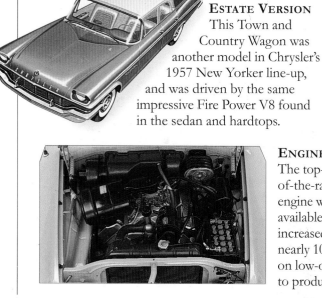

THE 1957 NEW YORKER
CONVERTIBLE COUPE

The car's glorious lines seriously alarmed Chrysler's competitors, especially since the styling was awarded two gold medals, the suspension was by newfangled torsion bar, and muscle was courtesy of one of the most respected engines in the world – the hemi-head Fire Power, which in the New Yorker cranked out 325 horses. Despite this, "the most glamorous cars of a generation" cost Chrysler a whopping $300 million and sales were disappointing. One of the problems was a propensity for rust, along with shabby fit and finish; another was low productivity – only a measly 10,948 four-door hardtop models rolled out of the Highland Park factory. Even so, the New Yorker was certainly one of the most beautiful cars Chrysler ever made.

INTERIOR
New Yorkers had the lot. Equipment included power windows, a six-way power seat, Hi-Way Hi-Fi phonograph, Electro-Touch radio, rear seat speaker, Instant Air heater, handbrake warning system, Air-Temp air-conditioning, and tinted glass – an altogether impressive array of features for a 1957 automobile.

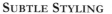

SUBTLE STYLING
The New Yorker has few styling excesses. Even the seven gratuitous slashes on the rear wing do not look over the top.

ESTATE VERSION
This Town and Country Wagon was another model in Chrysler's 1957 New Yorker line-up, and was driven by the same impressive Fire Power V8 found in the sedan and hardtops.

ENGINE
The top-of-the-range model had a top-of-the-range motor. The hemi-head engine was the largest production plant available in 1957. Bore and stroke were increased and displacement raised by nearly 10 per cent. It was efficient, ran on low-octane gas, and could be tickled to produce staggering outputs.

TYRES
Optional Captive-Aire tyres were available, with promises that they wouldn't let themselves down.

1957 CHRYSLER NEW YORKER

Chrysler stunned the world with their dart-like shapes of 1957. The unified design was created by the mind of one man – Virgil Exner – rather than by a committee, and it shows. Those prodigious rear wings sweep up gracefully, harmonizing well with the gently tapering roof line. The low belt line, huge expanse of glass, and slinky profile are commendably subtle.

REAR ASPECT
Rather than looking overstyled, the rear end and deck are actually quite restrained. The licence plate sits neatly in its niche, the tail pipes are completely concealed, the bumper is understated, and even the rear lights are not too heavy-handed.

PENNSYLVANIA
DSK 148
57 CHRYSLER

SPECIFICATIONS

MODEL 1957 Chrysler New Yorker
PRODUCTION 34,620 (all body styles)
BODY STYLE Four-door, six-seater hardtop.
CONSTRUCTION Monocoque.
ENGINE 392cid V8.
POWER OUTPUT 325 bhp.
TRANSMISSION Three-speed TorqueFlite automatic.
SUSPENSION *Front:* A-arms and longitudinal torsion bar; *Rear:* semi-elliptic leaf springs.
BRAKES Front and rear drums.
MAXIMUM SPEED 185 km/h (115 mph)
0–60 MPH (0–96 KM/H) 12.3 sec
A.F.C. 4.6 km/l (13 mpg)

1958 BUICK
Limited Riviera

1942 LIMITED BADGE,
USED AGAIN IN 1958

WHEN YOUR FORTUNES are flagging, you pour on the chrome. As blubbery barges go, the '58 Limited has to be one of the gaudiest. Spanning 5.78 m (19 ft) and tipping the scales at two tonnes, the Limited is empirical proof that 1958 was not Buick's happiest year. Despite all that twinkling kitsch and the reincarnated Limited badge, the bulbous Buick bombed. For a start, GM's Dynaflow transmission was not up to Hydra-Matic standards, and their brakes were disinclined to work. Furthermore, in what was a recession year for the industry, the Limited had been priced into Cadillac territory – $33 more than the Series 62. Total production for the Limited in 1958 was a very limited 7,436 units. By the late Fifties, Detroit had lost its way, and the '58 Limited was on the road to nowhere.

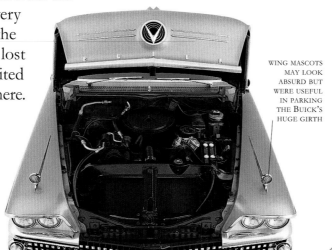

WING MASCOTS
MAY LOOK
ABSURD BUT
WERE USEFUL
IN PARKING
THE BUICK'S
HUGE GIRTH

ENGINE
The Valve-in-Head B12000 engine kicked out 300 horses, with a 364 cubic inch displacement. These specifications were respectable enough on paper, but on the road the Limited was too heavy to be anything other than sluggish.

REAR DESIGN

The Buick's butt was a confused jumble of bosomy curves, slanting fins, and horizontal flashings. The boot itself was big enough to house a football team.

SCREEN

The large windscreen was served by "wide angle" wipers and an automatic windscreen washer.

1958 BUICK LIMITED RIVIERA

Buick's answer to an aircraft carrier was a riot of ornamentation that went on for half a block. At rest, the Limited looked like it needed a fifth wheel to support that weighty rear overhang. Air-Poise suspension was an extra-cost option that used pressurized air bladders for a supposedly smooth hydraulic ride. The system was, however, a nightmare to service and literally let itself down.

TRIMMINGS

Interiors were trimmed in grey cloth and vinyl or Cordaveen. Seat cushions had Double-Depth foam rubber.

SPECIFICATIONS

MODEL 1958 Buick Limited Riviera Series 700

PRODUCTION 7,436 (all body styles)

BODY STYLE Two- and four-door, six-seater hardtops, two-door convertible.

CONSTRUCTION Steel monocoque.

ENGINE 364cid V8.

POWER OUTPUT 300 bhp.

TRANSMISSION Flight-Pitch Dynaflow automatic.

SUSPENSION *Front:* coil springs with A-arms; *Rear:* live axle with coil springs. Optional air suspension.

BRAKES Front and rear drums.

MAXIMUM SPEED 177 km/h (110 mph)

0–60 MPH (0–96 KM/H) 9.5 sec

A.F.C. 4.6 km/l (13 mpg)

INTERIOR

Power steering and brakes were essential and came as standard. Other standard equipment included an electric clock, cigarette lighters, and electric windows.

GRILLE

The "Fashion-Aire Dynastar" grille consisted of no fewer than 160 chrome squares, each with four polished facets to give some serious sparkle.

DECORATION

Unique to the Limited were 15 utterly pointless chrome slashes down both rear wings.

1958 EDSEL
Bermuda

TRANSPORTATION FOR THE LARGEST OF FAMILIES

WITHOUT THAT INFAMOUS GRILLE, the Bermuda wouldn't have been a bad old barge. The rest looked pretty safe and suburban, and even those faddish rear lights weren't that offensive. At $3,155 it was the top Edsel wagon, wooing the WASPs with more mock wood than Disneyland. But Ford had oversold the Edsel big-time, and every model suffered guilt by association. Initial sales in 1957 were nothing like the predicted 200,000, but weren't disastrous either. The Bermudas, though, found just 2,235 buyers and were discontinued after only one year. By '58, people no longer believed the hype, and Edsel sales evaporated; the company ceased trading in November 1959. Everybody knew that the '58 recession killed the Edsel, but at Ford major players in the project were cruelly demoted or fired.

EDSEL MASCOT
The Edsel name was chosen from 6,000 possibilities, including Mongoose, Turcotinga, and Utopian Turtletop.

ENGINE
"They're the industry's newest – and the best", cried the advertising. Edsel engines were strong 361 or 410cid V8s, with the station wagons usually powered by the smaller unit.

E400 ON VALVE COVERS INDICATES AMOUNT OF TORQUE

INTERIOR
Never one of Edsel's strongest selling points, the Teletouch gear selector was operated by push-buttons on the steering wheel. It was gimmicky and unreliable.

TELETOUCH BUTTON SENT A SIGNAL TO THE CAR'S "PRECISION BRAIN"

FORD WHEELBASE
Edsel wagons were based on the 295 cm (116 in) Ford station wagon platform.

1958 EDSEL BERMUDA

Looking back, one wonders how one of
the most powerful corporations in the
world could possibly have signed off
on such a stylistic debacle. '58 Edsels
weren't just ugly, they were appallingly
weird. The Bermuda's side view,
however, is innocuous enough and
no worse than many half-timbered
shopping-mall wagons of the period.
Note how the roof is slightly kinked
to give the huge panel extra rigidity.

SPECIFICATIONS

MODEL 1958 Edsel Bermuda
PRODUCTION 1,456 (six-seater
Bermudas)
BODY STYLE Four-door,
six-seater station wagon.
CONSTRUCTION Steel body
and chassis.
ENGINE 361cid V8.
POWER OUTPUT 303 bhp.
TRANSMISSION Three-speed
manual with optional overdrive,
optional three-speed automatic
with or without Teletouch control.
SUSPENSION *Front:* independent
coil springs;
Rear: leaf springs with live axle.
BRAKES Front and rear drums.
MAXIMUM SPEED 174 km/h
(108 mph)
0–60 MPH (0–96 KM/H) 10.2 sec
A.F.C. 5.3 km/l (15 mpg)

LIGHTS
*Zany boomerang
rear clusters
contained turn
signal, stop, and
reverse lights.*

FRONT ASPECT
*Grille was so prominent
that it required separate
flanking bumpers.*

INTERIOR
*All wagons had four armrests,
two coat-hooks, dome lights,
and vinyl white headlining.*

COLOUR
*This Bermuda is painted
in Spring Green, but buyers
had a choice of 161 different
colour combinations.*

1958 LINCOLN
Capri

A RANGE OF ALL-NEW LINCOLNS WERE BROUGHT
OUT IN 1958 TO CHALLENGE CADILLAC

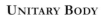

IN POSSIBLY ONE OF the most outrageous half-truths ever written, Lincoln copywriters insisted that the '58 Capri was "impressive without being ostentatious" and had a "tasteful, classic elegance". In reality, it was a stylistic nightmare, two-and-a-half tonnes of massive bumpers, sculpted wheel arches, and weirdly canted headlights. What's more, in the jumbo 430cid Continental V8 it had the largest engine available in an American production car at the time.

This visual anarchy and the '58 recession meant that sales halved from the previous year, and Ford realized that the Capri was as badly timed as the Edsel. Mind you, the luxury Lincoln had one solid advantage: it was quick *and* it handled. One magazine said, "it's doubtful if any big car could stick any tighter in the corners or handle any better at high speed", a homily helped by the unitary body, rear coil springs, and potent new brakes. The '58 Capri was one of the last driveaway dinosaurs. The door was closing on an era of kitsch.

UNITARY BODY
In '58, Lincoln switched to a unitary body, eliminating a chassis frame for the first time in 10 years. Suspension, drivetrain, and engine units were fastened to the body structure to minimize weight and offer a smoother ride. However, prototypes flexed so badly that all sorts of stiffening reinforcements were added, negating any weight savings.

STYLING
The Capri used every stylistic trick that Motown had ever learnt, but only desperate men would put fins on the rear bumper.

ENGINE
The big new 430cid V8 engine walloped out 375 horses, giving a power output second only to the Chrysler 300D. Lowered final drive ratios failed even to pay lip-service to fuel economy, with the Capri returning a groan-inspiring 3.5 km/l (10 mpg) around town.

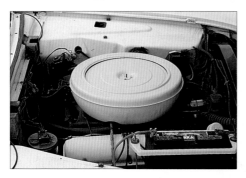

INTERIOR
For just under $5,000, standard features included electric windows with child-proof controls, a six-way Power Seat, a padded instrument panel, and five ashtrays, each with its own lighter. Seat belts and leather trim were optional.

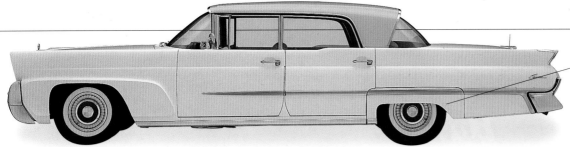

SUSPENSION
This was the first year that Lincolns had coil springs for rear suspension.

1958 LINCOLN CAPRI

Lincoln's dramatic restyle of '58 was not one of their happiest. The frivolous fins of '57 were trimmed down, but the sculpted bumpers and scalloped wings were still a mess. Ford's brief for the '58 Lincolns was to out-glitz Cadillac in every area, but somehow they didn't quite get it right. Instead, the Lincoln made the Caddy Eldorado look downright divine.

CABIN SPACE
The largest passenger car of the year, the Capri could accommodate six or even seven people, riding on an enormous, elongated 3.33 m (131 in) wheelbase.

FINS
By '58 the size of fins was falling, partly due to fashion, and also to reduce the risk of injuring pedestrians in road accidents.

WINDSCREEN
Tinted glass was a $50 option, along with translucent sun visors at $27.

SPECIFICATIONS

MODEL 1958 Lincoln Capri
PRODUCTION 6,859
BODY STYLE Four-door, six-seater sedan.
CONSTRUCTION Steel unitary body.
ENGINE 430cid V8.
POWER OUTPUT 375 bhp.
TRANSMISSION Three-speed Turbodrive automatic.
SUSPENSION Front and rear coil springs.
BRAKES Front and rear drums.
MAXIMUM SPEED 185 km/h (115 mph)
0–60 MPH (0–96 KM/H) 9 sec
A.F.C. 5 km/l (14 mpg)

TYRE SIZE
9x14 tyres couldn't cope with the Lincoln's prodigious weight. Cost-cutting and an obsession with a soft ride meant that most cars of the period wallowed around on potentially lethal undersized rubber.

1958 PACKARD
Hawk

SALES LITERATURE HERALDED THE ARRIVAL OF "A DISTINCTIVE, NEW, FULL-POWERED SPORTS-STYLED CAR"

DISTINCTIVE, BIZARRE, AND VERY un-American, the '58 Hawk was a pastiche of European styling cues. Which is why there were no quad headlights, no athletic profile, and no glinting chromium dentures on the grille. Inspired by the likes of Ferrari and Mercedes, it boasted tan pleated-leather hide, white-on-black instruments, Jaguaresque wing vents, a turned metal dashboard, gulping bonnet air-scoop, and a broad fibreglass shovel-nostril that could have been lifted off a Maserati. And it was supercharged.

But Packard's desperate attempt to distance themselves from traditional Detroit iron failed. At $4,000, the Hawk was overpriced, under-refined, and overdecorated. Packard had merged with Studebaker back in 1954, and although it was initially a successful alliance, problems with suppliers and another buy-out in 1956 basically sealed the company's fate. Only 588 Hawks were built, with the very last Packard rolling off the South Bend, Indiana, line on 13 July 1958. Today the Hawk stands as a quaint curiosity, a last-ditch attempt to preserve the Packard pedigree. It remains one of the most fiercely desired of the final Packards.

EURO STYLING
The door mirror was designed to replicate the knock-off hub spinners of wire wheels on European sports cars, but it looked out of place with the Hawk's discreet styling.

REAR ASPECT
Despite its European airs, no American car could escape the vogue for fins, and this car has two beauties. Nobody was too sure about the spare wheel impression on the boot, though, which was likened to a toilet seat.

TWIN EXHAUSTS
Standard on the Hawk, but fish-tail embellishers were an after-market accessory.

ENGINE
Flight-O-Matic automatic transmission and a hefty, supercharged 289cid V8 came as standard, hurling out 275 horses; 0–60 mph (96 km/h) took just under eight seconds. The Hawk's blower was a belt-driven McCulloch supercharger.

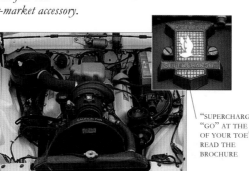

"SUPERCHARGED "GO" AT THE TIP OF YOUR TOE", READ THE BROCHURE

AIR VENTS
Front wing vents were shamelessly culled from British Mk IX and XK Jaguars.

1958 PACKARD HAWK

Uniquely, the Hawk had exterior vinyl armrests running along the side windows and a refreshing lack of chrome gaudiness on the flanks. The roof line and halo roof band are aeronautical, the belt line is tense and urgent, and the whole plot stood on 14-inch wheels to make it look lower and meaner.

STEERING
Power steering was a $70 factory option.

FRONT ASPECT
The Hawk was one of the few Packards that dared to sport single headlights and, along with that softly shaped front bumper and mailbox air intake, looked nothing like contemporary Americana.

SPECIFICATIONS

MODEL 1958 Packard Hawk
PRODUCTION 588
BODY STYLE Two-door, four-seater coupe.
CONSTRUCTION Steel body and chassis.
ENGINE 289cid V8.
POWER OUTPUT 275 bhp.
TRANSMISSION Three-speed Flight-O-Matic automatic, optional overdrive.
SUSPENSION *Front:* independent coil springs; *Rear:* leaf springs.
BRAKES Front and rear drums.
MAXIMUM SPEED 201 km/h (125 mph)
0–60 MPH (0–96 KM/H) 8 sec
A.F.C. 5.3 km/l (15 mpg)

INTERIOR
To stress the Hawk's supposed sporting bloodline, the interior was clad in soft hide with sports-car instrumentation. In addition, you could specify a raft of convenience options that included power windows and air-conditioning.

1958 RAMBLER
Ambassador

WHILE THE GOVERNMENT WAS telling consumers "You auto buy now", American Motors boss George Romney was telling the President that "Consumers are rebelling against the size, horsepower, and excessive styling of the American automobile".

Romney's Ramblers were the only industry success story for a recession-racked '58 when, for the first time ever, more cars were imported than exported. The Ambassador was Rambler's economy flagship, and road testers liked the speed, room, luxury, thrift, and high resale value. Also, it was reasonably priced, had a safety package option, "deep-dip" rustproofing, and a thoroughly modern monocoque shell. But buyers weren't buying. Motorists may have wanted economy and engineering integrity, but cars still had to be cool. The sensible Ambassador was an ugly, slab-sided machine for middle-aged squares.

THIS IS A
**DOUBLE – SAFE
SINGLE UNIT
BODY**
BUILT WITH AN ADVANCED METHOD OF BODY CONSTRUCTION IN WHICH THE BODY AND FRAME ARE COMBINED INTO A SINGLE ALL-WELDED STRUCTURAL UNIT
PIONEERED AND BUILT EXCLUSIVELY BY
AMERICAN MOTORS CORP.
DETROIT MICHIGAN

WHAT, NO CHASSIS?
Chassis-less body construction was a Nash/AMC tradition also used by many European nameplates, namely Jaguar. Few American manufacturers were interested in following suit. Despite modest dimensions, the Ambassador was accommodating; it had a very high roof line and could just about carry six passengers.

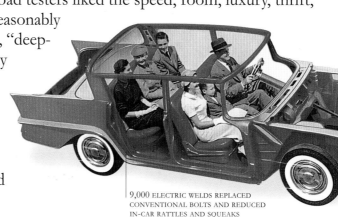

9,000 ELECTRIC WELDS REPLACED CONVENTIONAL BOLTS AND REDUCED IN-CAR RATTLES AND SQUEAKS

INTERIOR
The custom steering wheel was an option, along with power steering at $89.50. Flash-O-Matic automatic transmission could be column-operated or controlled by push-buttons on the dash. The Weather-Eye heater, another option, was reckoned to be one of the most efficient in the industry.

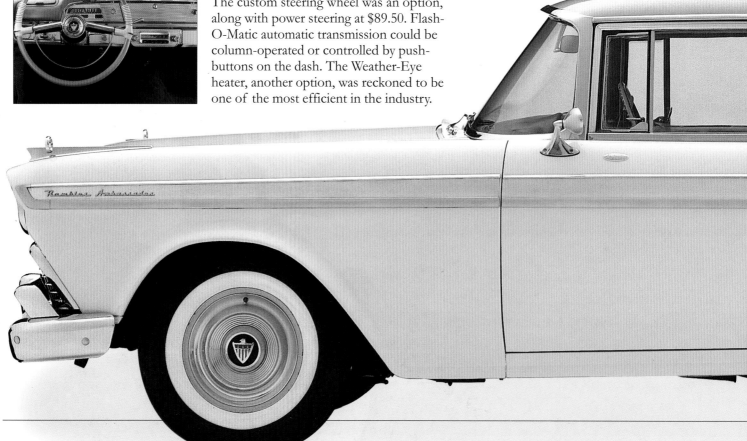

1958 RAMBLER AMBASSADOR

AMC stylist Ed Anderson did a good job with the '58 models, cleverly reskinning '56 and '57s with longer bonnets, different grilles, and tail-lights. But with modest tail fins and a plain rump, the Ambassador was no matinee idol and looked more like a taxi than an upmarket sedan. The six cars in the range included three station wagons.

SPECIFICATIONS

MODEL 1958 Rambler Ambassador
PRODUCTION 14,570 (all body styles)
BODY STYLE Four-door, six-seater sedan.
CONSTRUCTION Steel monocoque body.
ENGINE 327cid V8.
POWER OUTPUT 270 bhp.
TRANSMISSION Three-speed manual with optional overdrive, optional three-speed Flash-O-Matic automatic.
SUSPENSION *Front:* independent coil springs; *Rear:* coil with optional air springs.
BRAKES Front and rear drums.
MAXIMUM SPEED 169 km/h (105 mph)
0–60 MPH (0–96 KM/H) 10 sec
A.F.C. 6.4 km/l (18 mpg)

ENGINE

The cast-iron 327cid V8 motor gave 270 bhp and, despite a one-barrel carb, could reach 60 (96 km/h) in 10 seconds. The same engine had powered the '57 Rambler Rebel.

MODEST FINS

Sales literature championed the "sensible fin height" as an aid to safer driving by not obstructing rear vision.

SUSPENSION

Rear air suspension was an optional extra, but few buyers ordered it. Just as well, because reliability problems caused the industry to drop the whole concept soon after.

ORNAMENTATION

The sweepspear was one of the Ambassador's few concessions to ornamentation, and helped to break up an otherwise solid flank.

1959 CADILLAC
Eldorado

THE '59 CADILLAC ISN'T SO MUCH a car as a cathedral– a gothic monument to America's glory years. Over-long, over-low, and overstyled, it stands as the final flourish of the Fifties. We might marvel at its way-out space-age styling, those bizarre fins, and that profligate 390 cubic inch V8, but the most telling thing about the '59 is its sheer in-yer-face arrogance.

STAMP CELEBRATES THE CADILLAC'S MOST OUTSTANDING FEATURE

Back in the Fifties, the United States was the most powerful nation on earth. With money to burn, military might, arrow-straight freeways, and Marilyn Monroe, America really thought it could reach out and touch the Moon. But when the '59 Cad appeared, that nationalistic high was ebbing away. The Russians had launched Sputnik, Castro was getting chummy with Khrushchev, and there were race riots at home. A decade of glitz, glamour, and prosperity was coming to an end. America would never be the same again, and neither would her Cadillacs.

ENGINE
Base engine on the '59 was a five-bearing 390cid V8 with hydraulic lifters and high compression heads. Breathing through a Carter four-barrel, it developed 325 bhp, but with the Eldorado V8 and three Rochester two-barrels the '59 could muster an extra 20 bhp.

INTERIOR
Standard fare on the '59 Convertible was lavish – power brakes, power steering, auto tranny, power windows, two-speed windscreen wipers, and two-way power seat.

CADILLAC COUPE DE VILLE
The de Ville line-up was two sedans and a coupe, trimmed like the Series 6200 with the same standards plus electric windows and power seats. Sticker prices were $5,498 (Sedan) and $5,252 (Coupe).

AUTRONIC EYE
Automatic headlight-dipping came courtesy of the optional Autronic Eye, which could sense the lights of oncoming cars. At just $55, futuristic technology had never been so accessible.

UP-TO-DATE FEATURES
Options were amazingly modern, with air suspension, cruise control, remote boot lock, and bucket seats.

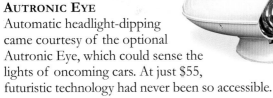

STAR QUALITY
Test drivers praised the '59's handling, ride, and superb power steering. Performance was sensational, delivered in utter silence with honey-like smoothness.

BOOT
The massive boot has enough room for a small golf tournament.

─ SPECIFICATIONS ─

MODEL 1959 Cadillac Eldorado
PRODUCTION 11,130
BODY STYLE Two-door, six-seater convertible.
CONSTRUCTION Steel body, X-frame chassis.
ENGINE 390cid V8.
POWER OUTPUT 325–345 bhp.
TRANSMISSION Three-speed Hydra-Matic automatic.
SUSPENSION All-round coil springs with optional Freon-12 gas suspension.
BRAKES Front and rear hydraulic power-assisted drums.
MAXIMUM SPEED 185 km/h (115 mph)
0–60 MPH (0–96 KM/H) 10.3 sec
A.F.C. 4.3 km/l (12.1 mpg)

1959 CADILLAC ELDORADO

Detroit's dream-makers produced visions of the future, and the '59 was the most florid of all. For one hysterical model year it was the pre-eminent American automobile, and at close on $6,000 you really had to have some serious juice to own one. 11,130 Series 62 convertibles were built in '59 and cost $5,455. Quality was patchy though, with too many rattles and a distinctly un-Cadillac propensity for rust. Even so, enthusiasts rank the '59 as King of the Cads.

MORTGAGE MODEL
The rare Biarritz Convertible had a sticker price of $7,401, the cost of an extremely substantial house.

ULTIMATE FIN FASHION
The wackiest fins of any car ever, the '59s were elbow high. Cadillac's finny trademark was an aviation cliché, calculated to lend lifeless steel the allure of speed, modernity, and escape.

CONTROVERSIAL FINS, KNOWN AS "ZAP", WERE LATER RIDICULED

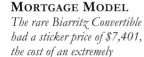

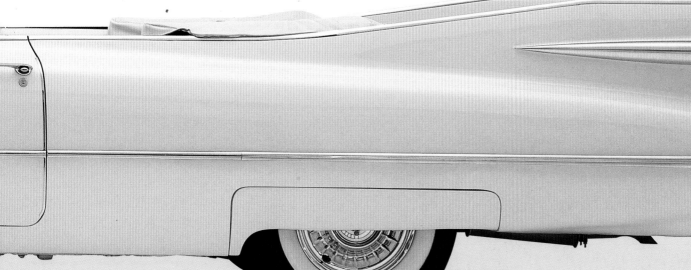

1959 DODGE
Custom Royal Lancer

TWO-DOOR CUSTOM ROYAL HARDTOP
STICKERED AT $3,151 IN '59

LICKING ITS WOUNDS FROM the '58 recession, Detroit came up with more metal, muscle, and magnificence than ever before. As always, Chrysler's offerings were the gaudiest, and their '59 Custom Royal had fins and finery to spare. And boy, could it go. Engine options went all the way up to a 383cid D500 motor with twin Carter four-barrels that heaved out a whopping 345 bhp. "Level Flight" Torsion-Aire suspension was a $127 extra that "lets you corner without side sway, stop without brake dive". There was no doubt that the copywriters were having a ball.

With a Forward Look profile, chromed eyebrows, four enormous tail-lights set in yet more chrome, and topped by towering duotone fins, the Custom Royal was a stylistic shambles. The brochure has a mailman beaming approvingly at the riotous '59 Custom with a catchline that runs, "reflects your taste for finer things". Complete garbage maybe, but that's the way they sold cars in '59.

LANCER BADGE
The Lancer name actually referred to an upmarket trim level that was standard on all hardtops and convertibles. The Custom Royal was Dodge's top offering.

FORWARD LOOK POLICY
In 1957 Chrysler introduced a new type of styling to their whole range. Cars should be longer, sleeker, and have exuberant tail fins. It was a resounding success until about 1960, when poor quality control – due in part to overwhelming demand – saw a dramatic decline in sales.

PUSH-BUTTON THREE-SPEED
TORQUEFLITE TRANSMISSION
COST A PRINCELY $227

INTERIOR
The cabin had plenty of toys, including an "Indi-Colour" speedometer that changed colour as speed increased, variable-speed windscreen wipers, padded dash, automatic headlight dimming, and swivelling seats in Jaquard fabric and vinyl.

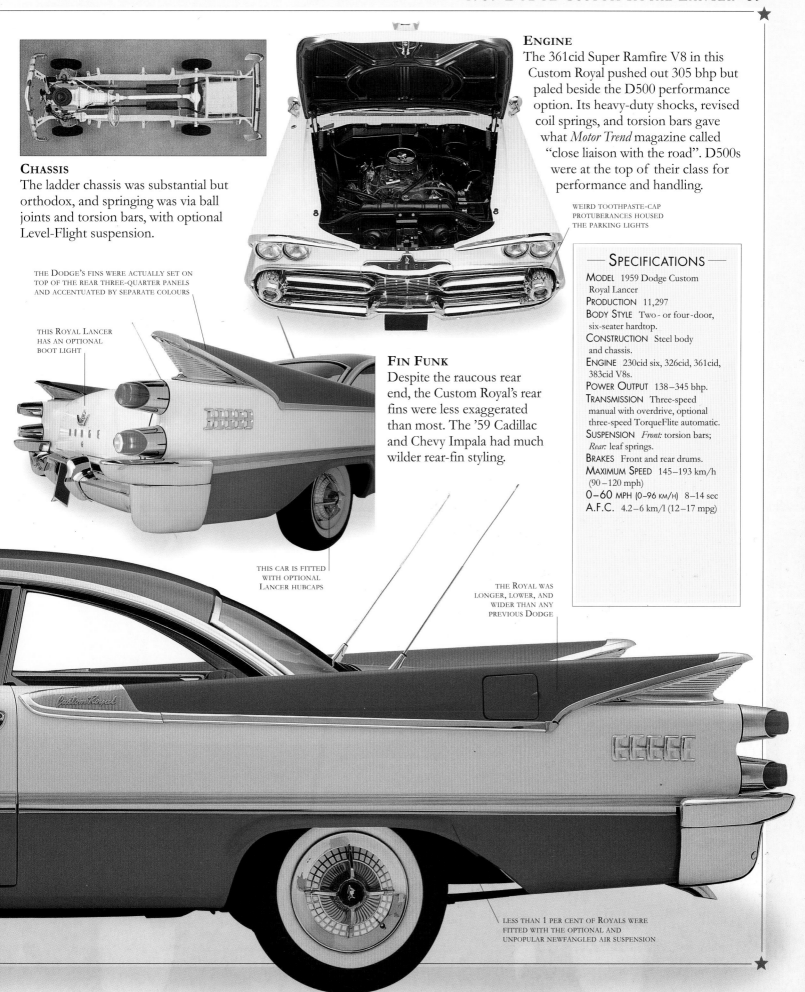

CHASSIS

The ladder chassis was substantial but orthodox, and springing was via ball joints and torsion bars, with optional Level-Flight suspension.

ENGINE

The 361cid Super Ramfire V8 in this Custom Royal pushed out 305 bhp but paled beside the D500 performance option. Its heavy-duty shocks, revised coil springs, and torsion bars gave what *Motor Trend* magazine called "close liaison with the road". D500s were at the top of their class for performance and handling.

WEIRD TOOTHPASTE-CAP PROTUBERANCES HOUSED THE PARKING LIGHTS

THE DODGE'S FINS WERE ACTUALLY SET ON TOP OF THE REAR THREE-QUARTER PANELS AND ACCENTUATED BY SEPARATE COLOURS

THIS ROYAL LANCER HAS AN OPTIONAL BOOT LIGHT

FIN FUNK

Despite the raucous rear end, the Custom Royal's rear fins were less exaggerated than most. The '59 Cadillac and Chevy Impala had much wilder rear-fin styling.

THIS CAR IS FITTED WITH OPTIONAL LANCER HUBCAPS

THE ROYAL WAS LONGER, LOWER, AND WIDER THAN ANY PREVIOUS DODGE

LESS THAN 1 PER CENT OF ROYALS WERE FITTED WITH THE OPTIONAL AND UNPOPULAR NEWFANGLED AIR SUSPENSION

SPECIFICATIONS

MODEL 1959 Dodge Custom Royal Lancer

PRODUCTION 11,297

BODY STYLE Two- or four-door, six-seater hardtop.

CONSTRUCTION Steel body and chassis.

ENGINE 230cid six, 326cid, 361cid, 383cid V8s.

POWER OUTPUT 138–345 bhp.

TRANSMISSION Three-speed manual with overdrive, optional three-speed TorqueFlite automatic.

SUSPENSION *Front:* torsion bars; *Rear:* leaf springs.

BRAKES Front and rear drums.

MAXIMUM SPEED 145–193 km/h (90–120 mph)

0–60 MPH (0–96 KM/H) 8–14 sec

A.F.C. 4.2–6 km/l (12–17 mpg)

THE RISE AND FALL OF THE GREAT AMERICAN FIN

WORLD WAR II GAVE AMERICA its fins, and it was an aeroplane that did it – the Lockheed P-38. In 1941 Harley Earl and his coterie from the GM design staff visited the Selfridge Field Air Force base near Detroit. Sworn to secrecy, they were only allowed to view the P-38 from a distance, but were rapt by its pointed nose, contoured streamlining, greenhouse cockpit, and twin tail booms.

THE '49 CAD'S LITTLE BUMPS WERE THE ONES THAT STARTED IT ALL

Obsessed with this brave new styling metaphor, Earl grafted a dorsal fin onto the prototype '48 Cadillac. But when he presented his new motif to senior GM executives, it bombed. Earl's confidence was shaken and he stormed back to the studio, railing "take that goddam fin off, nobody wants it". The designer refused and Earl nearly fired him. Three days later, Earl returned, saying "that fin's okay, let's keep it on". A good move, as 1949 was one of Cadillac's best ever sales years.

Earl couldn't possibly have foreseen the fad he was starting. What was little more than a jumped-up tail-light progressively mushroomed to shoulder height. After Cadillac, Oldsmobile followed in '49, Buick in '52, Chrysler in '55, Hudson, Studebaker, and Nash in '56, and conservative old Uncle Henry held out until 1957. But by '59 the fin had become so grotesque that the Chevrolet Impala's razor-like rear looked sharp enough

This baby can flick its tail at anything on the road!
THE '57 DeSOTO FIREFLITE'S FINNY REAR

1959 DODGE
Custom Royal Lancer

IMPOSING BACKSIDE
Vestigial rear screen pillars are so thin that the roof seems to float above the body. Combined with the high boot line and low roof line, it makes for a chunky rear aspect.

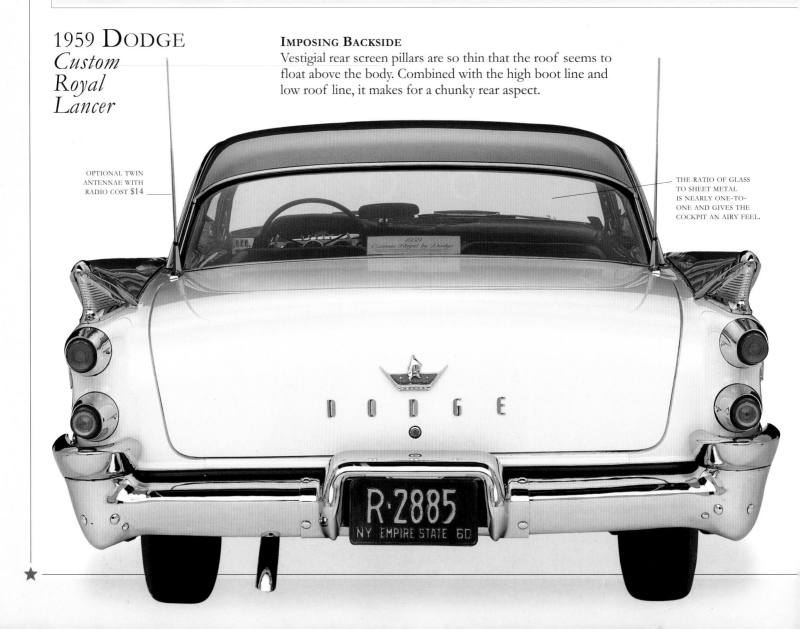

OPTIONAL TWIN ANTENNAE WITH RADIO COST $14

THE RATIO OF GLASS TO SHEET METAL IS NEARLY ONE-TO-ONE AND GIVES THE COCKPIT AN AIRY FEEL.

D O D G E

R·2885
NY EMPIRE STATE 60

to draw blood. Satirists laid into the fin with vicious glee. John Keats, in his book *The Insolent Chariots*, likened the American car to an overweight concubine. "With all the subtlety of a madam affecting a lorgnette, she put tail fins on her overblown bustle and spouted wavering antennae from each fin."

BELIEVE IT OR NOT, THE FINS ON THE '60 CHEVY IMPALA WERE ACTUALLY TONED DOWN FROM '59

Surprisingly, Virgil Exner, Chrysler's design guru, bravely attempted to argue that fins had a practical advantage. Using a scale model of a DeSoto in a wind tunnel, he claimed that roadholding was improved and steering corrections in strong cross-winds reduced by up to 20 per cent. But in reality it was impossible to argue with conviction that this absurd stylistic excess had a serious function. After fins had shrunk in the early Sixties, no-one reported worse handling or steering vagaries.

The fin was really the first of a cornucopia of visual novelties that gave consumers a reason for changing their cars every year. Cynically, the industry knew that these appalling appendages were just a tool to hasten the process of dynamic obsolescence, but a gullible public identified the fin with luxury and prestige, taking it as the punctuation mark of a well-styled car. It is endlessly fascinating to think that such a simple styling device managed so completely to entrance an entire decade of American car buyers.

THE EXPERIMENTAL CADILLAC CYCLONE TOOK THE FIN MOTIF TO NEW EXTREMES

FADDISH FRONT

The front end was the auto industry's idea of high style in '59. Quad headlights had ridiculous hooded chrome eyebrows, and the grille was outrageously overwrought. Such ostentation was merely a crutch for hobbling from one expensive restyle to the next.

WINDSCREEN IS SOLEX TINTED, AN $18 OPTIONAL EXTRA

VARIABLE-SPEED WINDSCREEN WIPERS AND WASHERS COST $18.25 EXTRA BACK IN '59

THE ABSURD OVER-CHROMED OVERRIDERS HOLD PARKING LIGHTS

R·2885 NY EMPIRE STATE 60

1959 EDSEL
Corsair

STEERING WHEEL LOGO

BY 1959 AMERICA HAD LOST her confidence; the economy nose-dived, Russia was first in space, there were race riots in Little Rock, and Ford was counting the cost of their disastrous Edsel project – close on 400 million dollars. "The Edsel look is here to stay" brayed the adverts, but the bold new vertical grille had become a country-wide joke. Sales didn't just die, they never took off, and those who had been rash enough to buy hid their chromium follies in suburban garages. Eisenhower's mantra of materialism was over, and buyers wanted to know more about economical compacts like the Nash Rambler, Studebaker Lark, and novel VW Beetle. Throw in a confusing 18-model line-up, poor build quality, and disenchanted dealers, and "The Newest Thing on Wheels" never stood a chance. Now famous as a powerful symbol of failure, the Edsel stands as a telling memorial to the foolishness of consumer culture in Fifties America.

― EDSEL HYPE ―

FORD HAD CANVASSED public opinion on a new design with which to challenge GM's dominance as far back as 1954, and named the new project the E ("experimental") Car. Officially christened the Edsel, it arrived in 1957 on the back of intense TV and magazine coverage. But by the time it hit the showrooms, the market had done a *volte-face* and wanted more than just empty chromium rhetoric. The main problem was that the Edsel's vision was never taken beyond yesterday or today. No input into the project considered the future, so by the time the Edsel did appear, it was a ridiculous leviathan, hopelessly out of kilter with its time.

REAR LIGHTS
Tail- and back-up lights were shared with the '58 Continental to save on tooling costs.

1959 EDSEL CORSAIR CONVERTIBLE
By 1959, the Corsair had become just a restyled Ranger, based on the Ford Fairlane. Corsairs had bigger motors and more standard equipment. But even a sticker price of $3,000 for the convertible didn't help sales, which were a miserable model year total of 45,000. Ford were desperate and tried to sell it as "A new kind of car that makes sense".

DECORATION
The dominating chrome and white sweepspear that runs the entire length of the car makes the rear deck look heavy.

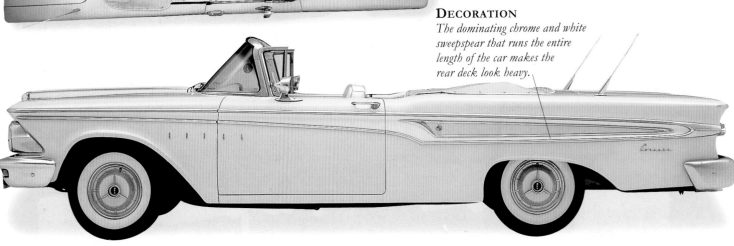

"GUARD RAIL" FRAME DESIGN WITH FULL-LENGTH SIDE RAILS

BALL JOINT FRONT SUSPENSION

SPECIFICATIONS

MODEL 1959 Edsel Corsair Convertible

PRODUCTION 1,343

BODY STYLE Two-door, five-seater convertible.

CONSTRUCTION Steel body and chassis.

ENGINE 332cid, 361cid V8s.

POWER OUTPUT 225–303 bhp.

TRANSMISSION Three-speed manual with optional overdrive, optional two- or three-speed Mile-O-Matic automatic.

SUSPENSION *Front:* independent with coil springs; *Rear:* leaf springs with live axle.

BRAKES Front and rear drums.

MAXIMUM SPEED 153–169 km/h (95–105 mph)

0–60 MPH (0–96 KM/H) 11–16 sec

A.F.C. 5.3 km/l (15 mpg)

INTERIOR

The dashboard was cleaned up for 1959 and the unreliable Teletouch transmission deleted in favour of a Mile-O-Matic two-speed with column shift. The eight-tube push-button radio was available at $64.95.

IN-CAR VINYL

This charming Philips record player is an after-market accessory fitted in the early 1960s.

MIRROR

The hooded chrome door mirror was remote-controlled, an extremely rare after-market option.

CHASSIS

The substantial steel girder chassis incorporated full-length side rails and five cross-members. It was hauled along by either an Edsel Express 332cid V8 producing 225 bhp or a Super Express 361cid V8 developing 303 bhp. 77 per cent of all 1959 Edsels were powered by V8s, with the Economy Six making up the numbers.

FRONT ASPECT

Roy Brown, the Edsel's designer, claimed that "The front theme of our newest car combines nostalgia with modern vertical thrust". Other pundits compared it to a horse collar, a man sucking a lemon, or even a toilet seat.

COLOUR

Petal Yellow was one of 17 possible exterior colours.

19 NEBRASKA 60
35·110
THE BEEF STATE

1959 FORD
Fairlane 500 Skyliner

THE '59 SKYLINER WAS 7½ CM (3 IN) SHORTER THAN THE '57–'58 MODELS

FORD RAISED THE ROOF in '57 with their glitziest range ever, and the "Retrac" was a party piece. The world's only mass-produced retractable hardtop debuted at the New York Show of '56 and the first production version was presented to a bemused President Eisenhower in '57. The Skyliner's balletic routine was the most talked-about gadget for years and filled Ford showrooms with thousands of gawping customers.

Surprisingly reliable and actuated by a single switch, the Retrac's roof had 185 m (610 ft) of wiring, three drive motors, and a feast of electrical hardware. But showmanship apart, the Skyliner was pricey and had precious little boot space or leg room. By '59 the novelty had worn off and division chief Robert McNamara's desire to end expensive "gimmick engineering" led to the wackiest car ever to come out of Dearborn being axed in 1960.

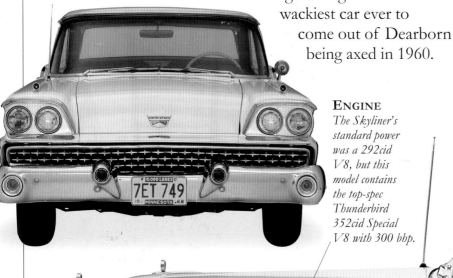

ROOF SEQUENCE
A switch on the steering column started three motors that opened the rear deck. Another motor unlocked the top, while a further motor hoisted the roof and sent it back to the open boot space. A separate servo then lowered the rear deck back into place. It all took just one minute, but had to be done with the gear shift in "Park" and the engine running.

ENGINE
The Skyliner's standard power was a 292cid V8, but this model contains the top-spec Thunderbird 352cid Special V8 with 300 bhp.

REAR STYLING
Fins were down for '59, but missile-shaped pressings on the higher rear wings were a neat touch to hide all that moving metalwork.

1959 FORD FAIRLANE 500 GALAXIE SKYLINER RETRACTABLE

The Skyliner lived for three years but was never a volume seller. Buyers may have thought it neat, but they were justifiably anxious about the roof mechanism's reliability. Just under 21,000 were sold in '57, less than 15,000 in '58, and a miserly 12,915 found buyers in '59. At two tonnes and $3,138, it was the heaviest, priciest, and least practical Ford in the range.

INTERIOR
Available options included power windows, tinted glass, four-way power seat, and Polar-Aire air-conditioning. The $19 Lifeguard safety package included padded instrument panel and sun visor.

The new **FORD SKYLINER** world's only Hide-Away Hardtop

SKYLINER COSTS
Ford spent $18 million testing the Skyliner's roof. Ironically, the Retrac's biggest fault wasn't electrical problems, but body rust.

SPECIFICATIONS

MODEL 1959 Ford Fairlane 500 Galaxie Skyliner Retractable
PRODUCTION 12,915
BODY STYLE Two-door hardtop with retractable roof.
CONSTRUCTION Steel body and chassis.
ENGINE 272cid, 292cid, 312cid, 352cid V8s.
POWER OUTPUT 190–300 bhp.
TRANSMISSION Three-speed manual, optional three-speed Cruise-O-Matic automatic.
SUSPENSION *Front:* coil springs; *Rear:* leaf springs.
BRAKES Front and rear drums.
MAXIMUM SPEED 169 km/h (105 mph)
0–60 MPH (0–96 KM/H) 10.6 sec
A.F.C. 5.4 km/l (15.3 mpg)

MANUAL OPERATION
If the electrics failed, there was a manual procedure for getting the roof down, but it was rarely needed.

FUEL TANK
This was located behind the rear seat, not for safety, but because there was nowhere else to put it.

1959 PLYMOUTH
Fury

Fury

A BOLD AND BRASSY NAME FOR
PLYMOUTH'S KITSCH CLASSIC

AMAZINGLY, THE '59 FURY was aimed squarely at middle-class, middle-income America. Amazingly, because it was as loud as Little Richard and as sexy as Jayne Mansfield. One of the most stylistically adventurous cars on the road, the futuristic Fury was pure "Forward Look". Plymouth's ads bellowed that it was "three full years" ahead of its time, and the '59 model was the most strident of the lot. That razor-edged profile made Plymouth a nameplate to kill for, especially if it was the top-line Sport Fury, which came with a personalized aluminium plaque that read "Made Expressly For..."

Sales of Plymouth's suburban trinket boomed in '59, with 89,114 Furys helping Plymouth rank third in the industry and celebrate the company's 11 millionth vehicle. With serious power and looks to stop a speeding train, the Fury wowed God-fearing America. But that rakish impudence couldn't last, and by '61 the Fury's fins were tragically trimmed. In the annals of kitsch, this one goes down as a real honey.

HEAVY-METAL VILLAIN
Stephen King's 1983 black comedy *Christine* used a '58 Fury as a demonic monster that suffocates its victims and eludes destruction by magically reconstituting itself. On screen, the Fury certainly looks like one of the baddest cars on the block.

ENGINE
The 318cid V8 pushed out just 230 horses, but Chrysler were starting to beat the performance drum as hard as they could. Top speed hit three figures, and acceleration was also brisk. The sheer bulk of the car plus those skinny tyres must have made things a touch scary at the limit.

INTERIOR
Inside was comic-book spaceship, with push-buttons galore. Swivelling front seats on Sport Furys were aimed at portlier buyers. The unlovely padded steering wheel was a $12 option.

REAR SPORT DECK
The optional boot-lid appliqué spare tyre cover was meant to take the line upmarket, but looked more like a trash-can lid.

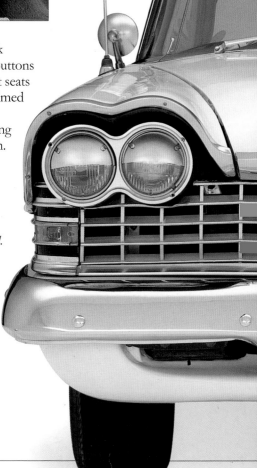

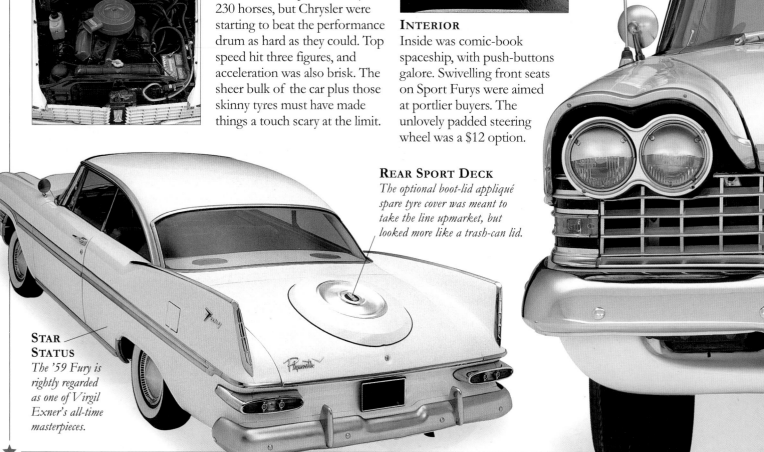

STAR STATUS
The '59 Fury is rightly regarded as one of Virgil Exner's all-time masterpieces.

FINS
Everyone had fins back in 1959, but the Fury's showed real class.

TASTEFUL FLAIR
Is that slogan tongue-in-cheek? Plymouth sold the Fury's bold lines as the perfect example of taste and discrimination. It could only happen in '59.

GOOD TASTE IS NEVER EXTREME

HEADLIGHTS
$40 optional electronic dipping for the headlights relieved the driver of yet one more little hardship.

LUXURY OPTIONS
Optional extras ranged from power brakes and the Golden Commando V8 to two-tone paint and contoured floormats.

1959 PLMOUTH FURY
Chrysler design chief Virgil Exner liked to see classic lines bolted onto modern cars, and the boot-lid spare tyre cover on the Fury is one example of this. The profile of this two-door hardtop shows off the Fury's fine proportions. The shape is dart-like with a tense urgency of line. The sloping cockpit and tapering rear window melt deliciously into those frantic fins.

FIERCE FRONT GRILLE
Cross-slatted grille was all-new for '59 and made the front end look like it could bite.

SPECIFICATIONS

MODEL 1959 Plymouth Fury

PRODUCTION 105,887 (all body styles and including Sport Furys)

BODY STYLE Two-door hardtop.

CONSTRUCTION Steel body and chassis.

ENGINE 318cid V8 (360cid V8 optional for Sport Fury).

POWER OUTPUT 230 bhp (Sport Fury 260 bhp, or 305 bhp with 360cid V8).

TRANSMISSION Three-speed manual with optional overdrive, optional three-speed TorqueFlite automatic, and PowerFlite automatic.

SUSPENSION *Front:* torsion bars; *Rear:* leaf springs.

BRAKES Front and rear drums, optional power assistance.

MAXIMUM SPEED 169–177 km/h (105–110 mph)

0–60 MPH (0–96 KM/H) 11 sec

A.F.C. 6 km/l (17 mpg)

1959 PONTIAC
Bonneville

THE BONNY WAS *MOTOR TREND*'S 1959 "CAR OF THE YEAR"

IN THE LATE '50s, Detroit was worried. Desperately trying to offer something fresh, manufacturers decided to hit the aspirational thirty-somethings with a new package of performance, substance, and style. Pontiac's "Wide Track" Bonneville of '59 was a sensation. General Manager Bunkie Knudsen gave the line an image of youth and power and Wide Track became all the rage. *Car Life* picked the Bonneville as its "Best Buy" and so did consumers. By 1960, soaring sales had made Pontiac the third most successful company in the industry.

The prestige Bonneville was also a dream to drive. The 389cid V8 pushed out up to 345 horses and, when the Tri-Power mill was fitted, top speeds hit 201 km/h (125 mph). At 1.93 m (6 ft 4 in) wide, the Custom two-door hardtop wouldn't fit in the car wash. But nobody cared. In 1959, America spent $300 million on chewing gum, the supermarket was its temple, and the jingling advert its national anthem. A self-obsessed utopia of comfort and convenience was about to go horribly wrong.

WILD AND WACKY
Garish three-colour striped upholstery was meant to give the Bonneville a jaunty carelessness and appeal to the young at heart. Warehouse-like interior dimensions made it a true six-seater.

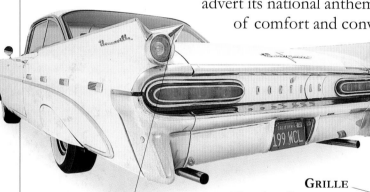

DOUBLE FINS
With consumers crying out for individuality, Pontiac gave the Bonneville not two fins, but four.

GRILLE
The split grille was new for '59. After reverting back to a full-length grille for just one year, it became a Pontiac trademark in the early '60s.

INTERIOR
The riotous interior had as much chrome as the exterior and buyers could specify Wonderbar radio, electric antenna, tinted glass, padded dash, and tissue dispenser. The under-dash air-conditioning unit is a later, after-market accessory.

SPECIFICATIONS

MODEL 1959 Pontiac Bonneville
Sport Coupe
PRODUCTION 27,769
BODY STYLE Two-door,
six-seater coupe.
CONSTRUCTION Steel body
and chassis.
ENGINE 389cid V8.
POWER OUTPUT 260–345 bhp.
TRANSMISSION Three-speed
manual, optional four-speed
Super Hydra-Matic automatic.
SUSPENSION Front and rear
coil springs.
BRAKES Front and rear drums.
MAXIMUM SPEED 177–201 km/h
(110–125 mph)
0–60 MPH (0–96 KM/H)
9–11.5 sec
A.F.C. 5.3 km/l (15 mpg)

1959 PONTIAC BONNEVILLE SPORT COUPE

Flushed with success, Pontiac claimed that they were
the maker of "America's Number One Road
Car". Adverts for the Bonneville were
thick with hyperbole, suggesting that
"when you arrive, bask for a minute in
the respectful spotlight of admiration
that's always focused on this striking,
tasteful car". The broad-shouldered
appearance was macho, tough, and
suggestive, and appealed to the public;
27,769 Sport Coupes like this were sold in 1959.

CHASSIS
*The chassis was known as
Spread-Tread and gave much
crisper cornering than was
possible in previous models.*

1958 BONNEVILLE
Pontiac's '58 Bonnevilles
were 23 cm (9 in) shorter and
13 cm (5 in) narrower than
the Wide Track '59s. The
most obvious difference was
in the grille, which was a one-
piece affair on the '58 model.
Sales literature from that year
crooned that the Bonneville
"sets a new pattern of
dynamic luxury for those
who like their motoring
rare and exciting".

BRAKES
*Early Bonnevilles had lousy
brakes, but '59s had finned drums
and 10 per cent more lining area.*

The Sixties

If the Fifties changed the way America looked, the Sixties changed the way Americans thought. Assassinations, demonstrations, confrontations, a youth with a conscience, and a war nobody wanted made the nation take a long hard look at itself.

AWAY FROM THE UNREST and upheaval of the decade, America still found time to enjoy life. The economy was in rude health, average earnings were $150 a week, and attendances at amusement parks boomed. JFK promised a new order and there were new distractions like felt-tip pens, non-dairy creamer, and a dance called the Twist.

FORD FALCON COMPACT

And there were drugs, lots of them. A Harvard researcher called Timothy Leary dabbled with recreational pharmaceuticals and became a cult hero by appearing on stage in 1967, dressed in white with flowers in his hair. He told half a million stoned followers to "turn on to the scene, tune in to what's happening, and drop out of everything", neatly articulating the mantra of the Sixties.

Pampered, comfortable, and bored out of their brains, the college-age young represented 10 per cent of the population and had the time and the power to pursue their own agendas. They rejected parental values of rising early, working hard, and saving money, and instead lashed into capitalism and the establishment. Anyone who was into change, high ideals, and a new order was determinedly pursued by hordes of wide-eyed devotees. The popularity of cult icons like Jack Kerouac, Martin Luther King Jr., and JFK soared to a new high.

Main Street America may have smiled nervously at Ken Kesey's best-selling novel, *One Flew Over the Cuckoo's Nest*, but the

THE LEGENDARY JFK
The youngest President ever elected was sworn in on 20 January 1961. Saying "the torch has been passed to a new generation of Americans", he promised strong leadership and hope for the Sixties.

	1960	1961	1962	1963	1964
AUTOMOTIVE	• **Chevrolet** trounce **Ford** in model year production • **Edsel** dropped after three disastrous years • Compact **Chevrolet** Corvair, **Ford** Falcon, **Mercury** Comet, and **Plymouth** Valiant appear • Car production double that of 1950 • Steel strike means aluminium on grilles and hubcaps gains popularity • 10 million families own cars	• **DeSoto** nameplate disappears • **Ford** and **Chevrolet** introduce new cast-iron engines • **Lincoln** introduce dazzling new Continental • **Dodge** launch compact Lancer • **Pontiac** launch Tempest, with transmission at rear to eliminate gearbox hump in interior • **Oldsmobile** introduce F-85 • Industry introduces lifetime chassis lubrication and self-adjusting brakes	• Fins and two-tone paint fade from most ranges • New class of intermediate model born in the **Chevy** Nova, **Ford** Fairlane, and **Mercury** Meteor • **Ford** and **Chrysler** offer V8s with 400 bhp • **Buick** offer new V6 • Calendar sales reach 6.8 million • Drag racing between **Ford**, **Chevrolet**, **Dodge**, **Mercury**, and **Pontiac** re-accelerates horsepower race	• New personal sports cars debut: **Buick** Riviera, **Studebaker** Avanti, and Corvette Sting Ray • **GM** introduce Tilt-Away steering wheel • **Chrysler** offer a new 50,000-mile warranty • Detroit agrees to install seat belts on '64 models • Car production hits record 7.3 million	• **Ford** release Mustang at New York World Fair; best-selling new car in history • **Studebaker** end US production • **GM** suffer massive strike • **Pontiac** GTO debuts  1964 OLDSMOBILE STARFIRE
HISTORICAL	• John F. Kennedy announces he's running for President • JFK and Nixon hold live TV debate • Russians shoot down US spy plane • 10 blacks shot dead in worst-ever race riot in Mississippi • *Ben Hur* wins a record 10 Oscars and *Psycho* opens	• Kennedy sworn in as President • US breaks diplomatic ties with Cuba • Bay of Pigs • JFK sends 100 "advisers" to Vietnam • Berlin Wall goes up • Yuri Gagarin is first man in space THE TWIST	• More US aid for South Vietnam • JFK embargoes Cuban imports • John Glenn orbits the earth • Martin Luther King Jr. jailed for illegal march in Georgia • Telstar satellite beams pictures around the world • Supreme Court outlaws prayer in schools • Marilyn Monroe dies from a drugs overdose • Decca record company turns down the Beatles	• Cuban missile crisis brings world to brink of nuclear war • JFK assassinated • Khrushchev warns the world that Russia has 100 megatonne A-bomb • 200 arrested at Mississippi University race riot • Five US helicopters shot down in Mekong Delta • Alcatraz closes • Tennessee Williams' *Sweet Bird of Youth* premieres	• LBJ signs sweeping Civil Rights Act • US escalates action against North Vietnam • Malcolm X forms Black Nationalist Party • First flight of 3,200 km/h (2,000 mph) B-70 bomber • Sidney Poitier becomes first black actor to win an Oscar • The Beatles appear on the *Ed Sullivan Show*

FAREWELL TO FINS
In the Sixties, Cadillacs shed their fins with indecent haste. Gone were the ridiculous tail feathers of the '59 (left), replaced by the clean, horizontal lines of the '65 (below).

subtext of cultural radicalism went straight over their heads. Artists like Warhol and Lichtenstein, with their Campbell's soup cans and cartoon blow-ups, may have appeared to be painting a democratic canvas, but in reality they were chipping away at establishment values. The problem was that only the radical youth could be bothered to listen.

While the old order blockaded Cuba, and sent "advisers" to Vietnam and John Glenn into orbit, the new order marched 200,000-strong to Washington to demonstrate over civil rights, listened to four mop-topped Englishmen called the Beatles, and joined Malcolm X's Black Nationalist Party. The Surgeon General blamed cigarettes for lung cancer, JFK was cruelly cut down in Dallas, and

SPACE MANIA
Ford's advertising campaign for '63 tapped into the national obsession with the space race: "A small spaceman makes big discoveries about Ford interiors."

Lyndon Johnson turned up the heat in Vietnam. America was changing, big-time.

Hordes of middle-class students, who wouldn't normally have drawn a rebellious breath, were out demonstrating to save themselves, and the Vietnamese. Many of their colleges and universities were sucked into the war machine. Suddenly, sacrosanct freedoms like experimental sex, drugs, hair, music, and clothing were under attack as unpatriotic, immoral, subversive, and unhygienic. And, as always, it was capitalism that was to blame for fuelling America's great engine of war.

A pall of paranoia fell over the nation. Everybody was chasing everybody else in the hit TV series *The Fugitive*, the CIA was blamed for the assassination of JFK, and bugs were found in the US Embassy in Moscow. The FBI tried not to investigate the murder of three civil rights workers in Mississippi and Malcolm X was gunned down in New York.

1965	1966	1967	1968	1969
• **Cadillacs** finally lose their tail fins • **American Motors** lose $13 million • **GM** make $1.54 billion • Ralph Nader's *Unsafe at Any Speed* published	• **Oldsmobile** launch big new sports car, the Toronado • Seven safety items added to all new cars • LBJ signs Traffic Safety Act • **Lincoln** get standard 462cid engine • Average big car price is $7,500, average compact is $3,100 • Extras add 40 per cent to price of average sedan • Model year production romps towards nine million cars	• 17 new safety standards incorporated into all US cars; prices rise by 21 per cent • **Pontiac** launch Firebird to fight Mustang and Camaro • **Cadillac** launch new Eldorado	• Model year production peaks at 8.4 million units • **Chrysler** adopt long-bonnet-short-boot philosophy with restyled **Dodge** Charger • **Lincoln** launch Continental Mark III • Three per cent price hike is biggest for 10 years • **Cadillac** get 472cid engine	• Side marker lights are new Federal safety requirement • Mustang, Camaro, and Firebird all get face-lifts

MALCOLM X

1967 CHEVROLET CAMARO RS

THE VIETNAM WAR ESCALATES

1965	1966	1967	1968	1969
• Malcolm X shot in New York • Nixon visits USSR • New York abolishes death penalty • First US astronaut walks in space • Julie Andrews wins Oscar for *Mary Poppins*	• US troops launch 8,000-strong offensive in Vietnam; bombers strafe Hanoi • American H-bomb goes missing after mid-air crash • Ronald Reagan becomes Governor of California • Black student shot in back at University of Mississippi • Bob Dylan records his first music using electric guitar • Film actress Hedy Lamarr arrested for shoplifting	• North Vietnam rejects US offer of peace talks; UN calls for an end to the Vietnam War • 200,000 protest in New York and San Francisco against War • Muhammad Ali refuses draft • Paratroops called in to quell race riots in Detroit • Stalin's daughter defects • First heart transplant • First microwave oven on market • Rolling Stones in court on drugs charges	• LBJ sends 50,000 more troops to Vietnam • LBJ signs Civil Rights Bill • Anti-war riots in Chicago • Nixon elected President and calls for Vietnam conflict to be scaled down • Bobby Kennedy assassinated • Jackie Kennedy marries Onassis • Martin Luther King Jr. assassinated in Memphis • Dustin Hoffman stars in *The Graduate*	• Biggest anti-war demonstration of the decade is called the "Vietnam Moratorium" • 400,000 attend Woodstock Festival • Man lands on moon • Premieres of *Midnight Cowboy* and *Easy Rider*

Even Defense Secretary Robert McNamara was dubbed a "mother of invention". It took the Beatles to sum up America's malaise in one word: "Help!".

Ford and Pontiac tried to cheer things up with the new Mustang, Camaro, and Firebird, helped by mini skirts, The Monkees, *Mission Impossible*, and *The Munsters*. With more disposable income than ever before, Easy Street stretched from one side of America to the other. Four out of five households now owned a car, multi-car families totalled 12 million, and between them they were consuming millions of gallons of gas a year.

The Pressure Builds

The music industry put on a happy face with *Good Vibrations*, *Feelin' Groovy*, *California Dreaming*, and *All You Need is Love*. But in the background the soundtrack of protest still tinkled away with *Alice's Restaurant*, Dylan's *The Times They Are A-Changin'*, and the veiled satire of *Rowan & Martin's Laugh-In*. But the laughing stopped abruptly when Tricky Dick Nixon announced that he was running for President. The shocks never seemed to end.

Things came to a head in 1968. Anarchy was so near that many people genuinely felt America was about to disintegrate. Assassins took out Martin Luther King Jr. and Robert Kennedy, race riots flared everywhere, and the police quelled anti-war protests with savage and needless brutality. The hot, violent summer of '68 in Chicago was like a civil

war. It was the catalyst America needed, and the machinery of change shifted up a gear.

Nixon began withdrawing troops from 'Nam, a fairer "lottery-style" draft system came into effect, and the US and USSR started talking to each other at the first of the Strategic Arms Limitation Talks. Neil Armstrong took those few giant steps for mankind and the establishment shrugged its shoulders and allowed Woodstock to happen. Public protest had succeeded, and the new order was here to stay. Peace and love to all.

Meanwhile, the auto industry was actually listening to what was going on. Manufacturers quickly purged their cars of futuristic frivolity and tail fins because they too couldn't ignore the cries of protest. The youth

A NEW BREED
Muscle cars like this '67 Camaro Z-28 answered the consumer's cri de coeur for distinction. The rock 'n' roll subculture of the Fifties had spread into a broad and profitable youth market that wanted to express its rebellious identity through its cars, and manufacturers were responding.

ANTI-WAR SENTIMENTS
In 1968, anti-war demonstrations in Chicago got out of hand and the National Guard had to be called in. Demonstrators taunted soldiers, who reacted with shocking violence. Novelist Norman Mailer was among more than 250 arrested on that day.

market was rebelling against everything, including dinosaurs in their driveways. What they wanted were machines with charisma and optimism, like the fun-loving Volkswagen Beetle.

The Birth of Auto Individuality

First came the socially responsible compacts (the Lark, Valiant, and the Falcon), then the personality pony cars (the Barracuda, Mustang, and Camaro), followed by the rebellious muscle iron (the GTO, Charger, and Trans Am). Business was now brisk because, for once, the motor mandarins were offering excitement, low prices, and a new deal – auto individuality. Sixties Detroit was at its most imaginative and culturally receptive and, despite war, labour unrest, and domestic turmoil, production peaked in '69 at an amazing 8.4 million cars.

And in the age of the individual there was no better sales ploy than to offer an individualized car. Sixties option lists read like the Declaration of Independence. Buyers could create custom-made cars by ticking boxes from a litany of permutations of engines, carburettors, transmissions, brakes, wheels, seats, interiors, and even colour-coded wing mirrors. By plugging into the culture of difference

and defiance, Detroit cynically stoked the fires of youthful rebellion. In 1966, Dodge launched its "Rebellion" promotion, featuring a woman standing beside a Charger holding a bomb behind her back. Buick advertised its Skylark GS as a muscle car "that will rattle your faith in the established order". Uncannily, during the Sixties, America's social and cultural changes were nearly always reflected in her automobiles. Both Washington and Detroit went through their own kind of revolution, but where Washington resisted caving in to the new order, Detroit embraced it like a new-found friend. To its credit, Motown gave customers what they wanted, machines with personality and distinction that were fun to drive, look at, and listen to.

But the status quo wouldn't stay stable for long. Left on its own, Detroit might well have continued selling mass-produced motoring mescaline through the next two decades without a hiccup, but it wasn't to be. Greed, Federal meddling, and the inability to create excitement in a non-creative atmosphere brought the industry to its knees. Bad news was just around the corner, and it was called the Seventies.

FLYING FALCON
1968 was one of the best years for the car industry and auto makers spent $1.5 billion bringing in new models. This '68 Ford Falcon was one of many cars that boasted better safety features and a longer warranty.

1960 CHEVROLET
Impala

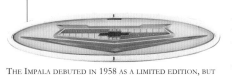

THE IMPALA DEBUTED IN 1958 AS A LIMITED EDITION, BUT WENT ON TO BECOME THE MOST POPULAR CAR IN '60s USA

IN THE SIXTIES, unbridled consumerism began to wane. America turned away from the politics of prosperity and, in deference, Chevrolet toned down its finny Impala. The '59's gothic cantilevered batwings went, replaced by a much blunter rear deck. WASP America was developing a social conscience and Fifties excess just wasn't cool anymore.

Mind you, the '60 Impala was no shrinking violet. Tired of gorging on gratuitous ornamentation, American motorists were offered a new theology — performance. Freeways were one long concrete loop, premium gas was cheap, and safety and environmentalism were a nightmare still to come. For $333, the Sports Coupe could boast a 348cid, 335 bhp Special Super Turbo-Thrust V8. The '59 Impala was riotous and the '60 stylistically muddled, but within a year the unruliness would disappear altogether. These cross-over Chevrolets are landmark cars — they ushered in a new decade that would change America and Americans forever.

INTERIOR
Inside, the Impala was loaded with performance metaphor: central speedo, four gauges, and a mock sports steering wheel with crossed flags. This car has power windows and dual Polaroid sun visors.

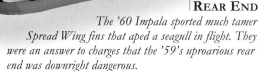

ENGINE
Two V8 engine options offered consumers seven heady levels of power, from 170 to 335 horses. Cheapskates could still specify the ancient Blue Flame Six, which wheezed out a miserly 135 bhp. Seen here is the 185 bhp, 283cid V8. Impalas could be invigorated with optional Positraction, heavy-duty springs, and power brakes.

REAR END
The '60 Impala sported much tamer Spread Wing fins that aped a seagull in flight. They were an answer to charges that the '59's uproarious rear end was downright dangerous.

SPECIFICATIONS

MODEL 1960 Chevrolet Impala
Sports Coupe
PRODUCTION Not available
BODY STYLE Two-door coupe.
CONSTRUCTION Steel body,
separate chassis.
ENGINE 235cid straight six, 283cid,
348cid V8s.
POWER OUTPUT 135–335 bhp
(348cid turbo V8).
TRANSMISSION Three-speed
manual, optional four-speed
manual, two-speed Powerglide
automatic, Turboglide automatic.
SUSPENSION *Front:* upper and
lower A-arms, coil springs;
Rear: coil springs with live axle.
BRAKES Front and rear drums.
MAXIMUM SPEED 145–217 km/h
(90–135 mph)
0–60 MPH (0–96 KM/H) 9–18 sec
A.F.C. 4.2–5.7 km/l
(12–16 mpg)

RACING IMPALA

The Impala impressed on circuits all over the world. This '61 model was deemed hot enough to dice with European track stars like the Jaguar Mark II, driven here by Graham Hill.

WHEELS

At $15 a set, wheel discs were a mandatory fashion accessory. Slick whitewalls were yours for just $36.

1960 CHEVROLET IMPALA SPORTS COUPE

Triple tail-lights and a vertically ribbed aluminium rear beauty panel helped to sober up the Impala's rear end. It was still a class act and a lot glitzier than the Bel Air's plainer tail. As for the front, it was meant to be quiet and calm and a million miles from the deranged dentistry of mid-Fifties grille treatments. The jet-fighter cockpit and quarter-panel missile ornaments were eerie portents of the coming decade of military intervention.

1960 CHRYSLER

300F

CHRYSLER'S LETTER SERIES STARTED IN 1955

"RED HOT AND RAMBUNCTIOUS" is how Chrysler sold the 300F. It may be one of the strangest straplines of any American auto maker, but the 300F really was red hot and a serious flying machine that could better 225 km/h (140 mph). The rambunctious refers to the ram-air induction on the bad-boy 413cid wedge-head V8. Ram tuning had long been a way of raising torque and horsepower for drag racing, and it gave the 300F a wicked performance persona.

One of Virgil Exner's happier designs, the 300F of '60 had unibody construction, a French Pont-A-Mousson four-speed gearbox, and front seats that swivelled towards you when you opened the doors. It also boasted an electro-luminescent instrument panel and Chrysler's best styling effort since 1957. But at $5,411, it was no surprise that only 964 Coupes found buyers. Nevertheless, it bolstered Chrysler's image, and taught them plenty of tuning tricks for the muscle-car wars that were revving up just around the corner.

SERIOUS COMFORT
More a coupe than a saloon, the 300F's four bucket seats were contoured in black, red, or white terracotta leather as here.

SWIVELLING SEAT
Self-activated swivelling seats were new for 1960 and pivoted outwards automatically when either door was opened. It's ironic that the burly 300F's typical owner was reckoned to be a flabby 40-year-old.

THIS MAGNIFICENT BLOCK SECURED THE FIRST SIX PLACES FOR 300Fs IN THE 1960 FLYING MILE COMPETITION AT DAYTONA, WITH A TOP SPEED OF 233 KM/H (145 MPH)

ENGINE
The 375 bhp 413cid V8 breathed through two Carter four-barrels with 30-inch rams and was a real gem of an engine. Chrysler carefully calculated optimum inlet manifold length and placed carburettors on the end of the tubes rather than the traditional inline, to give a steady build-up of power along the torque curve.

SOLEX TINTED GLASS WAS A $43 OPTION

WITH THE WINDOWS ROLLED DOWN, THE 300F HAD A PILLARLESS LOOK

DASHBOARD

The "Astra-Dome" instrumentation was illuminated at night by electro-luminescent light, giving a soft, eerie glow that shone through the translucent markings on the gauges. It was technically very daring and boasted six different laminations of plastic, vitreous, and phosphor.

TACHOMETER CAME AS STANDARD

THE ONLY BLEMISH

The much-criticized fake spare-tyre embellishment on the boot was variously described as a toilet seat or trash-can lid. Possibly the 300F's only stylistic peccadillo, it was dropped in '61.

SPECIFICATIONS

MODEL 1960 Chrysler 300F
PRODUCTION 1,212 (both
 body styles)
BODY STYLE Two-door coupe
 and convertible.
CONSTRUCTION Steel unitary body.
ENGINE 413cid V8.
POWER OUTPUT 375–400 bhp.
TRANSMISSION Three-speed push-
 button automatic, optional four-
 speed manual.
SUSPENSION *Front:* torsion bars;
Rear: leaf springs.
BRAKES Front and rear drums.
MAXIMUM SPEED 225 km/h
 (140 mph)
0–60 MPH (0–96 KM/H) 7.1 sec
A.F.C. 4.2 km/l (12 mpg)

HUMONGOUS BOOT

The two-door shape meant that the rear deck was the size of Indiana, and the cavernous boot was large enough to hold four wheels and tyres.

THIS PARTICULAR MODEL HAS SURE-GRIP DIFFERENTIAL, A $52 OPTION

LENGTHY FINS

You could argue that the 300F's fins started at the front of the car and travelled along the side, building up to lethal, dagger-like points above the exquisitely sculptured tail-lights. Within two years fins would disappear completely on the Chrysler letter series 300.

POWER ANTENNA WAS A $43 OPTION AND THIS CAR ALSO HAS THE GOLDEN TONE radio ($124) WITH REAR SEAT SPEAKER ($17)

NYLON WHITEWALLS CAME AS STANDARD

EVOLUTION OF THE CHRYSLER 300 LETTER SERIES

THE 300 SERIES started life in 1955 when Chrysler came up with the first production sedan to kick out 300 bhp. The following year it was given the designation "B" and horsepower was hiked to 340. In '57 it became the 300C, pushing out 375 horses and by '59, the "D" was producing 380 bhp. The only 300 without a letter was the '63, which would have read as a rather confusing 300I. Otherwise, the series followed in alphabetical order, the distinguished line culminating in the 360 bhp 300L of 1965.

ADVERTISING FOR THE 300F CALLED IT "THE SIXTH OF A FAMOUS FAMILY" AND "LEADER OF THE CLAN"

1955

AMERICA'S ORIGINAL muscle machine debuted as the C300, an image car to lock horns with the Corvette and T-Bird. Chrysler couldn't afford a two-seater, so instead stuffed everything they could into a New Yorker body. With a special Hemi and twin WCFB carbs, it was the fastest production car in the world and became known as "the car that swept Daytona".

KEY FEATURES
- Hand-built cars
- Oversize exhaust and solid valve lifters
- Only available in black, red, or white
- Base price of $4,055
- Options list runs to only 10 features

1956

THE 300B WAS THE first of the letter cars that gave buyers a choice of engine and transmission options. The base 354cid kicked out 340 horses, but mid-year a 355 bhp motor was offered, along with three different transmissions. The 300B, not Chevy's fuelie 283, was the first American engine to offer a genuine one horsepower per cubic inch.

KEY DEVELOPMENTS
- Revised rear end with new bumper and tail-lights
- Two-speed PowerFlite, TorqueFlite, and three-speed manual offered from mid-year
- Base price of $4,312
- Air-conditioning, record player, and clock set in steering wheel become options

1960 CHRYSLER *300F*

BADGE
The brazen red, white, and blue 300F badge on the rear wing left nobody in any doubt that this was really a thunderbolt in drag.

AIR-CONDITIONING COST A HEFTY $510 EXTRA

AUTOMATIC TRANSMISSION WAS ACTUATED BY PUSH-BUTTONS ON THE DASH

SHARP END
The 300F's razor-sharp rear fins were cited by Ralph Nader in his book *Unsafe at Any Speed* as "potentially lethal". In 1963, a motorcyclist hit the rear bumper of a 300F at speed and was impaled on the fin.

QUESTIONABLE REAR DECK TREATMENT WAS KNOWN AS "FLIGHT-SWEEP" AND WAS ALSO AVAILABLE ON OTHER CHRYSLERS

1960 CHRYSLER 300F

1957	1958	1961	1965

THE THIRD LETTER CAR in the 300 series was confusingly known as the 300C, confusing since the '55 had been tagged the C300. But that was where the similarity ended. Blessed with Virgil Exner's elegant rear finnery, it had quad headlights, a big trapezoidal grille, a convertible option, and a howling all-out maximum of 241 km/h (150 mph).

KEY DEVELOPMENTS
- Silentfan drive
- Stiffer torsion bars
- Optional high-lift cams boost horsepower to 390
- Base price $4,929
- Now available in five exterior colours

THE 300D WASN'T that different from the "C". With a simpler grille and slightly changed rear lights, it pushed out 380 horsepower and came with fuel injection as a $400 option. Power brakes were now standard, and the Hemi mill was gently reworked. At Bonneville, a 300D set a new speed record of 251 km/h (156 mph).

KEY DEVELOPMENTS
- Compression and horsepower up
- New valve timing, pistons, and cam
- Electrojector fuel injection is first use of a computer in a Chrysler product; only 16 cars fitted with fuel injection
- Last year of Firepower Hemi engine

THE 300G LOOKED much like the 300F, but the much-lambasted toilet seat was dropped from the rear deck and the front end wore Chrysler's new slanted headlights. This would be the last year of Exner's fins. 1,617 "G"s left showrooms in 1961, by which time prices, swollen by a handful of options, were homing in on a very considerable $7,000.

KEY DEVELOPMENTS
- Standard ram manifolding
- Short-ram high-output engine available
- Power windows, autopilot, and undercoating standard
- 15-inch wheels now fitted

THE ELEVENTH AND LAST year of the letter series, the 300L rode on racing tyres and shocks with a 413cid lump. Four-speed manual stick shift was a no-cost option and, in common with other '65 Chryslers, it retained unibody construction. But the 300L was not as quick as its forebears and is the least special of Chrysler's limited editions.

KEY DEVELOPMENTS
- Longer wheelbase
- New corporate C-body
- Last year for 413cid engine
- Column lever replaces push-buttons on TorqueFlite
- Bigger drum brakes

POWER AND BEAUTY

The 300F was one of America's most powerful cars, and a tuned version recorded a one-way run of an amazing 304 km/h (189 mph) on the Bonneville salt flats. But despite the prodigious performance, it was deliberately understated compared with many contemporary Detroit offerings.

THE PHRASE "BEAUTIFUL BRUTES" WAS COINED TO DESCRIBE THE 300 SERIES

WING MIRROR WAS REMOTE-CONTROLLED

FRONT TORSION BAR SUSPENSION AND EXTRA-STRENGTH LEAF SPRINGS MEANT THE 300F HANDLED WELL

1962 FORD
Falcon

THE FALCON, WITH ITS SIMPLE, ULTRA-CONSERVATIVE STYLING, WAS DUBBED BY FORD "THE EASIEST CAR IN THE WORLD TO OWN"

FORD CHIEF EXECUTIVE Robert McNamara had a soft spot for the Volkswagen Beetle and wanted Dearborn to turn out a small compact of its own. Obsessed with gas mileage and economy, McNamara wanted a four-cylinder, since it was $13.50 cheaper to make, but was persuaded that a six-pot would sell better. On 19 March 1958, Ford approved its small car programme and the Falcon, the first of the American compacts, was launched in 1960.

The press were unimpressed, calling it a modern version of the Tin Lizzy. One auto writer said of McNamara: "He wears granny glasses and has put out a granny car." But cash-strapped consumers liked the new-sized Ford, and the Falcon won over 435,000 sales in its first year. The ultimate throwaway car, the Falcon may have been mechanically uninteresting and conventional in looks but it was roomy, smooth-riding, and delivered an astonishing 10.6 km/l (30 mpg).

INTERIOR
The austere interior could be upgraded with an $87 Deluxe trim package, which became the Deluxe model in its own right from 1962. A padded dash and visors cost an extra $16, and front safety belts $21. Transmission choices were standard column-shift three-speed synchro manual or two-speed Ford-O-Matic automatic.

NEW BARGAIN COMPACT
Ford introduced "a wonderful world of savings in the new-sized Ford Falcon". Base Falcons stickered at just $1,974 in 1960.

GROWING SERIES
The Falcon range gradually expanded to station wagons, a neat-looking pick-up, the Falcon Sedan Delivery, the Econoline Van range, and the sporty Futura coupe. The Futura Sprint, convertible or hardtop, came with a zesty 260cid V8.

"BIG-CAR" ENGINE
The Falcon's standard mill was a 144cid six, which the adverts boasted was a "brand-new powerplant specifically designed to power the Falcon over America's hills and highways with big-car performance and safety".

FRONT GRILLE
The aluminium-stamped radiator grille changed every year. This "electric shaver" convex shape with vertical bars denotes a '62 Falcon.

SLIM DIMENSIONS
Prototypes had to be considerably widened and lengthened after Henry Ford himself complained they were too narrow.

SPECIFICATIONS

MODEL 1962 Ford Falcon

PRODUCTION 396,129

BODY STYLE Two- or four-door hardtops, station wagons, and convertible.

CONSTRUCTION All-steel unitary construction.

ENGINE 144cid, 170cid sixes, 260cid V8.

POWER OUTPUT 85–174 bhp.

TRANSMISSION Three-speed column-shift synchro manual, optional two-speed Ford-O-Matic automatic.

SUSPENSION *Front:* coil springs; *Rear:* leaf springs.

BRAKES Front and rear drums.

MAXIMUM SPEED 145–177 km/h (90–110 mph)

0–60 MPH (0–96 KM/H) 12–18 sec

A.F.C. 8.8–10.6 km/l (25–30 mpg)

1962 FORD FALCON
Half-a-bonnet shorter than full-size Fords, the slab-sided two- or four-door Falcon could comfortably seat six. Its styling was as simple as its engineering, with roly-poly rounded edges, creased body sides, and big, circular tail-lights. The Falcon series just about made it to the end of the decade, superseded in 1970 by the compact Maverick – based on the Falcon's chassis – and then by the even tinier and thriftier Pinto ranges.

ROOF STYLING
Mid-'62 two- and four-door Falcons had a T-Bird-style roof line.

ROOMY INSIDE
Ford's marketing men boasted that the Falcon offered "honest-to-goodness six-passenger comfort – plenty of room for six and their luggage!". For once the hype was true and the interior did actually have room for occupants over 1.8 m (6 ft) tall.

1962 FORD
Galaxie 500XL Sunliner

500 DESIGNATION STOOD FOR
THE INDY 500-MILE RACES

IN '62, FORD WERE SELLING their range as "America's liveliest, most carefree cars". And leading the lively look was the bright-as-a-button new Galaxie. This was General Manager Lee Iacocca's third year at the helm and he was pitching for the young-guy market with speed and muscle. Clean cut, sleek, and low, the Galaxie range was just what the boys wanted and it drove Ford into a new era. The new-for-'62 500XL was a real piece, with bucket seats, floor shift, a machine-turned instrument panel, and the option of a brutish 406cid V8. XL stood for "extra lively", making the 500 one of the first cars to kick off Ford's new Total Performance sales campaign.

The 500XL Sunliner Convertible was billed as a sporting rag-top and cost an eminently reasonable $3,350. Engines were mighty, rising from 292 through 390 to 406cid V8s, with a Borg-Warner stick-shift four-speed option. Ford learnt an important lesson from this car. Those big, in-yer-face engines clothed in large, luxurious bodies would become seriously hip.

INTERIOR
The interior was plush and palatial, with Mylar-trimmed, deep-pleated buckets flanking the centre console. Seats could be adjusted four ways manually and six ways electronically. The dashboard was padded, and front seat belts were an option.

MIRROR-LIGHT
The spotlight-mirror was a factory option; on a clear day, the light could emit a beam 800 metres (½ mile) ahead.

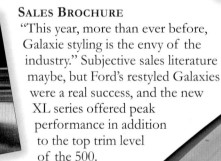

SALES BROCHURE
"This year, more than ever before, Galaxie styling is the envy of the industry." Subjective sales literature maybe, but Ford's restyled Galaxies were a real success, and the new XL series offered peak performance in addition to the top trim level of the 500.

Galaxie 500/XL sunliner

STYLISH CHROME
The arrow-straight side flash is a far cry from the florid sweepspears that adorned most Fifties models.

HIDDEN FILLER
The fuel filler-cap lurks behind this hinged section of the anodized beauty panel. The panel itself highlights the car's width.

LIGHTS
Large, round, rear-light cluster aped the T-Bird and appeared on the Falcon as well as the Fairlane, also debuting in 1962.

ENGINE
Stock Galaxies lumbered around with a 223cid six or 292cid V8. The 500XL could choose from a range of Thunderbird V8s that included the 390cid Special, as here, and a 405 bhp 406cid V8 with triple Holley carbs, which could be ordered for $379.

SPECIFICATIONS

MODEL 1962 Ford Galaxie 500XL Sunliner Convertible
PRODUCTION 13,183
BODY STYLE Two-door convertible.
CONSTRUCTION Steel body and chassis.
ENGINE 292cid, 352cid, 390cid, 406cid V8s.
POWER OUTPUT 170–405 bhp.
TRANSMISSION Three-speed Cruise-O-Matic automatic, optional four-speed manual.
SUSPENSION *Front:* coil springs; *Rear:* leaf springs.
BRAKES Front and rear drums.
MAXIMUM SPEED 174–225 km/h (108–140 mph)
0–60 MPH (0–96 KM/H) 7.6–14.2 sec
A.F.C. 5.7–6.4 km/l (16–18 mpg)

1962 FORD GALAXIE 500XL SUNLINER

The slab-sided Galaxie body was completely new for '62 and would set something of a styling trend for larger cars. Lines may have been flat and unadorned, but buyers could choose from 13 colours and 21 jaunty two-tones. The hardtop version of the 500XL Sunliner was the Club Victoria, $250 cheaper than the convertible and twice as popular, with 28,000 manufactured in '62.

HEAVY-RIBBED FLOOR

WIDE-CONTOURED FRAME WITH DOUBLE-CHANNEL SIDE RAILS

BODY INSULATION
The Galaxie had an especially quiet ride because it was soundproofed at various points. Sound-absorbent mastic was applied to the inside surfaces of the doors, bonnet, boot lid, wings, and quarter panels, while thick fibreglass "blankets" insulated the roof.

TOP UP
Unlike this example, the rarest Sunliners have a wind-cheating Starlift hardtop, which was not on the options list.

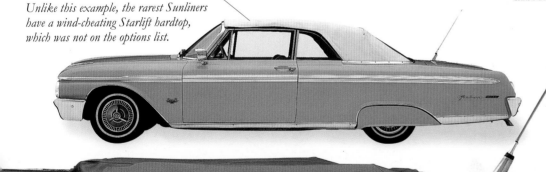

1962 FORD
Thunderbird

IT WAS NO ACCIDENT THAT THE third-generation T-Bird looked like it was fired from a rocket silo. Designer Bill Boyer wanted the new prodigy to have "an aircraft and missile-like shape", a subtext that wasn't lost on an American public vexed by the Cuban crisis and Khrushchev's declaration of an increase in Soviet military spending.

THUNDERBIRDS
ARE GO

The Sports Roadster model was the finest incarnation of the '61–'63 Thunderbird. With Kelsey-Hayes wire wheels and a two-seater fibreglass tonneau, it was one of the most glamorous cars on the block and one of the most exclusive. Virile, vast, and expensive, the Big Bird showed that Detroit still wasn't disposed to make smaller, cheaper cars. GM even impudently asserted that "a good used car is the only answer to America's need for cheap transportation". And anyway, building cars that looked and went like ballistic missiles was far more interesting and profitable.

INTERIOR
Aircraft imagery in the controls is obvious. The interior was designed around a prominent centre console that split the cabin into two separate cockpits, delineating positions of driver and passenger. T-Bird drivers weren't that young, and a Swing-Away steering wheel *(left)* aided access for the more corpulent driver.

STANDARD POWER
STEERING NEEDED
JUST THREE-AND-A-
HALF TURNS LOCK-
TO-LOCK

CONSTRUCTION WAS "DUAL-UNITIZED",
WITH SEPARATE FRONT AND REAR SECTIONS
WELDED TOGETHER AT THE COWL

TINTED GLASS, POWER SEATS AND
WINDOWS, AND AM/FM RADIO
WERE THE MOST POPULAR OPTIONS

ROOF FUN
With the top down, the streamlined tonneau made the Sports Roadster sleek enough to echo the '55 two-seater Thunderbird.

ENGINE
The M Series 390cid V8 was an option that could crack 60 (96 km/h) in eight seconds and run all the way to 193 km/h (120 mph). It had three Holley two-barrels and five main bearings. The biggest unit on offer was the 427cid V8 with 425 bhp.

THUNDERBIRD LANDAU
New for this model year was the swish Landau with a black or white vinyl top, designed to look like a leather-padded carriage top of yore. The roof was decorated in classic style, with chrome Landau irons on the sides. Leather upholstery was a plush extra at $106.

SPECIFICATIONS

MODEL 1962 Ford Thunderbird Sports Roadster
PRODUCTION 1,427
BODY STYLE Two-door, two-/four-seater convertible.
CONSTRUCTION Steel body and chassis.
ENGINE 390cid V8.
POWER OUTPUT 330–340 bhp.
TRANSMISSION Three-speed Cruise-O-Matic automatic.
SUSPENSION *Front:* upper and lower A-arms and coil springs; *Rear:* leaf springs with live axle.
BRAKES Front and rear drums.
MAXIMUM SPEED 187–201 km/h (116–125 mph)
0–60 MPH (0–96 KM/H) 9.7–12.4 sec
A.F.C. 3.9–7.1 km/l (11–20 mpg)

INTERIOR DESIGNER ART QUERFIELD SPENT MORE TIME ON THE T-BIRD'S CABIN THAN ON ANY OTHER CAR IN HIS 40 YEARS AT FORD

T-BIRDS WERE FINISHED IN 18 SINGLE SHADES OR 24 TWO-TONE COMBINATIONS

OVERHEAD
The Sports Roadster could also be a full four-seater. Trouble was, there was no space in the trunk for the tonneau, so it had to stay at home. *Motor Trend* magazine said: "Ford's plush style-setter has plenty of faults... but it's still the classic example of the prestige car."

THREE SETS OF FIVE CAST-CHROME SLASH MARKS UNMISTAKABLY SUGGEST TOTAL POWER

LESSER T-BIRDS COULD OPT FOR THE ROADSTER'S WIRE WHEELS AT $343

1962 FORD THUNDERBIRD

EVOLUTION OF THE FORD THUNDERBIRD

THE BEACH BOYS were in good company as they sang the T-Bird's praises. Along with the Mustang and 'Vette, the Thunderbird has a special place in the American psyche. Purists maintain that proper T-Birds flew only between '55 and '66, but after a few duff models in the '70s and '80s, the latest incarnation is actually quite a graceful car and still true to its original concept. Sadly, the '97 T-Bird marks the end of a remarkable 43-year run, with production scheduled to come to a close.

1955

FORD TOOK JUST 20 months to come up with an answer to Chevy's creaking Corvette, and didn't they do well? The 1955 to 1957 model years saw 40,000 of the original Thunderbirds leaving showrooms. While not a huge figure by Detroit's standards, this was a massive total for a new and unknown market for the American sports car.

KEY FEATURES
- First T-Bird rolls off the line on 9 September 1954
- Introduced on "T-Day" (22 October 1954) to triumphant accolades
- Startlingly low price of $2,695
- 4,000 orders taken on first day of sale

1959

SWAPPING TWO SEATS for four in 1958 showed the powerful influence of Ford's accountants. In a search for greater sales volume, the Thunderbird nameplate was taken upmarket to lose its youthful verve and become a prestige cruiser. Now, for the first time, T-Birds offered room for four, and the entire family could join the party.

KEY DEVELOPMENTS
- Ads sell T-Bird as "America's Most Becoming Car"
- 430cid Thunderbird Special V8 available
- New radical fan and revised rear suspension
- T-Bird finishes second in '59 Daytona

1964

WHILE THE THIRD-generation model (1961–63) was warmly received and sold well, the fourth generation from '64 saw the Thunderbird acquiring a middle-age spread. The subtle curves disappeared, replaced by a riot of planes and angles. With the car now weighing nearly two tonnes, things had got rather flabby. No prizes for charisma here.

KEY DEVELOPMENTS
- Complete restyle with longer bonnet and shorter roof
- Sports Roadster model dropped
- Five new rear axle options
- *Car and Driver* magazine lambasts T-Bird for "ego gratification"

1962 FORD *Thunderbird*

WITH THE BONNET DOWN, THE BIG BIRD WAS ONE OF THE MOST ATTRACTIVE AND STIFFEST CONVERTIBLES FORD HAD EVER MADE; THE HEAVY UNITARY-CONSTRUCTION BODY ALLOWED PRECIOUS FEW SHAKES, RATTLES, AND ROLLS

REAR ASPECT
Ford cleaned up the rear of their prestige offering after the demise of the '58 to '60 Squarebird. Lights were a simple rounded cluster, and the bumper was of the straight and plain school of design.

REAR OVERHANG WAS PRODIGIOUS, BUT PARKING COULD BE MASTERED BY USING THE REAR FIN AS A MARKER

LARGE TONNEAU PANEL CAME OFF EASILY BUT REQUIRED TWO PEOPLE TO HANDLE IT

19 SCENIC 68
2513
NEW HAMPSHIRE

1966

WITH A SHARPER FRONT, egg-crate grille, and full-width tail-lights, the '66 looked even neater; underneath the glitter, things were basically the same. A Town Hardtop and Town Landau were added to the range. *Car Life* called the '66 T-Bird a "flying carpet on autopilot" and marvelled at its speed, silence, and refinement.

KEY DEVELOPMENTS
• 345 bhp 428cid V8 available
• Prices reduced for '66
• Plush Landau is best-selling T-Bird for '66
• Last year of convertibles

1970

FORD'S ANSWER TO JAGUAR, the fifth-generation T-Bird from 1967 now had four doors and a tin top. Enthusiasts wailed that the most prized and individual of automobiles had turned into a truncated Galaxie, with all the trimmings. These Thunderbirds may have been groaning with every option available, but they lacked personality.

KEY DEVELOPMENTS
• New front end styling and reworked tail-lights
• Longer, lower, and wider
• New suspension and radial tyres give "uncanny" control
• T-Bird gains 0.7 per cent of total new car market

1978

1978 SAW FEW CHANGES from the '77 downsized model and, despite the car's economical pretensions, sales were a healthy 352,000 units. To add kudos to its now-emasculated Bird, Ford added a Diamond Jubilee model, calling it the "most exclusive Thunderbird you can buy". In reality the T-Bird was a pale facsimile, but the public didn't care.

KEY DEVELOPMENTS
• 351cid V8 tweaked for more performance
• Fuel consumption averages 5.3 km/l (15.1 mpg)
• Lighter power steering pump and better torque converter
• New Sports Decor option package at $466

1994

AFTER A FEW STYLE revisions in the '80s, which culminated in the classy 1989 rear-drive personal coupe that won *Motor Trend*'s Car of the Year, the revamped 1994 Thunderbird continued the fine return to form. It was now regarded as a world-class model and seen as a genuine contender with the established luxury German marques.

KEY DEVELOPMENTS
• Front and rear ends get smoother treatment
• Restyled "organic" interior with analogue gauges
• Dual airbags now standard
• Base model now stickers at $16,830

DIVINE DESIGN
Sales literature suggested that the T-Bird was the result of the combined efforts of Ford and God.

FRONT ASPECT
The front bears an uncanny resemblance to the British Ford Corsair. This link is neither surprising nor coincidental, since the Corsair was also made by Uncle Henry.

ODD STYLING CREASE RAN FROM WING TO DOOR AND IS THE MODEL'S LEAST BECOMING FEATURE

LONG-LIVED V8 GAVE 12 PER CENT MORE TORQUE THAN PREVIOUS MODEL

1963 STUDEBAKER
Avanti

AVANTI IS THE ITALIAN WORD FOR FORWARD

THE AVANTI WAS A BIG deal for Studebaker and the first all-new body style since 1953. The last car design of the legendary Raymond Loewy, it rode on a shortened Lark chassis with a stock Studey 289cid V8. The Avanti's striking simplicity of shape was just one of Loewy's celebrated confections. From his voguish Coca-Cola dispenser to the chaste Lucky Strike cigarette packet, Loewy's creations were instant classics, and the brilliant Avanti was a humdinger.

Studebaker's prodigy was fairly audacious too, with a fibreglass body, anti-sway bars, optional Paxton supercharger, and wind-cheating aerodynamics. Dealers, however, could not meet the huge wave of orders and this, combined with other niggles like flexing of the fibreglass shell, resulted in impatient buyers defecting to the Corvette camp instead. Fewer than 4,650 Avantis were made, and production ceased in December 1963, the Avanti concept being sold to a couple of Studebaker dealers. They went on to form the Avanti Motor Corporation, which successfully churned out Avantis well into the Eighties.

INTERIOR
The Avanti's dashboard is a study in simplicity, with Mercedes-type gauges and very little chrome extravagance. The centre console would look more at home in a light aircraft. Standard equipment included internal boot and bonnet releases and vinyl bucket seats.

BODY STYLING
The slippery shape was not wind-tunnel tested, but a piece of guesswork by Loewy. His calculations were spot-on, because in 1962 an Avanti R3 broke 29 Bonneville speed records, travelling faster than a standard American car had ever done before.

ENGINE
The 289cid was the best Studebaker V8 ever made, developing 240 bhp in standard R1 tune. Supercharged R2 and R3 boasted 290 and 335 bhp respectively, while the experimental fuel-injected R5 produced a howling 575 bhp.

1963 STUDEBAKER AVANTI

More European than American, the Avanti had a long neck, razor-edged front wings, and no grille. Early sketches show Loewy's inspiration, with tell-tale annotations scribbled on the paper that read "like Jaguar, Ferrari, Aston Martin, Mercedes". Lead time for the show Avanti was a hair-raising 13 months, with a full-scale clay model fashioned in only 40 days. Production estimates were as optimistic as 1,000 a month, but in the whole of 1964 Studebaker managed to churn out only 800 Avantis.

REAR VIEW
Hardly dated at all, the rear aspect is clean, uncluttered, and very modern. Note the ageless rear light treatment.

FRONT VIEW
Unmistakable from any angle, early '63 Avantis had round headlights, but most later '64 models sported square ones.

SPECIFICATIONS

MODEL 1963 Studebaker Avanti
PRODUCTION 3,834
BODY STYLE Two-door, four-seater coupe.
CONSTRUCTION Fibreglass body, steel chassis.
ENGINE 289cid, 304cid V8s.
POWER OUTPUT 240–575 bhp (304cid R5 V8 fuel-injected).
TRANSMISSION Three-speed manual, optional Power-Shift automatic.
SUSPENSION *Front*: upper and lower A-arms, coil springs; *Rear*: leaf springs.
BRAKES Front discs, rear drums.
MAXIMUM SPEED 193 km/h (120 mph)
0–60 MPH (0–96 KM/H) 7.5 sec
A.F.C. 6 km/l (17 mpg)

1964 BUICK
Riviera

BUICK'S '63 RIV WAS HAILED
AS A CONTEMPORARY CLASSIC

IN '58, SO THE STORY GOES, GM's design supremo Bill Mitchell was entranced by a Rolls-Royce he saw hissing past a London hotel. "What we want", said Mitchell, "is a cross between a Ferrari and a Rolls". By August 1960, he'd turned his vision into a full-size clay mock-up.

One of the world's most handsome cars, the original '63 Riviera was GM's attempt at a "Great New American Classic Car". And it worked. The elegant Riv was a clever amalgam of razor edges and chaste curves, embellished by just the right amount of chrome. Beneath the exquisite lines was a cross-member frame, a 401cid V8, power brakes, and a two-speed Turbine Drive tranny. In the interests of exclusivity, Buick agreed that only 40,000 would be made each year. With ravishing looks, prodigious performance, and the classiest image in town, the Riv ranks as one of Detroit's finest confections.

INTERIOR
The sumptuous Riv was a full four-seater, with the rear seat divided to look like buckets. The dominant V-shaped centre console mushroomed from between the front seats to blend into the dashboard. The car's interior has a European ambience uncharacteristic for the period.

DIMENSIONS
Relatively compact, the Riviera was considerably shorter and lighter than other big Buicks.

CONWAY TWITTY
The crooner of tunes like *It's Only Make Believe* owned the '64 Riv featured on these pages. Aimed at GM's most affluent customers, the Riviera soon became the American Jaguar.

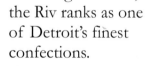

ENGINE
'64s had a 425cid Wildcat V8 that could be tickled up to 360 horses courtesy of dual four-barrels. *Car Life* magazine tested a '64 Riv with the Wildcat and stomped to 60 (96 km/h) in a scintillating 7.7 seconds. Buick sold the tooling for the old 401 to Rover, who used it to great success in their Range Rover.

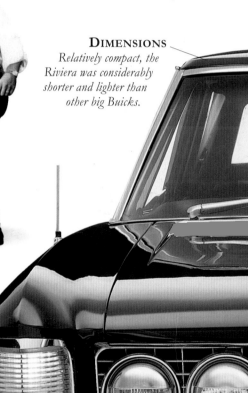

SMART FRONT
The purposeful W-section front could have come straight out of an Italian styling house.

BOOT SPACE
The substantial boot could take two sets of golf clubs with ease, testimony to the leisured lifestyle of the average Riviera owner.

1964 BUICK RIVIERA

The Riv was America's answer to the Bentley Continental, and pandered to Ivy League America's obsession with aristocratic European thoroughbreds like Aston Martin, Maserati, and Jaguar. The grille was inspired by the Ferrari 250GT, and the hard-edged wing line pre-dated the angular Rolls-Royce Silver Shadow by three years. The rear aspect was a study in simplicity, with an unembellished boot and delicate rear lights.

DECORATION
Ineffectual side scoops weren't there to cool the rear brakes; they are the Riviera's only concession to vanity and disappeared in '65.

BOOT LID
One optional extra was a remote-controlled boot lid, which was pretty neat for '64.

SPECIFICATIONS

MODEL 1964 Buick Riviera
PRODUCTION 37,958
BODY STYLE Two-door hardtop coupe.
CONSTRUCTION Steel body and chassis.
ENGINE 425cid V8.
POWER OUTPUT 340–360 bhp.
TRANSMISSION Two- or three-speed automatic.
SUSPENSION Front and rear coil springs.
BRAKES Front and rear drums.
MAXIMUM SPEED 193–201 km/h (120–125 mph)
0–60 MPH (0–96 KM/H) 8 sec
A.F.C. 4.2–5.7 km/l (12–16 mpg)

HEADLIGHTS
'63 and '64 Rivs have classic exposed double headlights. For reasons best known to themselves, Buick gave '65 cars headlights that were hidden behind electrically operated, clam-shell doors.

1964 LINCOLN
Continental

CONTINENTAL ORNAMENT
WAS A MARK OF ESTEEM

THERE'S AN UNSETTLING irony in the fact that John F. Kennedy was shot in a '61 Lincoln Continental. Like him, the revamped '61 Continental had a new integrity. Substantial and innovative, it was bristling with new ideas and survived for nine years without major change. The car fit for Presidents was elegant, restrained, and classically sculptured, perfect for Camelot's new dynasty of liberalism. Ironic, too, that JFK rather liked the Lincoln – he often used a stock White House Continental for non-official business.

Nearly $7,000 bought one of the most influential and best-built American cars of the Sixties. Not only did it carry a two-year, 24,000-mile warranty, but every engine was bench-tested and each car given a 200-category shake-down. WASP America approved and production doubled in the first year. Even the Industrial Design Institute was impressed, awarding its coveted bronze medal for "an outstanding contribution of simplicity and design elegance".

PRESIDENTIAL WHEELS

THE DARK BLUE '61 Continental phaeton, watched by the world in Dealey Plaza, Dallas, was on loan to the White House from Ford's Special Vehicles Division for $500 a year. It had rear seats that could be raised or lowered automatically, two-way radio telephone, and thick steel-plating along the front and rear side rails. After the November '63 assassination, it was still kept in harness, serving both the Johnson and Nixon administrations. Later fitted with a permanent solid roof, it was eventually retired to the Henry Ford Museum in Dearborn, where it still resides.

JFK IN THE PRESIDENTIAL CONTINENTAL ON THE DAY OF
HIS ASSASSINATION IN DALLAS, TEXAS

GAUGES SHOWING FUEL SUPPLY, OIL
PRESSURE, WATER TEMPERATURE, AND
BATTERY CHARGE WERE NEW FOR '64

INTERIOR
Every Continental had power steering and windows, walnut cappings, a padded dashboard, lush carpets, and vacuum-powered door locks as standard. The locks operated automatically as soon as the car started to move.

SUSPENSION
DAMPING WAS
CONSIDERED
THE BEST ON
ANY CAR

ENGINE
Power was supplied by a huge 430cid V8 that generated 320 bhp. Each engine was tested at near maximum revs for three hours and then stripped down for inspection. Many mechanical parts were sealed for life.

MASSIVE
SCREEN
GAVE
EXCELLENT
ALL-ROUND
VISION

TO SPREAD COSTS, THE CONTINENTAL SHARED SOME OF ITS FACTORY TOOLING WITH THE '61 THUNDERBIRD

LINEAR PROFILE

Apart from the gentle dip in the waistline at the back of the rear doors, the roof and wing lines form two uninterrupted, almost parallel lines.

STATE-OF-THE-ART HOOD

11 relays and a maze of linkages made the Continental's hood disappear neatly into the boot. The electrics were completely sealed and never needed maintenance.

CONVERTIBLE RARITIES

Rag-top Continentals were really "convertible sedans" with standard power tops. The '64 rag-tops were stickered at only $646 more than the four-door sedans, yet they remain much rarer models: only about 10 per cent of all '61–'67 Lincolns produced were convertibles.

SPECIFICATIONS

MODEL 1964 Lincoln Continental Convertible
PRODUCTION 3,328
BODY STYLE Four-door, five-seater convertible.
CONSTRUCTION Steel body and chassis.
ENGINE 430cid V8.
POWER OUTPUT 320 bhp.
TRANSMISSION Three-speed Turbo-Drive automatic.
SUSPENSION *Front:* control arms and coil springs; *Rear:* leaf springs with live axle.
BRAKES Front and rear drums.
MAXIMUM SPEED 185 km/h (115 mph)
0–60 MPH (0–96 KM/H) 11 sec
A.F.C. 5 km/l (14 mpg)

EASY ACCESS

The "suicide" rear-hinged doors hark back to classic pre-war coach-building. On older Continental Convertibles, opening all four doors at once can actually flex the floor and chassis.

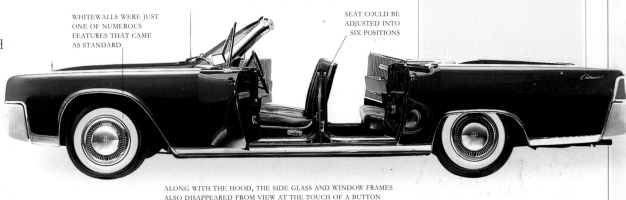

WHITEWALLS WERE JUST ONE OF NUMEROUS FEATURES THAT CAME AS STANDARD

SEAT COULD BE ADJUSTED INTO SIX POSITIONS

ALONG WITH THE HOOD, THE SIDE GLASS AND WINDOW FRAMES ALSO DISAPPEARED FROM VIEW AT THE TOUCH OF A BUTTON

EVOLUTION OF THE LINCOLN CONTINENTAL

THE REVOLUTIONARY Continental of 1961 ranks as one of Detroit's greatest achievements. Chiselled good looks, enviably perfect build quality, and an exclusive bloodline made it the most desirable Lincoln since the pre-war K-Series. Sixties Continentals were the pre-eminent American luxury car and had an aura of distinction that stood out from the garish autos of the Fifties. Today it stands as evidence that, when they tried, Detroit could match the best in the world.

1940

1940 WAS THE FIRST YEAR of the Continental, a European shape based on the Lincoln Zephyr. With both coupe and convertible retailing at just under $3,000, the nation sighed in admiration at Ford's new dreamboat. By 1941 the Continental became a model in its own right. One of America's most prestigious brands had been born.

KEY FEATURES
• First cars powered by Lincoln's unreliable L-head V12
• Push-button exterior door handles in '41
• New 305cid V12 in '42, along with face-lift that gives Continental longer, higher wings, and new nose
• Headlights now flanked by parking lights

1956

OFFERED ONLY AS a two-door model with a stratospheric price tag of $10,000, nobody expected the Mark II of 1956 to sell seriously. The comely Continental was a flagship car intended to bless other Ford products with a halo of association. And it worked. In its day the Mark II was distinguished, beautiful, and made by Uncle Henry.

KEY DEVELOPMENTS
• Launched at the 1955 Paris Auto Show to universal acclaim
• Special Continental Division created to market the Mark II
• All options standard except air-conditioning
• Only 2,994 sold

1961

LINCOLN BUILT YET another landmark car with the '61 Mark III. Bold, stylish, and influential, it scooped every award going. Bristling with quality and oozing class, the Camelot Continental set new standards of US automobile engineering integrity. Lincoln wisely kept the classic shape current, with only gentle styling changes up until 1969.

KEY DEVELOPMENTS
• Automatic transmission, radio, power brakes, steering, and windows all standard
• Mild styling tweaks until major face-lift in '65, but retains basic '61 shape
• '66 sees tail-lights no longer wrapping round bumper
• Gentle redesign in '68, with new bonnet

1964 LINCOLN *Continental*

IN '61, LINCOLN WERE THE ONLY MANUFACTURER TO OFFER A FOUR-DOOR CONVERTIBLE

LEAST POPULAR OPTION IN '64 WAS THE ADJUSTABLE STEERING WHEEL

QUALITY NOT QUANTITY
The '61 restyle reflected the new philosophy that big was not necessarily better. The previous Conti was a leviathan, but not so the '61. Lincoln historian James Wagner described the '61 Continental as "more like a Mercedes-Benz than a product of General Motors".

1972

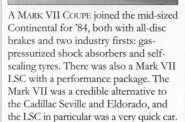

LONGER, LOWER, wider, and heavier than the Mark III Continental, the Mark IV, from '70 on, still had the same sharp shape. As before, it was based on the T-Bird and that big 460cid lived upfront, albeit detuned to a paltry 200 bhp due to emission controls. In spite of the energy crisis, it sold even better than the Mark III, averaging 50,000 to 60,000 each year.

KEY DEVELOPMENTS
• New criss-cross pattern grille
• New roof design with oblong opera window
• Increased leg and shoulder room for rear-seat passengers
• Cartier electric clock as standard

1984

A MARK VII COUPE joined the mid-sized Continental for '84, both with all-disc brakes and two industry firsts: gas-pressurized shock absorbers and self-sealing tyres. There was also a Mark VII LSC with a performance package. The Mark VII was a credible alternative to the Cadillac Seville and Eldorado, and the LSC in particular was a very quick car.

KEY DEVELOPMENTS
• Auto-levelling electronic air suspension standard in '84
• Two-door coupe joins line-up in '84
• LSC gains high output V8 for '85
• ABS standard in '86
• 302cid V8 gets sequential fuel injection in '86

1988

THE ALL-NEW CONTINENTAL for '88 was the first Lincoln with front-wheel drive and a six-cylinder mill. Weight was down but length was up. The only available engine was the 232cid V6 with four-speed overdrive automatic, not really powerful enough for such a big old tank. Computer-controlled suspension adjusted for changes in the road.

KEY DEVELOPMENTS
• Increased interior and boot space
• Now a genuine six-seater
• Electronic dash attracts criticism and is revised in '89
• His and her airbags for '89
• Dual exhausts for '89

1995

AFTER A MODERATE restyle in '94, '95 saw a major overhaul. Aside from the exterior design changes and a new 260 bhp V8, a dazzling array of high-tech features included the ability to programme ride, transmission, handling, and interior set-up to suit each individual driver. This was truly a car to take Lincoln into the 21st century.

KEY DEVELOPMENTS
• New unibody design
• New 32-valve InTech™ V8 is first Ford block to be placed in transverse mounting position
• New non-synchro four-speed automatic gearbox allows quicker shifting
• 100,000 mile (161,000 km) tune-up interval

COMPETITION BEATER
Low, wide, and mighty, the '60s Continental was considered the epitome of good taste and discrimination, and a patriotic alternative to the less sophisticated and poorly-built Jaguar Mark 10 sedan.

TINTED GLASS WAS A $53 OPTIONAL EXTRA

EVEN IN '64 YOU COULD HAVE CRUISE CONTROL, FOR A MERE $96 EXTRA

HEADLIGHTS COULD SENSE ONCOMING TRAFFIC AND DIM AUTOMATICALLY

NEW YORK
KTS 340
LINCOLN

1964 OLDSMOBILE
Starfire

IN 1964, LBJ SIGNED A tax-cut bill, *Peyton Place* was a TV hit, and Coca-Cola launched a new single-calorie soda called Tab. While America was on a roll, the auto industry was busy telling customers that bucket seats and centre consoles would enrich their lives. Oldsmobile trumpeted that their sporting Starfire Coupe offered "high adventure that starts right here!".

'64 OLDSMOBILES WERE MARKETED WITH THE SLOGAN, "WHERE THE ACTION IS"

Lame copy apart, the Starfire was quick, with Olds' most powerful lump, a 394cid V8 that could knock on the door of 193 km/h (120 mph). A terrifying thirst for gas didn't deter buyers, especially since these were big, softly-sprung mile-eaters, groaning with convenience options. Elegant and unadorned, the Starfire was one of a new breed of suburban starlets designed to make the WASP middle classes look as confident as they felt. And it worked.

CONVERTIBLE OPTION
The Starfire was easy on the hands, with power everything. Detroit knew that the "little woman" was becoming increasingly important in buying decisions and started to pitch their products at the shopping mall. Early Starfires were only available in convertible form and came with a special engine and de luxe interior.

ENGINE
Standard on the Starfire Coupe and Convertible was the mighty cast-iron block 394cid V8 with Rochester four-barrel carb, which churned out a hefty 345 bhp. Performance on original '61 models was positively exhilarating, but three years down the line the effect of all those sybaritic creature comforts and added weight meant that the Starfire wasn't that quick, and speed figures ended up this side of ordinary.

WEIGHT
The Starfire was no featherweight; all those luxury add-ons pushed the kerb weight to nearly two tonnes.

INTERIOR
Oldsmobile gave the Starfire plenty of creature comforts. Standard kit included Hydra-Matic automatic transmission, bucket seats, safety padded dash, centre console, tachometer, leather trim, plus power steering, brakes, and windows. The power seat could be adjusted into six positions and the Tilt-Away steering wheel into seven.

TILT STEERING WAS AN OPTION AT $43

1964 OLDSMOBILE STARFIRE

Based on the body shell of the Dynamic 88, the Starfire never looked special enough to win big sales. *Motor Trend* said: "What the Starfire misses most is a distinctive exterior like the Thunderbird." Mind you, they did describe the 193 km/h (120 mph) oily bits as "superior and sensational". The car's simple, extruded look was typical of the period and very few traces of jukebox styling remained by the mid-Sixties. Lines were clean and assertive, appealing to the affluent society's new-found sophistication.

ANTI-SPIN OPTION
Positive-traction rear axle was a factory-fitted option.

SPECIFICATIONS

MODEL 1964 Oldsmobile Starfire
PRODUCTION 25,890
BODY STYLE Two-door, five-seater coupe and convertible.
CONSTRUCTION Steel body and chassis.
ENGINE 394cid V8.
POWER OUTPUT 345 bhp.
TRANSMISSION Three-speed Hydra-Matic automatic.
SUSPENSION Front and rear coil springs.
BRAKES Front and rear drums.
MAXIMUM SPEED 193 km/h (120 mph)
0–60 MPH (0–96 KM/H) 9 sec
A.F.C. 4.2 km/l (12 mpg)

FINS
By '64, fins were getting more truncated by the day and had almost completely disappeared by '65.

HEADLIGHTS
Guide-Matic headlights automatically dimmed for oncoming cars.

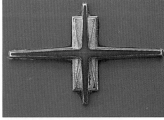

OLDSMOBILE BADGE
The Starfire name originally belonged to a jet fighter, and GM sold it as a limited edition up-market personal car. Sales began to dwindle by 1965, when it was eclipsed by the Buick Riviera. By 1967, the Starfire had been replaced by the Oldsmobile Toronado.

WHEELBASE
The Starfire was based on the Dynamic 88 and shared its 312 cm (123 in) wheelbase.

1964 PLYMOUTH
Barracuda

Barracuda

ROAD AND TRACK MAGAZINE SAID, "FOR SPORTS CAR PERFORMANCE AND PRACTICALITY, THE BARRACUDA IS PERFECT"

THE BIG THREE WEREN'T slow to cash in on the Sixties' youth boom. Ford couldn't keep their Mustang project secret and the Chrysler Corporation desperately wanted a piece of the action. To get the drop on Uncle Henry, they had to work fast. They took their existing compact, the Plymouth Valiant, prettied up the front end, added a dramatic wrap-around rear window, and called it the Barracuda. It hit the showroom carpets in April 1964, a fortnight before the Mustang.

A disarming amalgam of performance, poise, and refinement, Plymouth had achieved a miracle on the scale of loaves and fishes – they made the Barracuda fast, yet handle crisply and ride smoothly. The 273cid V8 made the car quicker than a Mustang, faster still if you specified the Formula S package. But that bizarre rear window dated fiercely and Mustangs outsold Barracudas ten-to-one. Plymouth believed the long-bonnet-short-boot "pony" formula wouldn't captivate consumers like a swooping, sporty fastback. Half a million Mustang buyers told them they'd backed the wrong horse.

Did you know

that the 1965 Plymouth Barracuda has an optional Formula 'S' sports package that includes a Commando 273-cu.-in. V-8 engine; heavy-duty shocks, springs, and sway bar; a tachometer; wide-rim (14-in.) wheels, special Blue Streak tires, and simulated bolt-on wheel covers?

You do now.

THE FORMULA S OPTION
Despite the fact that the Formula S offered a V8 block plus race trimmings, this was still rather tame by Plymouth standards. The '61 Fury, for example, had a 318cid unit that pushed out 230 bhp.

BARRACUDA EXTRAS
Although not as extensive as Mustang options, you could still add air-conditioning, TorqueFlite automatic transmission, and sport wheel covers with chrome lugs to the Barracuda's $2,500 base price.

ENGINE
The 'Cuda's base engine was a 170cid slant-six. Other mills were the 225cid six and two-barrel 273cid V8. Optional was Chrysler's new Hurst-linkage manual transmission along with new Sure-Grip differential.

THIS IS THE 225CID STRAIGHT SIX BLOCK THAT PRODUCED 145 BHP

OPTIONAL POWER STEERING MEANT THAT LOCK-TO-LOCK WAS ONLY THREE-AND-A-HALF TURNS

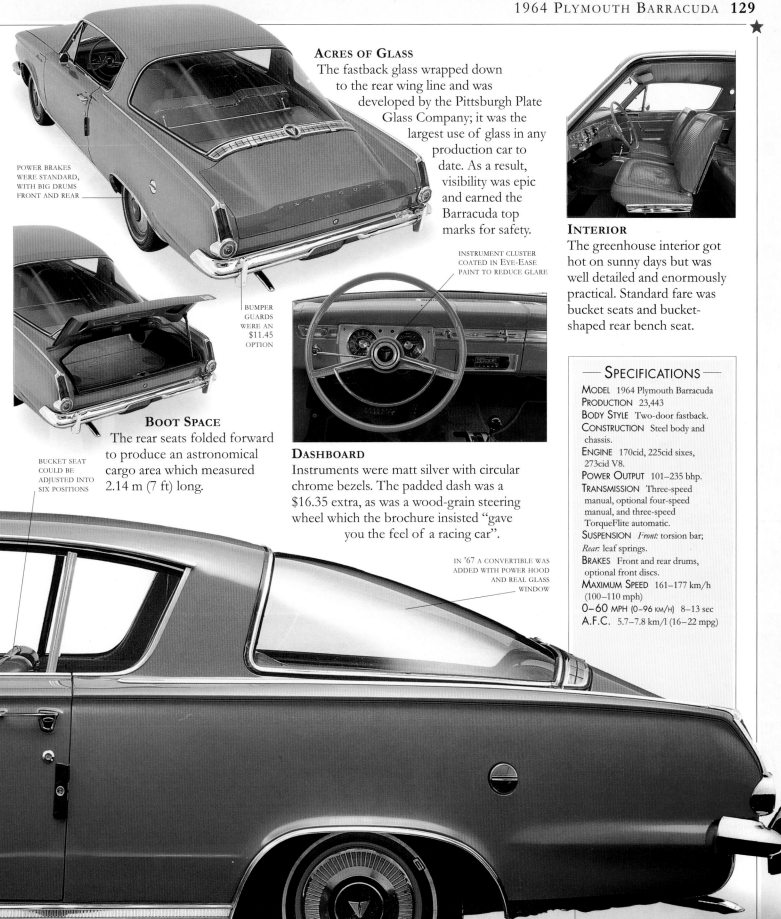

ACRES OF GLASS
The fastback glass wrapped down to the rear wing line and was developed by the Pittsburgh Plate Glass Company; it was the largest use of glass in any production car to date. As a result, visibility was epic and earned the Barracuda top marks for safety.

POWER BRAKES WERE STANDARD, WITH BIG DRUMS FRONT AND REAR

INSTRUMENT CLUSTER COATED IN EYE-EASE PAINT TO REDUCE GLARE

BUMPER GUARDS WERE AN $11.45 OPTION

INTERIOR
The greenhouse interior got hot on sunny days but was well detailed and enormously practical. Standard fare was bucket seats and bucket-shaped rear bench seat.

BOOT SPACE
The rear seats folded forward to produce an astronomical cargo area which measured 2.14 m (7 ft) long.

BUCKET SEAT COULD BE ADJUSTED INTO SIX POSITIONS

DASHBOARD
Instruments were matt silver with circular chrome bezels. The padded dash was a $16.35 extra, as was a wood-grain steering wheel which the brochure insisted "gave you the feel of a racing car".

IN '67 A CONVERTIBLE WAS ADDED WITH POWER HOOD AND REAL GLASS WINDOW

SPECIFICATIONS
MODEL 1964 Plymouth Barracuda
PRODUCTION 23,443
BODY STYLE Two-door fastback.
CONSTRUCTION Steel body and chassis.
ENGINE 170cid, 225cid sixes, 273cid V8.
POWER OUTPUT 101–235 bhp.
TRANSMISSION Three-speed manual, optional four-speed manual, and three-speed TorqueFlite automatic.
SUSPENSION *Front:* torsion bar; *Rear:* leaf springs.
BRAKES Front and rear drums, optional front discs.
MAXIMUM SPEED 161–177 km/h (100–110 mph)
0–60 MPH (0–96 KM/H) 8–13 sec
A.F.C. 5.7–7.8 km/l (16–22 mpg)

ONE OPTIONAL EXTRA WAS UNDERSEALING, A WISE INVESTMENT AT $15.70

MUSCLE AND PONY MANIA

BY THE EARLY SIXTIES, buyers were bored with over-chromed barges, petrol was cheap, and the economy was thumping. Two types of badly needed automotive narcotic were about to emerge – the pony car and the muscle car. The first real muscle cars were the '62 Plymouths and Dodges with their wedge-head V8s, but the machine that really defined the breed was John DeLorean's hip '64 Pontiac GTO. Stripped-to-the-bone, it was a street-legal screamer with blistering straight-line heave, and sales went absolutely ballistic.
Ford got in on the act with their hot Fairlane and Shelby Mustang, Oldsmobile placed

THE FIRST BARRACUDAS WERE ACTUALLY QUITE GENTEEL

a performance package in the F-85 and called it the 442, and Chrysler followed by stuffing Hemi engines into everything they could. The muscle car was hot news on the street because it promised not only horsepower, but individuality too. With a landslide of performance options, auto makers let buyers kid themselves that their cars were almost custom-made. One ad for the Dodge Challenger boasted, "this is a car you buy when you decide you don't want to be like everyone else".

Plymouth were too late with the '64 Barracuda to cash in on the muscle-car mania, but by '68 things were really cooking with special performance packages and a monster 440cid mill

EARLY MUSTANG PROTOTYPE WAS A PROMISE OF PERFORMANCE TO COME

PRESENTING THE *Mustang* by Ford Engineers and Stylists

1964 PLYMOUTH
Barracuda

THE BARRACUDA WAS A PLYMOUTH VALIANT FROM THE ROOF LINE DOWN AND SHARED ITS POWER AND SUSPENSION

VEHICLE NUMBER
This was located on a plate on the front left door post and became visible when the door was opened.

YOUTH MARKET
Based on the mass-market, best-selling Valiant, the Barracuda was aimed at a completely new market – rich young things with a desire to look cool.

a year later. By 1970 they had launched the Rapid Transit System and shortened the name of their pony prodigy to the tough-sounding 'Cuda. From then on, every manufacturer worth a damn was following Chrysler's example and rolling out muscle metal like it was the elixir of youth.

In '65, there was another automotive revolution in the Ford Mustang. A tamer form of rebellion, Ford's pony car had performance, handling, style, and youthful optimism. Built from off-the-shelf Falcon and Fairlane components with every option possible, Ford's new form of auto opium could be made all things to all men, or indeed women. It was a stomping success and sold a whopping 417,000 in its launch year. Despite churning out a frenetic 1,740 cars a day, Mustang demand always ran way ahead of supply.

Then with GM's '67 Firebird and Camaro came a rash of pony-car imitators, Mustang clones with similarly long bonnets and gaping mouths. But Detroit could never leave well alone, and both the pony car and the muscle car grew

BY '67, THE BARRACUDA HAD A STING IN ITS TAIL

gradually longer, fatter, and slower. By '71, both the Barracuda and the Mustang had ballooned in proportions, and sales gradually evaporated. Ironically, both the pony and muscle car had lost their *raison d'être* – they no longer showed individuality. Come 1972, the social tenor of America had matured and Detroit quietly drew the curtain on two of its most imaginative motoring genres.

THE '64 OLDSMOBILE 4-4-2 CUTLASS WAS SWIFT BUT NOT TRIM

OBSCENELY QUICK '70 HEMI 'CUDA OFFERED LEGALIZED MISCHIEF

BOLD STYLING
Compared with the Mustang, the Barracuda's front was busy, cluttered, and lacked symmetry, but it was a brave and bold design. Had the Mustang not been launched in the same month, things might have been very different.

PRISMATIC DAY-AND-NIGHT MIRROR COULD BE ADJUSTED TO DEFLECT ANNOYING HEADLIGHT GLARE AT NIGHT

INTERIOR COLOURS AVAILABLE WERE GOLD, BLUE, BLACK, OR THIS SMART RED

REMOTE-CONTROLLED OUTSIDE WING MIRROR WAS A $12 CONVENIENCE OPTION

PLYMOUTH

19 400TH ANNIVERSARY 65
1W166142
FLORIDA

1965 CHRYSLER
300L

THE FAMOUS 300 NAMEPLATE THAT HAD FIRST
MADE ITS MARK IN THE LATE FIFTIES WAS NOW IN ITS FINAL YEAR

BACK IN '55, CHRYSLER debuted their mighty 300 "Letter Car". The most powerful automobile of the year, the 300C kicked off a new genre of Gentleman's Hot Rod that was to last for more than a decade. Chrysler cleverly flagged annual model changes with letters, running from the 300B in 1956 all the way through – the letter I excepted – to this 300L in 1965.

And '65 was the swan-song year for the Letter Series speciality car. The 300L sat on high-performance rubber and suspension, and was powered by a high-output 413cid 360 bhp mill breathing through a four-barrel Carter carb. By the mid-Sixties, though, the game had changed and Chrysler were pumping their money into muscle-car iron like the Charger and GTX, an area of the market where business was brisk. The 300L was the last survivor of an era when the Madison Avenue advertising men were still trying to persuade us that an automobile as long as a freight train could also be a sports car.

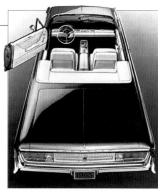

CONVERTIBLE FORM
A mere 440 two-door convertibles were produced, as well as 2,405 hardtops. Competition was particularly stiff in '65 and the 300L had to fight hard against the Oldsmobile Starfire, the agonisingly pretty Buick Riviera, and the market leader, Ford's flashy Thunderbird.

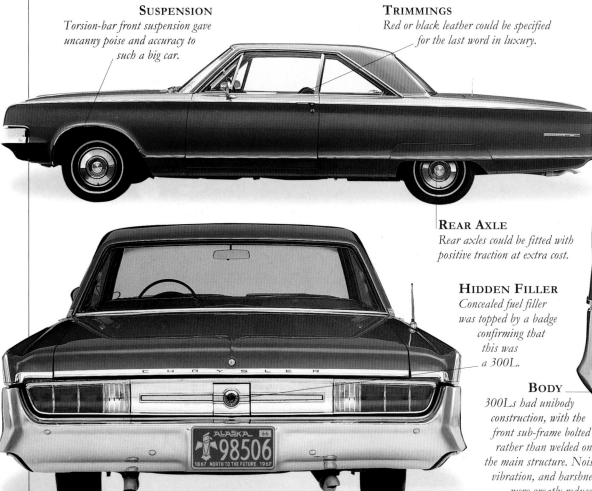

SUSPENSION
Torsion-bar front suspension gave uncanny poise and accuracy to such a big car.

TRIMMINGS
Red or black leather could be specified for the last word in luxury.

HEADLIGHTS
These live behind a horizontally etched glass panel.

REAR AXLE
Rear axles could be fitted with positive traction at extra cost.

HIDDEN FILLER
Concealed fuel filler was topped by a badge confirming that this was a 300L.

BODY
300Ls had unibody construction, with the front sub-frame bolted rather than welded onto the main structure. Noise, vibration, and harshness were greatly reduced.

ALASKA 66
98506
1867 NORTH TO THE FUTURE 1967

INTERIOR
Front buckets plus a centre console were standard on the L, as was column instead of push-button automatic gear shift. The rear seat was moulded to look like buckets but could accommodate three people.

1965 CHRYSLER 300L
Styling of the 300L was by Elwood Engle, who had replaced Virgil Exner as Chrysler's chief of design and had worked on the Lincolnesque '64 Imperial. Although Chrysler's advertising claimed that this was "The Most Beautiful Chrysler Ever Built", the "Crisp, Clean, Custom" look of '63–'64 had ballooned.

LUMINOUS LETTERING
The letter L in the centre of the grille lit up with the headlights.

ENGINE
The non-Hemi V8 was tough and reliable and gave the 300L very respectable performance figures. The L was quick, agile, and one of the smoothest-riding Letter Series cars made, with 45 bhp more than the standard 300's unit.

SPECIFICATIONS
MODEL 1965 Chrysler 300L
PRODUCTION 2,845
BODY STYLE Two-door hardtop and convertible.
CONSTRUCTION Steel unitary body.
ENGINE 413cid V8.
POWER OUTPUT 360 bhp.
TRANSMISSION Three-speed automatic, optional four-speed manual.
SUSPENSION *Front:* torsion bar; *Rear:* leaf springs.
BRAKES Front and rear drums.
MAXIMUM SPEED 177 km/h (110 mph)
0–60 MPH (0–96 KM/H) 8.8 sec
A.F.C. 4.2–5 km/l (12–14 mpg)

BADGING
The letter L in the centre of the grille was one of only a few places on the car where it could be distinguished from a standard 300.

1965 FORD
Mustang

THE MUSTANG
WAS THE FIRST "PONY" CAR

"A POOR MAN'S THUNDERBIRD for the working girl", the Mustang was compact, modern, young, and affordable. For a fraction of what the Edsel debacle cost, Ford Vice-President Lee Iacocca's offering captured the hearts and minds of a generation of American youth. Based on the humble Ford Falcon, the Mustang was technically unremarkable, but had square-jawed looks and carefree classlessness. Within two years of its '64 debut, one million had left showrooms.

But from a peak of 600,000 sold in 1966, sales evaporated to 150,000 by 1970. Heavier, longer, wider, and slower, the sleek horse had become a fat pig. As Iacocca later remarked, "our customers abandoned us, because we'd abandoned their car".

RACING MUSTANGS
Crisp handling and compact dimensions led to the Mustang becoming one of the first American cars to enjoy competition success on European racetracks.

INTERIOR
The base price was $2,372, but buyers ordered an average of $1,000 worth of the 70 options available. Interior trim could be personalized with a myriad of decor option packs, and extras such as full-length centre consoles and retractable seat belts jazzed up the basic model.

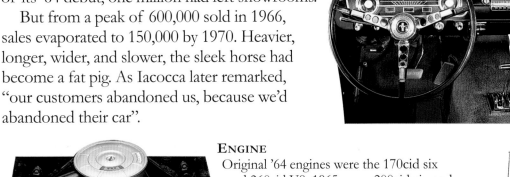

ENGINE
Original '64 engines were the 170cid six and 260cid V8. 1965 saw a 200cid six and 289cid Challenger V8 take over as base engines, with optional 225 bhp four-barrel Challenger and 271 bhp High Performance units on offer. About 73 per cent of Mustangs were fitted with the brilliant 289, which was a light, efficient, and gutsy mill.

COLOUR CHOICE
Honey Gold was one of 15 exterior colours on offer to Mustang buyers.

BRAKES
Power front disc brakes were a shrewd option on V8s and cost $58.

THE LEGENDARY 289
The 289cid Challenger V8 came into service in the Autumn of '64 and would remain part of the Mustang stable until it was dropped in performance-oriented 1969.

1965 FORD MUSTANG HARDTOP COUPE

The Mustang's styling was the work of Joe Oros, David Ash, and Gale Halderman. The basic formula of long-bonnet-short-boot was pioneered on the Mustang and became known as the "pony car" look, carrying on into the early '70s. When the Mustang debuted in April 1964, it was offered in two body styles: hardtop coupe and convertible. A few months later, the official 1965 range contained another model in a 2+2 fastback coupe. The hardtop coupe, also known as the notchback, was by far the most popular model throughout the Mustang's lifespan.

REAR STYLING
The notchback rear aspect has classically perfect proportions. The simple bumper and overriders are positively chaste compared to earlier Detroit confections.

SPECIFICATIONS

MODEL 1965 Ford Mustang
PRODUCTION 559,451
BODY STYLE Two-door, four-seater coupe, fastback, and convertible.
CONSTRUCTION Steel unitary body.
ENGINE 200cid six, 289cid V8.
POWER OUTPUT 120–271 bhp.
TRANSMISSION Three-speed manual, optional four-speed manual, and two-speed Cruise-O-Matic automatic.
SUSPENSION *Front:* coil springs; *Rear:* leaf springs with live axle.
BRAKES Front and rear drums; optional front discs
MAXIMUM SPEED 177–198 km/h (110–123 mph)
0–60 MPH (0–96 KM/H) 7.6–9 sec
A.F.C. 6 km/l (17 mpg)

USEFUL EXTRA
The $42 optional Equa-Lock limited slip differential helped keep rear wheels from burning rubber.

1966 CHEVROLET
Corvair Monza

Corvair

ANOTHER DESIGN TRIUMPH FROM
BILL MITCHELL'S GM STUDIO

BY 1960, SALES OF DINOSAURS were down, small-car imports were up, and Detroit finally listened to a market screaming for economy compacts. Then along came Chevrolet's adventurous answer to the Volkswagen Beetle, the pretty, rear-engined Corvair, which sold for half the price of a Ford Thunderbird.

But problems soon arose. GM's draconian cost-cutting meant that a crucial $15 suspension stabilizing bar was omitted, and early Corvairs handled like pigs. The suspension was redesigned in '65, but it was too late. Bad news also came in the form of Ralph Nader's book *Unsafe at Any Speed*, which lambasted the Corvair. The new Ford Mustang, which had become *the* hot compact, didn't help either. By 1969, it was all over for the Corvair. GM's stab at downsizing had been a disaster.

INTERIOR
The all-vinyl interior was very European, with bucket seats and telescopic steering column. The restrained steering wheel and deep-set instruments could have come straight out of a BMW.

MONZA MANIA
The early Corvair Monzas, with de luxe trim and automatic transmission, were a big hit. This 1961 example was one of over 143,000 sold that year, over half of the grand total.

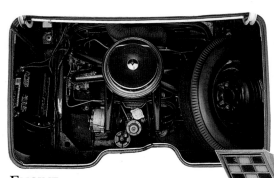

140 REPRESENTED
POWER OUTPUT

ENGINE
Corvairs had alloy, air-cooled, horizontal sixes. The base unit was a 164cid with four Rochester carbs developing 140 bhp. The hot turbocharged motors could push out 180 bhp.

END OF THE LINE
By the end of '68, sales of the handsome Monza coupe were down to just 6,800 units and GM decided to pull the plug in May '69. Those who had bought a '69 Corvair were given a certificate worth $150 off any other '69–'70 Chevrolet.

WHEELS
Wire wheel covers were a pricey $59 option on the Monza. White sidewalls could be ordered for an extra $29.

SUSPENSION
*The post-'65 Corvair
had Corvette-type fully
independent rear suspension
via upper and lower control
arms and coil springs.*

WINDOWS
*Side windows were made
of specially curved glass.*

HOOD
*Most tops
were manually
operated and
stowed behind
a fabric tonneau,
but this model
has the $54
power top option.*

1966 CHEVROLET CORVAIR MONZA CONVERTIBLE

After very few styling changes for the first five years, the
new body design for '65 had a heavy Italian influence with
smooth-flowing, rounded lines that impressed
the motoring press. *Car and Driver* magazine
called it "the best of established foreign and
domestic coachwork". The new longer, wider,
and lower Corvair initially sold well but
floundered from '66 in the face of the rival
Mustang and Nader's damning book.

SPECIFICATIONS

MODEL 1966 Chevrolet
Corvair Monza
PRODUCTION 60,447 (1966,
Monza only)
BODY STYLE Two- and four-door
four-seater coupe and convertible.
CONSTRUCTION Steel unitary body.
ENGINE 164cid flat sixes.
POWER OUTPUT 95–140 bhp.
TRANSMISSION Three-speed
manual, optional four-speed
manual, and two-speed
Powerglide automatic.
SUSPENSION Front and rear
coil springs.
BRAKES Front and rear drums.
MAXIMUM SPEED 169–193 km/h
(105–120 mph)
0–60 MPH (0–96 KM/H) 11–15.2 sec
A.F.C. 7 km/l (20 mpg)

1966 CHEVROLET
Corvette Sting Ray

1966 PRODUCED THE HIGHEST SALES OF THIS 'VETTE SERIES

THE ORIGINAL STING RAY Corvette of '63 to '67 is the most collectable of them all. With roots going back to the Sting Ray Special Racer and experimental XP720, production cars had a luscious fastback profile, split rear window, hidden headlights, and doors cut into the roof.

Underneath the body there was a new ladder-type frame, independent rear suspension with double-jointed driveshafts and, for the first time, a power steering option. Output ranged from 300 to 425 brake, with the big-block 427cid L88 pushing out a howling 530. The public went wild and the Sting Ray's reception in '63 caused as many ripples as the Jag XKE. In 1965, four-wheel discs became available, along with side-mounted exhausts. Among the fastest 'Vettes of all, hot 427s could run the quarter mile in 13.6 seconds and top a genuine 241 km/h (150 mph). Now highly prized, a fuel-injected, disc-brake '65 or big-block 427 will prove a highly entertaining and lucrative investment.

1963 SPLIT-SCREEN COUPE
Bill Mitchell, GM's head of styling, loved the 'Vette's split rear window, but humourless critics and the motoring press reckoned it was "dumb and blocked rear vision". Sadly, by 1964, it was history.

INTERIOR
Buyers could specify leather seats, tinted glass, headrests, shoulder harness, teak wood steering wheel, telescopic steering column, and air-conditioning, a very rare option on the convertible. Tachometer, seat belts, and electric clock came as standard.

LOGO
Sting Ray nomenclature was introduced in 1963, and became a synonym for American racing pedigree.

ENGINE
The 327cid Turbo-Fire cast-iron block V8 was the 'Vette's base power plant, producing 300 brake through a single four-barrel Holley carb. Three-speed manual transmission was standard, with optional two-speed automatic available at $195 and three types of four-speed manual shift also offered.

BRAKES
Optional four-wheel discs were unreliable and it took Chevrolet 17 years to redesign them.

FRONT VIEW
Hidden headlights, large bonnet bulge, and muscular wheel-arch lines give the 'Vette a mean look.

INTERIOR OPTIONS
Telescopic steering column and genuine teak steering wheel were options for '65 and '66.

SPECIFICATIONS

MODEL 1966 Chevrolet Corvette Sting Ray
PRODUCTION 27,720
BODY STYLE Two-door, two seater coupe and convertible.
CONSTRUCTION Ladder frame with fibreglass body.
ENGINE 327cid, 427cid V8s.
POWER OUTPUT 300–425 bhp.
TRANSMISSION Three-speed manual, optional four-speed manual, and two-speed Powerglide automatic.
SUSPENSION *Front:* coil springs; *Rear:* independent.
BRAKES Front and rear drums, optional front and rear discs.
MAXIMUM SPEED 190–241 km/h (118–150 mph)
0–60 MPH (0–96 KM/H) 4.7–8 sec
A.F.C. 3.5–6 km/l (10–17 mpg)

1966 CHEVROLET CORVETTE STING RAY

The '66 Sting Ray Roadster listed at $4,084 and weighed as much as a Camaro. 17,762 rolled off the St. Louis line in the '66 model year, almost double the number of Fastback Coupes. This was the penultimate year of the Sting Ray; 1968 saw the restyled Corvette introduced without the Sting Ray name. It reappeared in '69 as the Stingray (one word).

HARDTOP OPTION
Convertibles were offered with a beautiful, snug-fitting, detachable hardtop from 1964, rather than the soft top as here.

ENGINE
The fuel injection option ended in '65 because of high cost.

PERFORMANCE REAR
Positive Traction rear axle could be ordered for an extra $42.

1966 PONTIAC
GTO

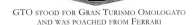

GTO STOOD FOR GRAN TURISMO OMOLOGATO
AND WAS POACHED FROM FERRARI

"THE GREAT ONE" was Pontiac's answer to a youth market with attitude and disposable cash. Detroit exploited a generation's rebellion by creating cars with machismo to burn. In 1964, John DeLorean, Pontiac's chief engineer, shoe-horned the division's biggest V8 into the timid little Tempest compact with electrifying results. He then beefed up the brakes and suspension, threw in three two-barrel carbs and a floor shift, and garnished the result with a name that belonged to a Ferrari. In 1966 it became a model in its own right, and Detroit's first "muscle car" had been born. Pundits reckon the flowing lines of these second-generation GTOs make them the best-looking of all. Engines were energetic performers too, with a standard 335 bhp 389cid V8 that could be specified in 360 bhp high-output tune. But by '67 GTO sales had tailed off by 15 per cent, depressed by a burgeoning social conscience and Federal meddling. The performance era was about to be legislated into the history books.

INTERIOR
GTOs were equipped to the same high standard as the Pontiac Tempest Le Mans. Items included ashtray lights, cigarette lighter, carpeting, and a power top for convertibles. Air-conditioning and power steering could be ordered at $343 and $95 respectively.

ENGINE
The base 335 bhp 389cid block had a high-output Tri-Power big brother that pushed out 360 bhp for an extra $116. The range was expanded in '67 to include an economy 255 bhp 400cid V8 and a Ram-Air 400cid mill that also developed 360 bhp, but at higher revs per minute.

BIG BLOCK
Pontiac were the first mainstream manufacturer to combine big-cube power with a light body. In tests, a '66 Convertible hit 60 mph (96 km/h) in 6.8 seconds.

INDICATORS
Indicators in the grille were meant to mimic European-style driving lights.

HEADLIGHTS
The stacked headlights were new for Pontiacs in '65 and were retained on GTOs until the end of the decade.

SPECIFICATIONS

MODEL 1966 Pontiac GTO Convertible

PRODUCTION 96,946 (all body styles)

BODY STYLE Two-door, five-seater hardtop, coupe, and convertible.

CONSTRUCTION Steel unitary body.

ENGINE 389cid V8s.

POWER OUTPUT 335–360 bhp.

TRANSMISSION Three-speed manual, optional four-speed manual, and three-speed Hydra-Matic automatic.

SUSPENSION Front and rear coil springs.

BRAKES Front and rear drums, optional discs.

MAXIMUM SPEED 201 km/h (125 mph)

0–60 MPH (0–96 KM/H) 6.6–9.5 sec

A.F.C. 5.3 km/l (15 mpg)

1966 PONTIAC GTO CONVERTIBLE

John DeLorean's idea of placing a high-spec engine in the standard Tempest body paved the way for a whole new genre and gave Pontiac immediate success in '64. Had Ford not chosen to release the Mustang in the same year, the GTO would have been the star of '64, and even more sales would have been secured. As it was, sales peaked in '66 with almost 100,000 GTOs going to power-hungry young drivers whose average age was 25. The Convertible was the most aesthetically pleasing of the range.

PERFORMANCE REAR
The GTO came with heavy-duty shocks and springs as standard, along with a stabilizer bar.

LENGTH
It might look long, but the GTO was actually 38 cm (15 in) shorter than Pontiac's largest models.

1967 FORD
Shelby Mustang GT500

GT500 NAME WAS ARBITRARY AND DID NOT REFER TO POWER

LOOKING BACK FROM OUR ERA of weedy political correctness, it's amazing to remember a time when you could buy this sort of stomach-churning horsepower straight from the showroom floor. What's more, if you couldn't afford to buy it, you could borrow it for the weekend from your local Hertz rent-a-car. The fact is that the American public loved the grunt, the image, and the Carroll Shelby Cobra connection. Ford's advertising slogan went straight to the point – Shelby Mustangs were "*The* Road Cars". With 289 and 428cid V8s, they were blisteringly quick and kings of both street and strip. By '67 they were civilized too, with options like factory air and power steering, as well as lots of gauges, a wood-rim Shelby wheel, and that all-important 140 mph (225 km/h) speedo. The little Pony Mustang had grown into a thundering stallion.

DASHBOARD
The special Shelby steering wheel was standard, along with Stewart-Warner oil and amp gauges and a tachometer red-lining at 8,000 rpm. Two interior colours were available – parchment and black.

CHUNKY FRONT
'67 Shelbys had a larger bonnet scoop than previous models, plus a custom-built fibreglass front to complement the stock Mustang's new longer bonnet.

WOOD-RIM STEERING WHEEL

— CARROLL SHELBY —

CARROLL SHELBY, the most charismatic ex-chicken farmer you could ever meet, smiled when he told me the Hertz story. "We delivered the first batch of black-and-gold cars to Hertz the day before a hailstorm. The cars had racing brakes that really needed carefully warming up. When the ice storm hit, dozens were totalled. My reputation with Hertz went down the tubes big time." But the Hertz connection was good for the Shelby, and there are tales of people renting 350s and 500s for the weekend and bringing them back with bald tyres and evidence of racing numbers on the doors. There was even one case of somebody lifting a 289 Hi-Po out of a Hertz Shelby and substituting the stock 289 from his aunt's notchback, hoping no-one would notice.

CARROLL SHELBY RECEIVES HIS TROPHY FOR WINNING THE RIVERSIDE GRAND PRIX IN 1960

INTERIOR DECOR WAS BRUSHED ALUMINIUM WITH MOULDED DOOR PANELS AND COURTESY LAMPS

SHELBY'S SPRINGING WAS SIMILAR TO THE MUSTANG WITH FRONT SWAY BAR, STIFF SPRINGS, AND GABRIEL SHOCKS

G.T. 500

ENGINE
The GT500 had the 428 Police Interceptor unit with two Holley four-barrel carbs. Oval, finned aluminium open-element air cleaner and cast-aluminium valve covers were unique to the big-block Shelby.

SHELBY PLATE
Carroll Shelby gave the early Mustangs his special treatment in a dedicated factory in Los Angeles. Later cars were built in Ionia, Michigan.

INTERIOR
All GT350s and 500s boasted the standard and very practical Mustang fold-down rear seat along with Shelby's own padded roll-bar. Shelbys came in fastback only; there were no notchbacks and convertibles were only available from '68.

SPECIFICATIONS

MODEL 1967 Ford Shelby Cobra Mustang GT500
PRODUCTION 2,048
BODY STYLE Two-door, four-seater coupe.
CONSTRUCTION Steel unitary body.
ENGINE 428cid V8.
POWER OUTPUT 360 bhp.
TRANSMISSION Four-speed manual, three-speed automatic.
SUSPENSION *Front:* coil springs; *Rear:* leaf springs.
BRAKES Front discs, rear drums.
MAXIMUM SPEED 212 km/h (132 mph)
0–60 MPH (0–96 KM/H) 6.8 sec
A.F.C. 4.6 km/l (13 mpg)

SCOOPS ACTED AS INTERIOR AIR EXTRACTORS

REAR DECK IS MADE OF FIBREGLASS TO SAVE WEIGHT

POPULAR CHOICE
Shelbys were a big hit in '67, with 1,175 350s and 2,048 500s sold. Prices were also about 15 per cent cheaper than in '66.

WHEELS ARE OPTIONAL KELSEY-HAYES MAGSTARS

1967 FORD SHELBY MUSTANG

EVOLUTION OF THE FORD MUSTANG

NO OTHER CAR HIT its target like the Mustang. Aimed at the 18–24 market, it was charismatic, youthful, and cheap; mass-produced individuality had never looked so good. With their litany of options, Mustangs could be everything from a secretary's economy compact to a street racer's howling banshee. Iacocca's prodigy may have spawned the Firebird and the Camaro, but its legacy is far greater than that. Thirty-odd years later, America still loves the galloping pony.

1962

THE MUSTANG'S ANTECEDENTS go back to the Project T5 styling study created in 1962 by engineer Herb Misch and design chief Eugene Bordinat. Meant to take on British Triumphs and MGs, it had independent springing, a tubular frame, integral roll-bar, and a 60-degree 1927cc V4 engine.

KEY FEATURES
• Ford backs sporty, compact Project T5
• Mustang styling exercises approved in just 21 days
• Target market is baby boomers
• Prototype debuts in time for US Grand Prix at Watkins Glen

1964

LAUNCHED IN APRIL 1964, the Mustang was such a colossal hit that production at the Dearborn factory couldn't cope and spilled over to the Ford plant in San Jose, California. By the end of the year the Pony had notched up 263,000 sales and the full calendar year production total for '65 of 418,000 units was an industry record.

KEY DEVELOPMENTS
• Early cars have 260cid V8s
• First batch has non-adjustable passenger seats
• Base price is an amazing $2,368
• Lee Iacocca makes the front cover of *Time* magazine

1969

THE MUSTANG QUICKLY put on weight and, far from being a compact, had grown into a luxury Grand Tourer. Mind you, power was up too, with screamers like the Mach One and whopping Boss 429. Moving away from the pony car philosophy wasn't one of Ford's best ideas, and '69 model year output fell to 190,727 units, down from 300,000.

KEY DEVELOPMENTS
• New sports roof fastback body style
• New ultra-high performance models Boss 302 and Boss 429
• Luxury Grandee model launched
• 81.5 per cent of all '69 'Stangs have a V8

1967 FORD *Shelby Mustang GT500*

FOR THE SHELBY, THE MUSTANG'S REAR LIGHTS WERE REPLACED WITH THE '65 T-BIRD'S SEQUENTIAL LIGHTS

MORE POWER AND CONTROL
Power steering and brakes on the '67 model meant that the once rough-riding Shelby had changed into a luxury slingshot.

SHELBY G.T. 500

19 GEORGIA STATE 67
USA 716
SHELBY

1971

THE MUSTANGS OF '71 grew in every dimension except for height. Heavier, wider, and more bloated than its lithe predecessors, the Mustang lost its way and sales plummeted to nearly a third of '65–'66 numbers. Everybody knew that this wasn't the way to go, but over the following three years things would get even worse.

KEY DEVELOPMENTS
• Boss 302 and 489 dropped in favour of Boss 351
• Standard base engine is now a 250cid six

1974

APOLOGETICALLY BILLED AS "the right car at the right time", the Mustang II wasn't worthy of bearing the hallowed name. With parts borrowed from the sub-compact Pinto, it was a knee-jerk reaction to the Arab oil embargo. Mind you, for all its ordinariness, sales were strong, with 385,000 Mustang IIs finding buyers in the first year.

KEY DEVELOPMENTS
• New body designed by Ghia
• Now billed as a "luxury sub-compact"
• Pared down four-model line-up
• Base engine is asthmatic 140cid four
• Mach One gets 171cid V6

1979

THE FIFTH GENERATION Mustangs were clean, taut, and crisply styled. On the down side, handling wasn't brilliant, interior space was limited, and build quality couldn't match the Japanese. The Iran-Iraq war meant that performance was out and economy was in, but the desire for power would soon return, and the Mustang would rise again.

KEY DEVELOPMENTS
• New colour-keyed urethane bumpers
• Heavy aerodynamic influence
• Wicked 302cid V8 option
• Cobra option has 2.3 turbo four

1993

1993 MUSTANGS WERE among the most civilized and refined of the breed. The 5-litre V8 was considered quick enough to make a highway patrol car, and the limited edition Mustang Cobra included GT40 heads and roller rockers. This incarnation kept the customers satisfied until the splendid all-new Mustang arrived on the scene in 1995.

KEY DEVELOPMENTS
• Three body styles available in LX 5.0 guise
• Base models run on 88 bhp four
• Driver's airbag standard
• GT Mustangs push out 225 bhp

FORCED CHANGES
The standard centre-grille high-beam headlights were forced to the sides in some states because of Federal legislation.

AT THE END OF '67, CARS WERE RENAMED SHELBY COBRAS, BUT FORD STILL HANDLED ALL PROMOTION AND ADVERTISING

SHELBY BODIES WERE NEW FOR '67, WITH A SHARK-LIKE FRONT GRILLE AND REVISED BONNET WITH RAM-AIR OPENINGS

RACING-STYLE LOCK PINS WERE STANDARD ON THE BONNET

428CID V8 STARTED LIFE IN THE ORIGINAL AC COBRA

APRIL GEORGIA STATE 1967
USA 716
SHELBY

1967 OLDSMOBILE
Toronado

THE FIRST BIG FRONT-DRIVING LAND YACHT since the Cord 810 of the Thirties, the Toronado was an automotive milestone and the most desirable Olds ever. With a 425cid V8 and unique chain-and-sprocket-drive automatic transmission, it had big-car power and outstanding road manners, and could crack 217 km/h (135 mph). Initial sales weren't brilliant, with sober buyers plumping for the more conventional Riviera, but by '71 the Riviera's design had lost its way and the Toronado really came into its own, selling up to 50,000 a year until the mid-Seventies. From then on, however, the more glamorous Cadillac Eldorado, also with front drive, outsold both the Riviera and the Toronado. Built on an exclusive slow-moving assembly line, Toronados had few faults, which was remarkable for such a technically audacious car. Even so, the press carped about the poor rear visibility, lousy gas mileage, and voracious appetite for front tyres. But time heals all wounds, and these days there's no greater collector's car bargain than a '66–'67 Toronado.

NARROW GRILLE WAS A TORO STYLING TRADEMARK

NOVEL FRONTAL STYLE
The concealed headlights and horizontal bar grille were genuinely innovative but would disappear in '68 for a heavier and less attractive front-end treatment. The Toronado's design arose in a free-expression competition organized by Olds in 1962. It became the marque's top model to date, and the equivalent of the Buick Riviera.

TOP-FLIGHT CREDENTIALS
The Toronado was brisk, poised, and accurate. Understeer and front-wheel scrabble were kept to a minimum, and the car handled like a compact. Acceleration was in the Jaguar sedan league, and flat out it could chew the tail feathers of a Hi-Po Mustang.

ENGINE
The torque converter was mounted behind the 425cid V8, and the gearbox under the left cylinder bank, with both connected by chain and sprocket. Hailed as unbreakable, this arrangement enabled the engine to be placed directly over the front wheels, resulting in near-perfect weight distribution.

FROM 1972 TORONADOS WERE BUILT EXCLUSIVELY IN LANSING

THE TORONADO NAME CAME FROM A 1963 CHEVROLET SHOW CAR AND HAS NO KNOWN MEANING

INTERIOR
Standard equipment included Turbo Hydra-Matic tranny, power steering and brakes, Strato-bench front seat, de luxe armrests, rear cigarette lighters, foam seat cushions, a special chrome moulding package, and interiors in vinyl, leather, or cloth.

THE TORONADO WAS MEANT TO COMBINE TRADITIONAL BIG-CAR POWER WITH OUTSTANDING HANDLING AND TRACTION

HIGH ENGINE TEMPERATURES AND THE HUGE ROCHESTER 4GC FOUR-BARREL CARB CAUSED MANY UNDER-BONNET FIRES

DOORS WERE HEAVY AND DIFFICULT TO OPEN; BUILT-IN ASSISTANCE CAME IN 1967

SPECIFICATIONS

MODEL 1967 Oldsmobile Toronado
PRODUCTION 21,790
BODY STYLE Two-door, five-seater coupe.
CONSTRUCTION Steel body and frame.
ENGINE 425cid V8.
POWER OUTPUT 385 bhp.
TRANSMISSION Three-speed Turbo Hydra-Matic automatic.
SUSPENSION *Front:* torsion bar; *Rear:* leaf springs with solid axle.
BRAKES Front and rear drums.
MAXIMUM SPEED 217 km/h (135 mph)
0–60 MPH (0–96 KM/H) 8.5 sec
A.F.C. 3.9 km/l (11 mpg)

INDIVIDUAL STYLE
The Toro was a dream car design. Despite sharing a basic body with other GM models like the Riviera and Eldorado, it still emerged very separate and distinctive. *Automobile Quarterly* called it "logical, imaginative, and totally unique", and *Motor Trade* nominated it Car of the Year in 1966.

GM'S FRONT-DRIVE FIRST
Offered only as a hardtop coupe, the Toronado was GM's break with the past and the first commitment to front-wheel drive, which would become a corporate theology by 1980.

C-PILLARS SWEEP GENTLY DOWNWARDS, WHILE ROOF FLOWS SMOOTHLY INTO RAKISH FASTBACK SHAPE

CURVED BODY IS EMPOWERED BY BOLDLY FLARED WHEEL ARCHES; UNADORNED FRONT AND REAR TUCK CLEANLY AWAY

GM
MARK OF EXCELLENCE

STANDARD RUBBER WAS 8.85/15

EVOLUTION OF THE OLDSMOBILE TORONADO

ONE OF THE MOST startling designs GM have ever come up with, and the first front-wheel drive car for 30 years, the Toronado didn't stay audacious for very long. As with so many other American machines of the era, it swelled, lost its individuality, and eventually lumbered into obscurity. But those first bewitching Toronados that left the Lansing plant in Michigan are a monument to a moment in time when the US auto industry could have led the world.

1967 OLDSMOBILE TORONADO

1966

THE INNOVATIVE Toronado was the result of a competition organized by Olds studio chief Stanley Wilen in 1962. He wanted his team to do something wild and exciting, to create a dream car. The winning design was penned by David R. North and approved by the legendary Bill Mitchell. The new Toro was nominated Car of the Year in 1966.

KEY FEATURES
• Unique retractable headlights
• Narrow horizontal grille
• Standard power steering and power brakes
• 425cid V8 standard
• Two trim levels – standard and de luxe
• Olds calendar year production peaks at 586,381

1970

THE FRONT-WHEEL drive Toronado was still the top-of-the-pile Olds, but since 1966 it had metamorphosed into an overstuffed luxury limo. Only 7 per cent of Toronados had bucket seats, yet 73 per cent had tilt steering wheels and 28 per cent cruise control, testament to the fact that Oldsmobile's spirited prodigy had become a fat-cat's slushmobile.

KEY DEVELOPMENTS
• 455cid 370 bhp V8
• Turbo Hydra-Matic transmission, power steering, and power brakes standard
• Interior trims in vinyl, cloth, or leather
• Custom Toro outsells basic 10-to-1
• Sticker price $5,216

1972

BIGGER, HEAVIER, AND longer, the '72 Toro still had front-wheel drive but laboured under the 1971 restyle, which made it look as if it had been squashed flat. The car was no longer sporty but pompous and plutocratic. It continued to sport the 455cid engine, but power was down to 250 bhp, and even more power emasculation was to follow.

KEY DEVELOPMENTS
• All Toronados now made exclusively in Lansing, Michigan
• Factory price $5,341
• Toronado Brougham sells 17,824
• Standard Toro sells 31,076
• 1972 is Oldsmobile's 75th year in the automobile business

1967 OLDSMOBILE *Toronado*

MARQUE LEADER
The supreme Olds of the Sixties, the Toro was sophisticated both in its styling and underpinnings.

ALTHOUGH AN ENORMOUS CAR, THE TORONADO WAS A RAKISH FASTBACK

PRONOUNCED FLARED WHEEL ARCHES ARE THE FOCAL POINT OF THE TORO'S CURVED FUSELAGE

ROOF LINE TUMBLES SMOOTHLY DOWN TO REAR DECK

1977

THIS WAS A HARD YEAR. The 55 mph (88 km/h) speed limit had been around since 1974, catalytic converters were law in California, and gas had doubled in price since '72. GM offered a limited run of full-size cars with airbags, but buyers weren't interested. Cars clearly had to get smaller, but the 1977 Toronado was still as big as they come.

KEY DEVELOPMENTS
• Unhappy T-Top roof available
• Sled-like dimensions cause buyer resistance
• Public sees Toronado as just another socially irresponsible leviathan
• Frontal aspect panned as a return to "Detroit's worst stylistic excesses"

1979

ALTHOUGH STILL LARGE, lumbering, and none too economical, Olds' luxury coupe was now a lot smaller than the previous behemoth. The fully independent suspension gave a smooth ride but was overly soft with too much sway and bounce, and handling was no great shakes. The Toro was now a traditional and conservative prestige cruiser.

KEY DEVELOPMENTS
• 252cid V6 and 307cid V8 the best engines
• 350cid diesel engine encounters huge buyer resistance
• Fuel consumption of 5.3 km/l (15 mpg) is criticized
• Toro now very similar to Buick Riviera, which also went front-wheel drive in '79

1986

THE ALL-NEW TORO descendant, though still front-wheel drive, proved a sales debacle. Loyal Toronado buyers hated the shrunken styling, closely resembling other GM models such as the Riviera and Eldorado. The trimmed-down Toro still pitched heavily and its steering was woolly. It was marketed as a six-seater, but the back seat only had room for two.

KEY DEVELOPMENTS
• 231cid fuel-injected V6 is widely praised
• Gas mileage is up, at 7 km/l (20 mpg) average
• Trunk criticized for being too shallow
• "Bustle back" rear styling wins few friends
• Maximum horsepower a miserable 170 bhp

1991

NEW BODY PANELS in 1990 increased the car's length, in a deliberate reskin to revive flagging sales. Anti-lock braking, an option since 1988, became standard and a new "3800" engine, also launched in '88, added 15 bhp. In 1990 Toros gained a stronger 170 bhp V6 with electronically controlled four-speed automatic. But by 1992 Oldsmobile had dropped the car.

KEY DEVELOPMENTS
• Optional dashboard visual information centre is panned by the press
• Driver's-side airbag introduced in 1990
• '90 body restyle improved looks, if not sales
• Fuel-injected V6 returns 7.8 km/l (22 mpg)
• Big recall in '92 for missing steering-rack bolts

UNFORTUNATE RESTYLE
It was a great shame that the Toronado lost its distinctive front. Bill Mitchell tried hard to defend its simplicity but lost out on the 1968 model, with its heavy rectangular grille.

STANDARD STICKER PRICE WAS $4,585; DE LUXE VERSIONS RAN TO $4,779

FRONT-WHEEL DRIVE WAS NOVEL IN 1966 BUT WOULD BECOME A COMPANY PHILOSOPHY FOR GM

1968 DODGE
Charger R/T

AN AGGRESSIVE, WARLIKE NAME FOR
THE ULTIMATE MACHOMOBILE

IN 1967, LYNDON JOHNSON was carpet-bombing Hanoi, and civil-rights unrest exploded in Detroit. Both abroad and at home, America was racked by confrontation. On the freeways, another battle was taking place – the horsepower wars of Ford, General Motors, and Chrysler.

The second-generation Dodge Charger from '68–'70 was the embodiment of aggression and marketed with bellicose abandon. Copywriters screamed that it was "American guts shaped like a Mach 2 jet on wheels". For $3,480 the Road and Track Charger came with beefed-up brakes and springs and an engine named after a gun – the Magnum 440 V8. Even the classic Coke-bottle shape had a predatorial meanness, with hooded lights and a sinister sneer. Bill Brownlie, Dodge's design chief, wanted "something extremely masculine that looked like it had been lifted off the Daytona track". One of the most handsome muscle cars of the Sixties, the Charger gave a generation of restless young Americans exactly what they wanted – a machine for waging war on the street.

THE BADDIES GET
AIRBORNE IN *BULLITT*

THE DODGE
CHALLENGER
IN *VANISHING
POINT*

1968 DODGE CHARGER R/T
The ads called the Charger "a beautiful screamer" and were aimed at "a rugged type of individual". The profile is all-aggression, with shoulder-padded lines, mock vents on the doors, and twin exhausts that roared. Long and low with an evil brutality, the Charger was a design masterpiece that looked dramatic even when standing still. Few other American cars of the period possessed such harmony, balance, and poise.

PERFORMANCE EXTRAS
The R/T came with twin drainpipe exhausts, heavy-duty brakes, and F70x14 tyres.

INSIDE STORY
Chargers were also for those who liked it "soft inside". All had a clock, heater, cigarette lighter, and illuminated ashtray as standard.

ENGINE

440cid V8s pushed out 375 bhp and could crack 60 mph (96 km/h) in under seven seconds. Ultra-potent 426cid Hemis could do it in five, courtesy of a staggering 425 bhp. The V8 engines were incredibly heavy, with the 426 weighing in at an outrageous 4,433 kg (9,765 lb).

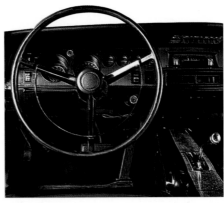

INTERIOR

The cockpit is stark, masculine, and all-vinyl. Epic performance was read from the large tachometer and speedo, and vital functions from the temperature, oil, and voltage gauges. TorqueFlite three-speed automatic was standard.

SPECIFICATIONS
MODEL 1968 Dodge Charger R/T
PRODUCTION 96,100 (all Chargers)
BODY STYLE Two-door, four-seater fastback.
CONSTRUCTION Steel body and chassis.
ENGINE 426cid, 440cid V8s.
POWER OUTPUT 375–440 bhp.
TRANSMISSION Three-speed TorqueFlite automatic, optional four-speed manual.
SUSPENSION *Front:* torsion bars; *Rear:* leaf springs with live axle.
BRAKES Front and rear drums.
MAXIMUM SPEED 182–251 km/h (113–156 mph)
0–60 MPH (0–96 KM/H) 4.8–7 sec
A.F.C. 4.2–5.3 km/l (12–15 mpg)

MEAN GRILLE

The concealed front lights disappear under hinged covers to create a mean-looking frontal aspect.

BONNET INDICATORS

Indicator repeaters facing the driver were built into the bonnet scoop.

POWER

The engine had buckets of stump-pulling torque that would rock the car from side to side when idle. The 426 Hemi unit cost an eminently reasonable $605.

1968 MERCURY
Cougar

THE '67 COUGAR ALSO CAME
OUT IN THIS DAN GURNEY
SPECIAL-EDITION MODEL

THAT THE COUGAR WAS SUCH A RUNAWAY success is empirical proof that the mid-Sixties "pony car" market really was turbocharged. After all, this was just an upscale, stretched Mustang, and nobody thought that the Lincoln-Mercury small dealer base could cope anyway. But cope they did, selling 150,000 Cougars in its debut year of '67 and 110,000 in '68, as a performance-hungry America rushed to get a slice of Mercury's "untamed luxury".

Mercury fielded three Cougar models for '67: the base, the GT, and the XR-7. GTs had the bad-boy 390cid V8, and XR-7s the 289cid V8 with plush hide trim. The Cougar scooped *Motor Trend*'s Car of the Year award for '67 and Lincoln-Mercury boasted that it was "the best-equipped luxury sports car money can buy". Admirably plugging the gap between the Mustang and the T-Bird, the Cougar had European styling, American power, and a luxury options list as long as a Sears catalogue.

INVIGORATING COUGAR
Lincoln-Mercury wanted to invigorate their image and return them to the hot-car days of the late Forties and early Fifties. The Cougar was a watershed car and revived their fortunes, blessing the rest of the range with an aura of performance and restrained luxury.

INTERIOR
All Cougars featured pony-car essentials like standard bucket seats, walnut-grain steering wheel, centre console, and floor shift. Bench seats were available but seldom specified.

ENGINE
Standard fare for the '68 was the 210 bhp 302cid V8. Power could be gently upped by specifying a 230 brake version, or boosted with a variety of blocks up to the massive 335 bhp 428cid GT-E V8. Three-speed manual was standard, with four-speed manual and three-speed automatic options.

SOUPED-UP COUGAR
Cougars were converted to Group 2 configuration for Trans-American sedan racing, and included high-performance modifications, a stripped out interior, and a four-speed Borg-Warner box.

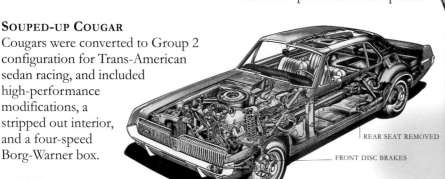

REAR SEAT REMOVED

FRONT DISC BRAKES

SIDE LIGHT
*One of the only differences
between the '67 and '68
models is the addition of
this side marker light.*

BRAKES
*The dual hydraulic brake system
allowed separate operation of front
and rear brakes "for even more
braking assurance". A warning light
on the dashboard indicated pressure
loss in either brake system.*

1968 MERCURY COUGAR

With their Remington shaver grilles, concealed headlights, and
fared-in bumpers, Cougars were good-looking cars. By 1972,
yearly sales of the top-line XR-7 exceeded those of the
cheapest Cougar, and in '74 the base model was dropped. For
real performance, buyers opted for the GT-E package, with
a colossal engine, twin bonnet scoops,
steel wheels, quadruple
exhausts, and heavy-
duty suspension.

SPECIFICATIONS

MODEL 1968 Mercury Cougar
PRODUCTION 113,726
BODY STYLE Two-door,
four-seater coupe.
CONSTRUCTION Steel unitary body.
ENGINE 302cid, 390cid, 428cid
V8s.
POWER OUTPUT 210–335 bhp.
TRANSMISSION Three-speed
manual, optional four-speed
manual, and three-speed
Merc-O-Matic automatic.
SUSPENSION *Front:* coil springs;
Rear: leaf springs.
BRAKES Front and rear drums;
optional front discs.
MAXIMUM SPEED 169–209 km/h
(105–130 mph)
0–60 MPH (0–96 KM/H)
17.3–10.2 sec
A.F.C. 5.7 km/l (16 mpg)

REAR VIEW
*Sequential tail-lights à la T-Bird were now
a standard Ford trademark, and the dual
exhausts added to the aggressive rear aspect.*

MALE MERCURY
"The relationship between a man and his
car is a very special thing", opined the '67
Mercury sales brochure – no real surprise
from a company that prided itself on
making "the man's car".

HEADLIGHTS
*The Cougar's disappearing headlights were hidden
behind vacuum-powered slatted covers that opened
automatically when the lights were turned on.*

1969 CHEVROLET
Corvette Stingray

CHEVROLET AND CHEQUERED FLAGS
REFLECT THE CAR'S RACING PEDIGREE

THE MOTORING PRESS REALLY lashed into the '69 Shark, calling it a piece of junk, a low point in Corvette history, and the beginning of a new trend towards the image-and-gadget car. Instead of testing the 'Vette, *Car and Driver* magazine simply recited a litany of glitches and pronounced it "too dire to drive", sending ripples of rage through GM. To be frank, the '69 was not the best 'Vette ever. Styling was boisterous, boot space vestigial, the seats had you sliding all over the place, and the general build was shoddy. Two great engines saved the day, the 327cid and three incarnations of the big-block 427. With the hottest L88 version hitting 60 mph (96 km/h) in five-and-a-half seconds and peaking at 257 km/h (160 mph), these were cars that were race-ready from the showroom floor. Despite the vitriol, the public liked their image, gadgets, and grunt, buying 38,762 of them, a production record unbroken for the next six years – empirical proof that, occasionally, car journalists do talk hot air.

ENGINE
If the stock 427 was not enough, there was always the 500 bhp ZL1, a 274 km/h (170 mph) racing option package. To discourage boy racers, no heater was installed in the ZL1; only two were ever sold to retail customers.

BIG DADDY
With the 427 unit, the 'Vette was the biggest, heaviest, fastest, thirstiest, cheapest, and most powerful sports car on the market.

SHARK-BASED DESIGN
GM chief Bill Mitchell was an admirer of sharks – "they are exciting to look at"– and wanted to design a car with similar lines. In 1960 a prototype car was made called the Mako Shark and the end result was the 1963 Sting Ray, reputedly Mitchell's favourite piece of work. A further prototype in 1966, the Mako Shark II, produced the 1968–72 generation of Stingray.

INTERIOR
A major drawback of the '69 was its sharply raked seats, which prevented the traditional Corvette arm-out-of-the-window pose. While the telescopic tilt column and leather trim were extras, the glove compartment had been introduced as standard in 1968.

STINGRAY BADGE
Chevy stopped calling its 'Vette the Sting Ray in 1968, but thought better of it in '69, reinstating the name as one word.

WHEELS
Wheel-rim width increased to 20 cm (8 in) in 1969, wide enough to roll an English cricket pitch.

HEADLIGHTS
The '69 retained hidden headlights, but instead of being electrically operated they now worked off a vacuum to give slow but fluid illumination. In 1984 the electric system was reintroduced.

SPECIFICATIONS

MODEL 1969 Chevrolet Corvette Stingray

PRODUCTION 38,762

BODY STYLE Two-seater sports and convertible

CONSTRUCTION Fibreglass, separate chassis.

ENGINE 327cid, 427cid V8s.

POWER OUTPUT 300–500 bhp.

TRANSMISSION Three-speed manual, optional four-speed manual, three-speed Turbo Hydra-Matic automatic.

SUSPENSION *Front:* upper and lower A-arms, coil springs; *Rear:* independent with transverse strut and leaf springs.

BRAKES Front and rear discs.

MAXIMUM SPEED 188–274 km/h (117–170 mph)

0–60 MPH (0–96 KM/H) 5.7–7.7 sec

A.F.C. 3.5 km/l (10 mpg)

1969 CHEVROLET CORVETTE STINGRAY
The Stingray filled its wheel arches very convincingly with an aggressive, menacing presence. Any similarity to the European sports cars that inspired the original Corvettes had by now withered away, to be replaced by a new, threatening personality. In the annals of motoring history, there is no car with more evil looks than this 1968–72 generation Corvette.

ROOF PANEL
Half of the '69 production were coupes with twin lift-off roof panels and a removable window – making this Stingray almost a convertible.

EXHAUST
The side-mounted exhaust system was an option only in 1969, but was withdrawn in 1970 because of excessive heat and noise.

The Seventies

Seventies America had more pressing concerns than protest. For the first time ever, the world's most affluent society was in the red. For a people weaned on plenty, the coming decade of debt would rattle America's confidence like nothing before.

FOR AMERICANS and their cars, the Seventies were the end of an era. Popular resentment seethed on the streets. Watergate, crime, welfare dependency, and bussing made many people anxious and angry. The United States, so powerful for so long, now seemed adrift, divided by race, class, sex, and war. As one pundit concisely put it: "Sometimes you get the feeling that nothing's gone right since John Kennedy died. We've had the Vietnam War, all the rioting, and now we can't even get any gas. Before America used to win everything, but now sometimes I think our sun has set."

Americans weren't worse off in the Seventies, it's just that their expectations of growing prosperity now seemed less well founded. The shining optimism of the Fifties and Sixties had waned, and nothing did more to blunt the nation's confidence than the economic malaise of '73–'74. Nixon

devalued the dollar, productivity sagged, inflation and unemployment ballooned, and Uncle Sam could no longer cut it in world markets. The once mighty industrial engine had stalled, and commercial America seemed to do little more than buy and sell burgers and root-beer floats.

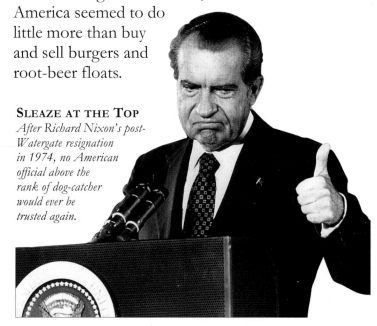

SLEAZE AT THE TOP
After Richard Nixon's post-Watergate resignation in 1974, no American official above the rank of dog-catcher would ever be trusted again.

	1970	1971	1972	1973	1974
A U T O M O T I V E	• **Ford** take over from **Chevrolet** as number one manufacturer, producing 2,096,184 cars in '70 model year • Congress passes Clean Air Act • **GM** lose $1 billion in profits because of 67-day strike • **Buick** bring out largest-ever 455cid V8 block for the Riviera • Lee Iacocca becomes President of **Ford** • **Cadillac** announce massive new 500cid V8	• Legislation demands that all new US cars must be able to run on unleaded fuel • New compact **Ford** Pinto • Nixon abolishes 7 per cent excise tax on cars and imposes 10 per cent surcharge on imported cars • **Ford** offer awesome power in Boss 351 Mustang	• **Chevrolet** back at number one, selling 2,420,564 cars • **Lincoln** Continental Mark IV unveiled • **AMC** unveil leisure off-roader, the Cherokee *1973 OLDSMOBILE H/O CUTLASS*	• 5 mph (8 km/h) impact bumpers are mandatory • Emission regulations force manufacturers to detune engines • **Chrysler's** one millionth car rolls off the line • **Cadillac** Eldorado Convertible is official Indy 500 pace car • US cars average only 4.8 km/l (13.5 mpg)	• Energy crisis triggers fuel shortages and spiralling prices • 55 mph (88 km/h) speed limit becomes law • Smaller **Ford** Mustang II debuts, redefining pony car *1974 FORD COUNTRY SQUIRE ESTATE*
H I S T O R I C A L	• Four students killed by National Guard at Kent State University • Nixon promises to remove all troops from Cambodia • Memorial to JFK unveiled in Dallas • Charles Manson on trial for mass murder • The Beatles split up • Jimi Hendrix dies of drug overdose • Charles de Gaulle dies	• Nixon pledges to end all US involvement in Vietnam • Charles Manson sentenced to death • 18-year-olds given the vote • Muhammad Ali cleared of draft dodging • Astronauts drive on Moon in lunar buggy • Disney World opens in Orlando, Florida	• Nixon wins second term; various aides are indicted over Watergate • J. Edgar Hoover resigns after 50 years • NASA launches Jupiter space probe *RICHARD NIXON MEETS MAO TSE TUNG*	• Nixon orders halt to Vietnam bombing; America and Vietnam exchange POWs • Federal prosecutors order fresh inquiry into Watergate; Nixon admits to installing bugs in Oval Office • Vice-President Spiro Agnew resigns in disgrace • Gerald Ford sworn in as new Vice-President • J. Paul Getty's grandson kidnapped	• Grand Jury says Nixon involved in Watergate cover-up; Supreme Court orders Nixon to hand over Watergate tapes • Nixon resigns; Vice-President Ford takes over as President • Students injured in racial fighting in Boston • Kidnapped Patti Hearst is caught on camera robbing a bank • *The Sting*, with Robert Redford and Paul Newman, wins seven Oscars

FACT AND FICTION
Sam Peckinpah's 1972 film The Getaway *was a violent orgy of non-stop car crashes, mirroring the rising tide of crime and amorality that deeply worried Seventies America.*

SLUGGISH 'STANG
The 1973 Mustang was big, fat, and slow. Sales had been sliding since '67 and the third-generation car did nothing to stop the rot. Ford's pony car had changed, and not for the better.

But the most painful blow of all was the energy crisis. The Yom Kippur War in 1973 saw Arab nations raise oil prices by 387 per cent, which, for a country like America that consumed so much of the stuff, was a nightmare best left undocumented. Petrol station queues snaked into the horizon and the last digit of licence plates – odd or even – determined the days of the week you could buy petrol. A blanket 55 mph (88 km/h) speed limit was a daily reminder that things were going horribly wrong. Retail prices hit the stratosphere, unemployment went off the clock, and inflation soared into double digits. A headline in the *Washington Post* articulated America's anxieties: "Things will get worse before they get worse."

While Watergate and Vietnam had shaken people's complacency, economic infirmity absolutely terrified them. The American Dream had been built on the foundations of prosperity and plenty, and without them that special vibrancy and energy that so characterized the post-war years simply evaporated. Economic progress had been America's opiate, helping to accelerate productivity, home ownership, education, and the consumer good-life. And for all its vulgarity, the much-lambasted consumer culture did more than just improve the comfort of Americans.

1975	1976	1977	1978	1979
• Petrol is double its 1972 price • Catalytic converters become law in California • Congress passes Energy Policy and Conservation Act • **Cadillac** offer fuel injection on 500cid V8 • **Chrysler** axe palatial Imperial • "Baby" **Cadillac** Seville appears, smallest Caddy for 50 years • Ill-fated **AMC** Pacer launched as **Chevy** Vega/**Ford** Pinto competition	• Bicentennial celebrations invigorate auto industry • **Chevrolet** launch all-new sub-compact Chevette • Last **Cadillac** Eldorado Convertible rolls off the line • Sumptuous **Lincoln** Mark V debuts • **Lincoln-Mercury** introduce upgraded Capri II	• **GM** downsize whole fleet as sop to superficial functionalism • **Ford** F-Series pick-up is best-selling American vehicle • **Chevrolet** withdraw the Vega • **Buick** launch scaled-down aeroback-styled Century • **GM** pilot airbags to a less-than-enthusiastic public • **Ford** introduce new T-Bird at $2,700 less than old model	• **Ford** celebrate 75th anniversary • Third-best car sales ever recorded • Lee Iacocca fired as **Ford** President; moves to Chrysler • Third-generation **Ford** Mustang appears • **Cadillac** include **Oldsmobile** diesel engine option on Seville • **Buick** offer turbo option • **Ford** launch Fairmont compact • **VW** first foreign manufacturer since 1930s to build cars in US	• Second energy crisis sends fuel prices through the roof • Car imports rise to 22.7 per cent of US domestic car market • **Honda** open first US plant
		SKATEBOARDING CRAZE		1979 DELOREAN
• Americans evacuate US embassy in Saigon • CIA claimed to have ordered Mafia contract to assassinate Fidel Castro • Soviet cosmonauts and American astronauts shake hands in space • Gerald Ford says he will run for President in '76, as does a former Governor of California, Ronald Reagan • Jack Nicholson stars in *One Flew Over the Cuckoo's Nest*	• One million people celebrate US bicentennial in Washington, DC • Jimmy Carter wins Democratic nomination • Gerald Ford and Jimmy Carter hold televised debate • Jimmy Carter elected President • US ambassador kidnapped and killed in Beirut • Concorde completes first commercial transatlantic supersonic flight	• Space Shuttle makes maiden flight • Gary Gilmore executed • Martin Luther King Jr. awarded posthumous Medal of Freedom • New York blacked out by massive power failure, leading to looting and rioting • Roman Polanski jailed for sex with a 13-year-old • Elvis Presley dies • *Rocky* wins Oscar for best film • *Star Wars* is highest-grossing film	• US and USSR discuss a strategic arms limitation treaty (SALT) • President Carter hosts Israeli-Egyptian summit • Bugs found in US embassy in Moscow • Arkady Shavchenko, highest-ranking Soviet official at UN, defects • 900 US cultists die in mass suicide in Guyana • *Superman* draws record crowds	• Atomic leak at Three Mile Island, Pennsylvania • Brezhnev and Carter sign SALT agreement • Iranian terrorists storm US embassy in Tehran • John Wayne dies • Muhammad Ali retires

KEEPING IT BIG
Detroit kept producing vast shopping carts like the monster '73 Ford Country Squire. Although groaning under the weight of energy-absorbing bumpers, the Squire was only fitted with radial tyres as an option.

FINAL FLOURISH
The 5.3 km/l (15 mpg) '75 Eldorado was Cadillac's final flourish before they succumbed to environmental pressures and fielded their compact new Seville, with a fuel-economy computer on board.

It also served to distract the nation from its social and political ills. With nothing to allay their angst, most Americans now lost faith in their institutions, politicians, security, and even their future. And the motor car, so long a barometer of America's health and a prescription for escape, was in the doldrums too. The mandarins of Motown had ignored the oil shocks and the rise of Japanese imports. The city of Detroit had deteriorated into urban anarchy and earned itself the soubriquet of "Murder City USA". The management and staff at GM's 15-storey headquarters went to and fro via secured entrances and exits that side-stepped the car capital's mean streets. What was going wrong for America was going wrong for the auto industry. Within a few years Honda would open its first American car factory in Ohio and GM would post its biggest loss in history – an astonishing $760 million. The automobile quickly became the symbol of all that was wrong with American

consumerism. Pressure began to mount for the Government to mandate changes in Detroit's dinosaurs. The offensive began with the Federal Clean Air Act of 1970, which demanded a 90 per cent reduction in three exhaust pollutants. Then, in 1975, Congress passed the Energy Policy and Conservation Act, demanding that auto makers achieved an ambitious corporate average fuel economy of 27.5 mpg (9.7 km/l) within 10 years. Worse still, bumpers had to withstand 5 mph (8 km/h) impacts without damage, a Federal bombshell that caused creative car design to come to a crashing halt.

The Manufacturers Respond

Safety and environmental responsibility shifted the traditional balance of power from design and styling to engineering and efficiency, the only way to meet the strictures of the grey-faced legislators. The Big Three increased their offerings in the compact and intermediate classes, and in '77 GM took the unprecedented step of downsizing their entire line-up. Americans believed that the country's problems could be solved if they consumed in a more responsible and frugal way. The square, stern lines of Seventies metal comforted them that they were doing the right thing. But it was a superficial and hollow functionalism. Cars like

CAR KEYS AND CLUTCH
While Starsky and Hutch did battle with dark forces on the streets in their red-and-white Ford Torino, the media beamed the decay of America's social fabric straight into the nation's living room. But wasn't Huggy Bear one cool dude?

DISCO ESCAPISM
Behind the disco throb of Robert Stigwood's '78 Saturday Night Fever *lay a subtext of aimless youth whose only escape from their daily tedium was dance. It highlighted the growing disaffection of a teenbeat generation trying to find some focus in a decade of unemployment and inflation.*

NUCLEAR FALLOUT
In 1979 the Three Mile Island nuclear power plant in Pennsylvania almost went into meltdown because of gas trapped inside a crippled reactor. A combination of defective equipment and operator error rocked America's confidence in her nuclear prowess.

the Mustang II, Dodge Aspen, Ford Torino, and Mercury Monterey were just pale facsimiles of the far superior imports from Germany and Japan.

For manufacturers accustomed to huge profit margins from epic cars, the anaemic returns on "econoboxes" seemed paltry and quality nose-dived as a result. GM had to recall 6.7 million cars for engine-mount problems, Ford Pintos exploded in a ball of flame when hit from behind, the Chevrolet Vega rusted so badly that it was nicknamed "the biodegradable car", and the gumdrop-shaped AMC Pacer had steering that would seize rock solid. Even the great white hope, General Motors' 350cid diesel, would break its crankshaft and crack its block, and the THM 200 automatic gearbox to which it was mated was the object of more consumer complaints than any other automotive transmission in history.

The Price of Intervention

Sadly, quality wasn't the only casualty in the Seventies. American cars lost their guts, glitz, and glamour. The chromium fantasy was under siege from a hurricane of killjoy legislative interference and meddling. Detroit had no choice but to turn its back on the usual extravagance, producing instead a gaggle of dreary intermediates, compacts, and sub-compacts with all the charisma of old shoes.

Detroit had been allowed to party unhindered for three decades and, left to its own devices, would have done precious little to improve exhaust emissions and fuel consumption. The massive governmental pressure of the Seventies caught car makers off guard and their engineering couldn't cope. The Seventies were all about short-term fixes to long-term problems, which is why the new generation of clean-air cars stalled, ran roughly, and were generally second-rate. The American automobile had hit rock bottom.

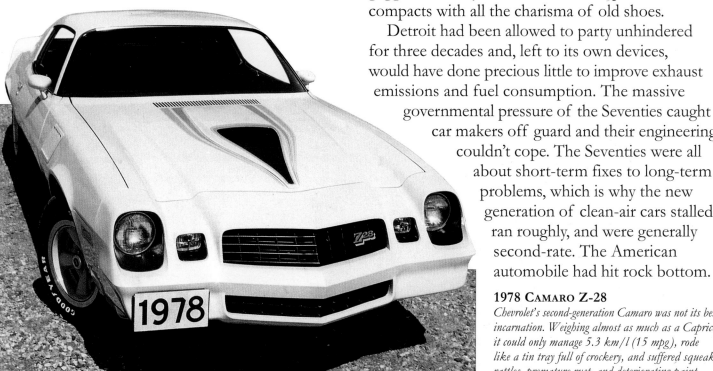

1978 CAMARO Z-28
Chevrolet's second-generation Camaro was not its best incarnation. Weighing almost as much as a Caprice, it could only manage 5.3 km/l (15 mpg), rode like a tin tray full of crockery, and suffered squeaks, rattles, premature rust, and deteriorating paint.

1970 CHEVROLET
Monte Carlo

CHEVROLET ADVERTS FOR THE MONTE CARLO PROMISED THAT "GOOD TASTE SPEAKS FOR ITSELF"

NOW THE WORLD'S LARGEST producer of motor vehicles, Chevrolet kicked off the Seventies with their Ford Thunderbird chaser, the 1970 Monte Carlo. Hailed as "action and elegance in a sporty personal luxury package", it was only available as a coupe and came with power front discs, Elm-Burl dash-panel inlays, and a choice of engines that ranged from the standard 350cid V8 to the Herculean SS 454.

At $3,123 in base form, it was cheap compared to the $5,000 needed to buy a Thunderbird. But the T-Bird had become as urbane as Dean Martin and the Monte couldn't match the Ford's élan. Even so, despite a six-week strike that lost Chevrolet 100,000 sales, no less than 130,000 Monte Carlos found buyers which, compared to a mere 40,000 T-Birds, made Chevy's new personal luxury confection a monster hit.

INTERIOR
The Monte Carlo's cabin was Chevrolet's most luxurious for the year, but was criticized for having limited front and rear legroom. Centre console and bucket seats were a $53 option, as was the special instrumentation package of tachometer, ammeter, and temperature gauge at $68.

RACE STYLING
The slippery aerodynamics and near perfect power-to-weight distribution turned the car into a fine high-performance machine.

ENGINE
The potent SS 454 option was a modest $147 and could catapult the Monte Carlo to 60 mph (96 km/h) in less than eight seconds, making it a favourite with short-track stock-car racers.

HIDDEN AERIAL
The radio aerial is hidden in the screen.

RACING IMAGE

The sporty chequered flag motif didn't really reflect the Monte's market-place. Owners were respectable, middle-aged types with five-bedroom houses in uptown neighbourhoods.

1970 CHEVROLET MONTE CARLO

The Monte Carlo used the same platform as the redesigned 1969 Pontiac Grand Prix. Stylistically, the long bonnet and short boot promised performance and power. The single headlights were mounted in square-shaped housings, and the grid-textured grille was simple and unfussy. The smooth-centred wheel trims were not popular with buyers and, in '71, prettier, chromed mock-wire wheels were offered. A year later, a mild facelift saw a wider grille and vertical parking lights placed inboard of the headlights.

SPECIFICATIONS

MODEL 1970 Chevrolet Monte Carlo

PRODUCTION 145,975

BODY STYLE Two-door, five-seater coupe.

CONSTRUCTION Steel body and chassis.

ENGINE 350cid, 400cid, 454cid V8s.

POWER OUTPUT 250–360 bhp.

TRANSMISSION Three-speed manual, optional two-speed Powerglide automatic, Turbo Hydra-Matic three-speed automatic.

SUSPENSION *Front:* coil springs; *Rear:* leaf springs.

BRAKES Front and rear drums.

MAXIMUM SPEED 185–211 km/h (115–132 mph)

0–60 MPH (0–96 KM/H) 8–14 sec

A.F.C. 5.3–7 km/l (15–20 mpg)

REAR STABILITY

Another option available, and fitted on this car, was rear anti-sway bars.

VINYL OPTION

Black vinyl top was a $120 option. Buyers could also choose blue, dark gold, green, or white.

PILLAR

Prodigious rear pillar made city parking literally hit-or-miss.

WHEELBASE

The Monte Carlo was built to the smaller Chevelle's wheelbase, but was several centimetres longer.

1970 PLYMOUTH
'Cuda

INTERIOR
'Cuda interiors were flamboyant, with body-hugging bucket seats, Hurst pistol-grip shifter, and wood-grain steering wheel. This model has the Rallye instrument cluster, with tachometer, oil pressure gauge, and 150 mph (241 km/h) speedo.

THE 440-6 WAS A $250 'CUDA ENGINE OPTION

THE TOUGH-SOUNDING '70s 'Cuda was one of the last flowerings of America's performance binge. Furiously fast, it was a totally new incarnation of the first '64 Barracuda and unashamedly aimed at psychopathic street-racers. Cynically, Plymouth even dubbed their belligerent model line-up "The Rapid Transit System".

'70 Barracudas came in three styles – the 'Cuda was the performance model – and nine engine choices, topped by the outrageous 426cid Hemi. Chrysler's advertising men bellowed that the Hemi was "our angriest body wrapped around ol' King Kong hisself". But rising insurance rates and new emission standards meant that the muscle car was an endangered species. By 1973 Plymouth brochures showed a 'Cuda with a young married couple, complete with a baby in the smiling woman's arms. The party was well and truly over.

STYLING
Plymouth stylists kept the shape uncluttered, with tapered-in bumpers, concealed wipers, flush door handles, smooth overhangs, and subtly flared wheel arches.

AIR CLEANER
Unsilenced air cleaners such as this weren't allowed in California because of drive-by noise regulations.

SHAKER HOOD
The distinctive shaker hood, allowing the air cleaner space to vibrate through the top of the bonnet, was a standard 'Cuda feature.

COLOUR CHOICE
'Cudas came in 18 strident colours, with funky names like "In Violet", "Lemon Twist", and "Vitamin C".

ENGINE
The 440cid "six-pack" Magnum motor cranked out 385 bhp and drank through three two-barrel Holley carbs, explaining the six-pack label. Base engine was a 383cid V8, which pushed out 335 horses.

1970 PLYMOUTH 'CUDA
The '70 'Cuda's crisp, taut styling is shared with the Dodge Challenger, and the classic long-bonnet-short-boot design leaves you in no doubt that this is a pony car. Government legislation and hefty insurance rates ensured that this was the penultimate year of the big-engined Barracudas; after '71, the biggest block on offer was a 340cid V8. By '74, total Barracudas sales for the year had slipped to just over 11,000, and it was axed before the '75 model year.

SPECIFICATIONS
MODEL 1970 Plymouth 'Cuda
PRODUCTION 19,515
BODY STYLE Two-door, four-seater coupe and convertible.
CONSTRUCTION Steel unitary body.
ENGINE 383cid, 426cid, 440cid V8s.
POWER OUTPUT 335–425 bhp.
TRANSMISSION Three-speed manual, optional four-speed manual, and three-speed TorqueFlite automatic.
SUSPENSION *Front:* torsion bars; *Rear:* leaf springs with live axle.
BRAKES Front discs, rear drums.
MAXIMUM SPEED 220–241 km/h (137–150 mph)
0–60 MPH (0–96 KM/H) 5.9–6.9 sec
A.F.C. 4.2–6 km/l (12–17 mpg)

PERFORMANCE PARTS
Super Stock springs and a heavy-duty Dana 60 rear axle were standard on all 440 'Cudas.

STRIPING
Optional inverted hockey stick graphics trumpeted engine size.

1971 BUICK
Riviera

THE '71 RIVIERA WAS A RADICAL MODEL FOR TRADITIONALLY CONSERVATIVE BUICK

THE '63 RIVIERA HAD BEEN one of Buick's best sellers, but by the late Sixties it was lagging far behind Ford's now-luxurious Thunderbird. Mind you, the Riviera easily outsold its stable-mate, the radical front-wheel drive Toronado, but for '71 Buick upped the stakes by unveiling a new Riviera that was a little bit special.

Handsome and dramatic, the "boat-tail", as it was nicknamed, had its stylistic roots in the split rear-screen Sting Ray of '63. It was as elegant as Jackie Onassis and as hard-hitting as Muhammad Ali. Its base price was $5,251, undercutting the arch-rival T-Bird by a wide margin. Designer Bill Mitchell nominated it as his favourite car of all time and, while sales of Rivieras hardly went crazy, at last Buick had a flagship coupe that was the envy of the industry.

INTERIOR
Although the Seventies cabin was plush and hedonistic, it was more than a little bit plasticky. After 1972, the rear seat could be split 60/40 – pretty neat for a coupe. The option list was infinite and you could swell the car's base sticker price by a small fortune. Tilt steering wheel *(left)* was standard on the Riviera.

ENGINE
The Riviera came with GM's biggest mill, the mighty 455. The even hotter Gran Sport option made the massive V8 even smoother and quieter, and offered big-buck buyers a stonking 330 bhp. One reviewer said of the GS-engined car, "there's nothing better made on these shores".

SUPREME STOPPING POWER
The Riviera drew praise for its braking, helped by a Max Trac anti-skid option. The Riv could stop from 96 km/h (60 mph) in 41 m (135 ft), 12 m (40 ft) shorter than its rivals.

PILLARLESS STYLE
With the side windows down, Buick's bruiser was pillarless, further gracing those swooping lines.

SOFT-RAY TINTED GLASS HELPED KEEP THINGS COOL

THIS IS THE 315 BHP ENGINE; A 330 BHP UNIT WAS AVAILABLE AT EXTRA COST

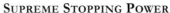

VENTS ARE PART OF THE AIR-CONDITIONING
SYSTEM AND UNIQUE TO '71 RIVIERAS

ELECTRIC BOOT RELEASES ARE
NOT A MODERN PHENOMENON –
THEY WERE ON THE '71 RIVIERA'S
OPTIONS LIST

SEATING COULD BE
ALL-VINYL BENCH
SEATS WITH CUSTOM
TRIM OR FRONT BUCKETS

OVERHEAD BEAUTY

The Riviera's styling may
have been excessive, but it
still made a capacious five-
seater, despite the fastback
roof line and massive
rear window. The 3.1 m
(122 in) wheelbase made
the '71 boat-tail longer
than previous Rivieras.

CHUNKY REAR

The muscular rear flanks flow
into the boat-tail rear. Only a
Detroit stylist would graft a huge
chrome point to the back of a car.

WHEEL ARCHES WERE WIDE OPEN
AND WENT AGAINST THE TREND
FOR SKIRTED WINGS

SPECIFICATIONS

MODEL 1971 Buick Riviera
PRODUCTION 33,810
BODY STYLE Two-door coupe.
CONSTRUCTION Steel body and
box-section chassis.
ENGINE 455cid V8.
POWER OUTPUT 315–330 bhp.
TRANSMISSION Three-speed Turbo
Hydra-Matic automatic.
SUSPENSION *Front:* independent
coil springs;
Rear: self-levelling pneumatic
bellows over shocks.
BRAKES Front discs, rear drums.
MAXIMUM SPEED 201 km/h
(125 mph)
0–60 MPH (0–96 KM/H) 8.4 sec
A.F.C. 4.2–5.3 km/l
(12–15 mpg)

EVOLUTION OF THE BUICK RIVIERA

THE RIVIERA TAG first appeared in 1949, when the Buick Roadmaster Riviera became the first pillarless hardtop convertible. During the Fifties, Buick spread the Riviera name all over the place, so, in 1955, for example, you could choose between a Buick Super Riviera, Roadmaster Riviera, Century Riviera, and Special Riviera. The name was steadily misapplied so that by 1971 the Riv had lost its special cachet and become just another land yacht.

1963

ONE OF THE ALL-TIME great automotive designs, in the same league as the '36–'37 Cord and the Continental Mark II, the Riviera was agile, sexy, and highly prized. The public loved it and it soon became the patriotic choice for Ivy League America. Even the Europeans raved. And with that 401cid V8 upfront, it could even worry a Jag.

KEY FEATURES
- Standard 325 bhp 401cid V8 with optional 340 bhp 425cid V8
- Two-speed automatic transmission
- Open headlights
- Optional leather interior

1969

BY THE TIME THIS 1969 model hit the streets, the Riviera had gone through a number of rebirths. Headlights were hidden in '65, then exposed with a 1966 fastback redesign that lengthened the car, only to be hidden once more in '68. A GS (Gran Sport) option was introduced from 1965, and a larger power unit made available from 1967.

KEY DEVELOPMENTS
- Three-speed transmission from 1964
- 1966 redesign made car longer, heavier, and more curvaceous
- 1968 redesign of front aspect
- 360 bhp 430cid V8 unit available from 1967

1970

THE "NOW YOU SEE THEM, now you don't" headlights saga continued in this 1970 revamp; two years after they had been hidden away, out they came once more. Not that it did anything for the looks of the Riviera – the once "classic" styling had now been replaced by ugly retro design touches. A new power unit boosted output to 370 bhp.

KEY DEVELOPMENTS
- New 370 bhp 455cid V8 unit as standard
- Electronic skid-control braking system
- Now sitting on shortened Electra chassis
- All-new "E" body by Donald C. Laskey

1971 BUICK *Riviera*

DARING LINES SUCH AS THESE HAD NEVER BEFORE BEEN SEEN ON A PRODUCTION CAR

VIEW FROM REAR-VIEW MIRROR WAS SLIGHTLY RESTRICTED

ONE-PIECE REAR WINDSCREEN CURVES DOWNWARDS

CONTROVERSIAL STYLING
The rear of the car was a Bill Mitchell "classic" that had his trademark stamped all over it, the GM supremo having also designed the rear of the '63 Sting Ray coupe. This time, however, critics were not so universal in their praise, and even Mitchell found himself having to defend the design.

LAND OF ENCHANTMENT
AMY ◆ 589
72 NEW MEXICO USA

1977	1979	1986	1995

1977

AFTER THE "BOAT-TAIL" had been replaced by a more conventional design in 1974, there was little change until this downsizing in '77, which placed the Riviera on the same chassis as the new Electra. By this time, sales had fallen from nearly 43,000 in 1967 to 20,500, with the Riviera now regarded as just another standard luxury coupe.

KEY DEVELOPMENTS
- 1971 redesign with radical "boat-tail" styling, blunted slightly in 1973
- 1974 redesign is far more conventional
- 1977 model downsized
- 455cid V8 has reduced output of 205 bhp
- "Mac-Trac" anti-wheelspin system

1979

THE FIRST FRONT-WHEEL drive Buick Riviera entered the market in '79 on GM's newly-downsized E-body platform. The body and mechanics were shared with the Cadillac Eldorado and Oldsmobile Toronado. Despite relatively minor styling changes from 1977, the public liked it and sales shot back up to nearly 53,000 units.

KEY DEVELOPMENTS
- Front-wheel drive
- Sporty T-type with a turbo V6 available
- Disc brakes all round
- Lightest Riviera yet

1986

SALES OF THE RIVIERA rose in 1981, then dropped back in '82. The first convertible was introduced in 1983, but poor sales saw it withdrawn after 1985. The standard Riviera had a slight frontal design change in 1984, and this was the prelude to a complete downsizing again in 1986. Hardly a successful move as sales plummeted 70 per cent.

KEY DEVELOPMENTS
- Four-speed automatic gearbox introduced as standard in 1984
- Riviera convertible available 1983–85
- Downsized in 1986

1995

SALES HIT AN ALL-TIME LOW of just over 15,000 units in 1987, crashing to 8,625 a year later. Realizing that downsizing was probably not a good idea, Buick gave the 1989 Riviera an extra 28 cm (11 in) and a plusher ride; sales doubled. After falling sales in the early 1990s, this 1995 model harks back to the 1971–73 "boat-tail" era with its unusual yet stylish rear aspect.

KEY DEVELOPMENTS
- Improved V6 in 1988
- 1989 redesign lengthened the car at back and added more comfort and chrome
- ABS as standard in 1991
- 1995 redesign with tapered tail and regular V6 (205 bhp) and supercharged V6 (225 bhp) engines

CLASSY THROUGHOUT
The lines of the boat-tail were not only beautiful at the rear, but were carried right through to the thrusting, pointed grille.

BUILT ON A REPUTATION
By 1971 the Riviera had become almost a caricature of itself, now bigger and brasher than it ever was before. It was the coupe in which to make a truly stunning entrance.

THE 455CID BLOCK COULD PUMP OUT 315 BHP AND REACH 60 (96 KM/H) IN 8.4 SECONDS

LAND OF ENCHANTMENT
AMY ☀ 589
72 NEW MEXICO USA

1971 CHEVROLET
Nova SS

ONE OF CHEVROLET'S SALES TRIUMPHS

THE NOVA NAME FIRST appeared in 1962 as the top-line model of Chevrolet's new Falcon-buster compact, the Chevy II. Evolving into a range in its own right, by '71 the Nova's Super Sport (SS) package was one of the smallest muscle cars ever fielded by Detroit. In an era when performance was on the wane, the diminutive banshee found plenty of friends among the budget drag-racing set. That strong 350cid V8 just happened to be a small-block Chevy, perfect for all those tweaky manifolds, carbs, headers, and distributors courtesy of a massive hop-up industry. Some pundits even went so far as hailing the Nova SS as the Seventies equivalent of the '57 Chevy.

Frisky, tough, and impudent, Chevy's giant-killer could easily double the legal limit and, with wide-profile rubber, body stripes, Strato bucket seats, and custom interior, the SS was a Nova to die for. Quick and rare, only 7,016 '71 Novas sported the magic SS badge. Performance iron died a death in '72, making these last-of-the-line '71s perfect candidates for the "Chevy Muscle Hall of Fame".

INTERIOR
Nova features included front armrests, anti-theft steering-wheel-column lock, and ignition key alarm system. The $328 SS package bought a sports steering wheel and special gauges, but air-conditioning and a centre console were extra-cost options.

STYLING
The Nova's shell would last for 11 years and was shared with Buick, Oldsmobile, and Pontiac.

TYRES AND WHEELS
Wide-profile, bias-belted, white-lettered E70x14 tyres were standard SS fare, but the handsome Sportmag five-spoke alloys were an $85 option.

PONY STYLING
Playing on the "long-hood-short-deck" phrase used so much in Sixties auto-writing, Nova ads in the Seventies ran the copyline "Long Hood, Short Price".

LIGHTS
Amber plastic lamp lenses were new for '71.

1971 CHEVROLET NOVA SS

Handsome, neat, and chaste, the Nova was a new breed of passenger car for the Seventies. Advertised as the "Not Too Small Car", it looked a lot like a scaled-down version of the Chevelle and debuted in this form in 1968 to rave reviews. Safety legislation hit Detroit hard and the Nova was forced to carry side marker-lights, shoulder harnesses, rear window defogger, dual-circuit brakes, and impact-absorbing steering column.

ENGINE
The two- or four-barrel 350cid V8 ran on regular fuel and pushed out 270 ponies. At one point, Chevrolet planned to squeeze the massive 454cid V8 from the Chevelle into the Nova SS, but regrettably dropped the idea.

BLOCK
In '71, the option of a four-cylinder block was withdrawn on the Nova. Not surprising, considering that out of 315,000 Nova sales in 1970, only 2,247 buyers chose a four.

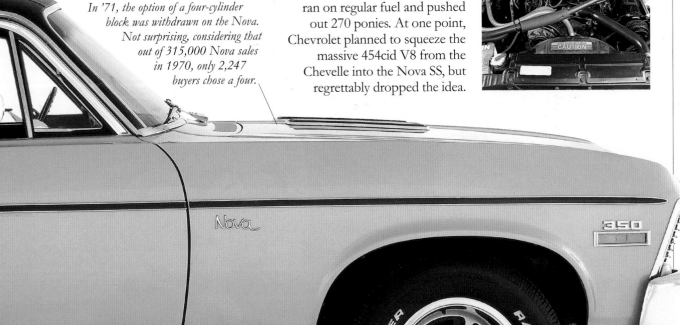

1971 OLDSMOBILE
4-4-2

INTERIOR
Despite the cheap-looking, wood-grain vinyl dash, the 4-4-2's cabin had a real race-car feel. Bucket seats, custom steering wheel, and Hurst Competition gear shift came as standard, but the sports console at $77 and Rallye pack with clock and tacho at $84 were extras.

1971 WAS THE LAST OF THE 4-4-2's glory years. A performance package *par excellence*, it was GM's longest-lived muscle car, tracing its roots all the way back to the heady days of '64 when a 4-4-2 combo was made available for the Oldsmobile Cutlass F-85. Possibly some of the most refined slingshots ever to come from any GM division, 4-4-2s had looks, charisma, and brawn to spare. The 4-4-2 nomenclature stood for a four-barrel carb, four-speed manual transmission, and two exhausts. Olds cleverly raided the store room, using hot-shot parts previously only available to police departments. The deal was cheap and the noise on the street shattering. At $3,551, the super-swift Hardtop Coupe came with a 455cid V8, Rallye suspension, Strato bucket seats, and a top whack of 193 km/h (120 mph). The 4-4-2 package might have run and run had it not hit the '71 fuel crisis bang on. Which proved a shame, because it was to be a long time before power like this would be seen again.

OLDS CHURNED OUT 558,889 CARS IN '71

ENGINE BLOCK
Oldsmobile never tired of proclaiming that their 455cid mill was the largest V8 ever placed in a production car.

FRONT REDESIGN
1971 saw a new two-piece grille with twin headlights as separate units.

ENGINE
"Factory blue-printed to save you money", screamed the ads. The monster 455cid V8 was stock for 4-4-2s in '71, but it was its swansong year and power output would soon dwindle.

SIDE LIGHTS
Huge dinner-plate side lights almost looked like front-end exhausts.

1971 OLDSMOBILE 4-4-2

From 1964 to '67, the 4-4-2 was simply a performance option that could be fitted into the F-85 range, but its growing popularity meant that in 1968 Olds decided to create a separate series for it in hardtop and convertible guises. Advertising literature espoused the 4-4-2's torquey credentials: "A hot new number. Police needed it, Olds built it, pursuit proved it." But despite legislation that curbed the 4-4-2's power output and led to the series being deleted after '71, the 4-4-2 had made its mark and put Oldsmobile well up there on the muscle-car map.

REAR DIFFERENTIAL
No less than eight rear-end ratios were offered, along with an optional anti-spin differential at $44.

REDUCED POWER
Sales literature pronounced that "4-4-2 performance is strictly top drawer", but in reality, unleaded fuel meant a performance penalty.

COLOUR CHOICES
In addition to this "Viking Blue", Oldsmobile added "Bittersweet", "Lime Green", and "Saturn Gold" to their 1971 colour range.

EXHAUST
Apart from the badge, the twin drain-pipe exhausts were the only clue that you were trailing a wild man.

SPECIFICATIONS

MODEL 1971 Oldsmobile 4-4-2

PRODUCTION 7,589

BODY STYLE Two-door coupe and convertible.

CONSTRUCTION Steel body and chassis.

ENGINE 455cid V8.

POWER OUTPUT 340–350 bhp.

TRANSMISSION Three-speed manual, optional four-speed manual, three-speed Turbo Hydra-Matic automatic.

SUSPENSION *Front:* coil springs; *Rear:* leaf springs.

BRAKES Front discs, rear drums.

MAXIMUM SPEED 201 km/h (125 mph)

0–60 MPH (0–96 KM/H) 6.4 sec

A.F.C. 3.5–5 km/l (10–14 mpg)

1972 CHEVROLET
Camaro SS396

6,562 CAMAROS HAD THE SS PACKAGE IN '72

AFTER A SUCCESSFUL DEBUT in '67, the Camaro hit the deck in '72. Sluggish sales and a 174-day strike at the Lordstown, Ohio, plant meant Camaros were in short supply and only 68,656 were produced that year. Worse still, 1,100 half-finished cars sitting on the assembly lines couldn't meet the impending '73 bumper impact laws, so GM were forced to junk the lot. There were some dark mutterings in GM boardrooms. Should the Camaro be canned?

1972 also saw the Super Sport (SS) package bow out. *Road & Track* magazine mourned its passing, hailing the SS396 as "the best car built in America in 1971". But the early Seventies were a bad trip for the automobile, and the Camaro would rise again; five years later it was selling over a quarter of a million units. This is one American icon that refuses to die.

CAMARO RACERS
NASCAR racing has always been an important showcase for manufacturers of performance iron. Chevy spent big bucks to become performance heavyweights, and the Camaro, along with the Chevelle, was a successful racing model in the early '70s.

STYLING
The Camaro was designed using computer technology; the smooth, horizontal surfaces blended together in an aerodynamically functional shape.

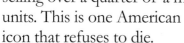

1972 CHEVROLET CAMARO SS396
The Camaro design survived an incredible 11 years without any serious alteration. It lured eyes and dollars away from the traditional European performance machines and became one of the most recognized American GTs of the Seventies. As well as the SS package, Camaros could also be specified in Rally Sport (RS) and Z-28 performance guise.

WHEELS
Camaros came with five wheel-trim options.

REAR SPOILER
The SS and Z-28 packages got a rear-deck spoiler; the RS did not. The black rear panel is unique to the SS396.

ENGINE

Camaros came with engines to suit all pockets. The entry-level V8 was just $96 more than the plodding straight six. This is the lively 396cid V8, but the legendary 454cid V8, with a mind-blowing 425 bhp, was definitely not for the faint-hearted.

INTERIOR

Interior revisions for '72 were mostly confined to the door panels, which now included map bins and coin holders under the door handles. The high-back seats are a clue that this is a post-'70 model.

GOOD PRICE

Individuality and power came cheap in '72 – the SS package cost just $306 – though extras were plentiful. Under 5,000 owners chose a six compared to nearly 64,000 who opted for one of the V8 options.

COOL INTERIOR
Air-conditioning for the Camaro cost an additional $397.

EXTRA GRIP
Chevy dealers would even sell you spray-on liquid Tire Chain to improve traction on your Camaro, drag-race style.

SPECIFICATIONS

MODEL 1972 Chevrolet Camaro SS396

PRODUCTION 6,562 (SS)

BODY STYLE Two-door coupe.

CONSTRUCTION Steel body and chassis.

ENGINE 350cid, 396cid, 402cid V8s (SS).

POWER OUTPUT 240–330 bhp.

TRANSMISSION Three-speed manual, optional four-speed manual, and automatic.

SUSPENSION *Front:* coil springs; *Rear:* leaf springs.

BRAKES Front power discs and rear drums.

MAXIMUM SPEED 201 km/h (125 mph)

0–60 MPH (0–96 KM/H) 7.5 sec

A.F.C. 5.3 km/l (15 mpg)

1972 LINCOLN
Continental Mark IV

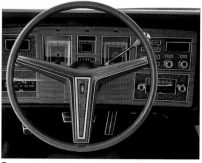

INTERIOR
Standard equipment included a Cartier electric clock, wood dash, and a six-way power Twin Comfort lounge seat. Even so, it all felt a bit tacky and didn't have the uptown cachet of European imports.

THE MARK IV WAS LONGER AND WIDER THAN THE MARK III

IN 1972, $10,000 BOUGHT you TV detective Frank Cannon's corpulent Mark IV Continental, the luxury car fit to lock bumpers with Cadillac's finest. As big as they came and surprisingly fast, the all-new hunch-flanked body had a Rolls-Royce-esque grille and distinctive, fake spare-wheel cover. Road-testers were unanimous in their praise for its power, luxury, and size, remarking that the Mark IV's bonnet "looks like an aircraft carrier landing-deck on final approach".

The list of luxury features was as long as a Chicago phone directory – air-conditioning, six-by-six-way power seats, power windows, antenna, and door locks. And all standard. The air-con was about as complex and powerful as a Saturn rocket and, to please the legislators, under a bonnet the size of a baseball field nestled a forest of emission pipery. America may have wanted to kick the smog habit, but trim its waistline? Never.

SPACE AND COMFORT
A two-door in name, the Continental had room enough for five. The baroque interior is typical of the period, and the tiny "opera" window in the huge rear pillar became a Lincoln styling metaphor.

ENGINE
At 460cid, the Continental's V8 may have been Olympian, but it was still eclipsed by Cadillac's jumbo 500cid power plant that was around at the same time. The Mark IV block's power output for '72 was 224 bhp, a stark contrast to the 365 horses pushed out only a year before. Federal restrictions on power output had a lot to answer for.

COLOUR CHOICE
The garish yellow is typical '70s, but all Mark IVs could be painted in a metallic hue for $127.

FRONT ASPECT
Shuttered headlights and heavyweight chrome bumper added to the car's presence.

SPECIFICATIONS

MODEL 1972 Lincoln Continental Mark IV
PRODUCTION 48,591 (1972)
BODY STYLE Two-door, five seater hardtop.
CONSTRUCTION Steel body and chassis.
ENGINE 460cid V8.
POWER OUTPUT 224 bhp.
TRANSMISSION Three-speed Select-Shift automatic.
SUSPENSION Helical coil front and rear.
BRAKES Front power discs, rear drums.
MAXIMUM SPEED 196 km/h (122 mph)
0-60 MPH (0-96 KM/H) 17.8 sec
A.F.C. 3.5 km/l (10 mpg)

1972 LINCOLN CONTINENTAL MARK IV

Rolls-Royce were mortally offended by the Continental's copy of their grille, but didn't actually litigate. They wished they had as the grille went on to become a Lincoln trademark. The Mark IV offered more space for rear passengers and was the first Continental to incorporate an "opera" window into the rear pillar, albeit at a cost of $81.84.

REAR EXTRAS
TractionLok differential and high-ratio rear axle were both on the options list.

LEATHER TRIMMINGS
Leather lounge seats were an option at $179.

ROOF
The vinyl, leather-look roof was standard on all Mark IVs.

CONTINENTAL COVER
This had been a Lincoln styling trait since the early Mark Is.

TYRES
Standard rubber was 225/15 radials.

1973 PONTIAC
Trans Am

WITH THE BRAWNY TRANS AM, PONTIAC KEPT THE BRUTE-FORCE PERFORMANCE FLAG FLYING

IN THE SEVENTIES, FOR THE FIRST time in American history, the Government stepped in between the motor industry and consumers. With the 1973 oil crisis, the Big Three were ordered to tighten their belts. Automotive design came to a screaming halt, and the big-block Trans Am became the last of the really fast cars.

The muscular Firebird had been around since 1969 and, with its rounded bulges, looked as if its skin had been forced out by the strength underneath. Gas shortage or not, the public liked the 1973 Trans Am, and sales quadrupled. The 455 Super Duty V8 had a socially unacceptable horsepower of 310 and, while Pontiac bravely tried to ignore the killjoy legislation, someone remarked that their High Output 455 was the largest engine ever offered in a pony car. The game was up, and within months modifications to comply with emission regulations had brought power down to 290 bhp.

The hell-raising 455 soldiered on until 1976, and that athletic fastback body until '82. But the frenetic muscle years of 1967–73 had irretrievably passed, and those wonderful big-block banshees would never be seen again.

ELITE ENGINE
The big-block Trans Ams were Detroit's final salute to performance. The 455 Super Duty gave "the sort of acceleration that hasn't been seen in years". Reaching 60 (96 km/h) took under six seconds, and the engine could run all the way to 217 km/h (135 mph).

ACTION-MAN MACHINE
The Trans Am was seriously macho. *Car & Driver* called it "a hard-muscled, lightning-reflexed commando of a car".

SD ENGINE
The Super Duty V8 had cylinder heads that moved more air than Chrysler's famous Hemi. The 1973 455 SD could cover a quarter mile (0.4 km) in 13.8 seconds at 174 km/h (108 mph).

RACY FEATURES INCLUDED BONNET SCOOP AND FRONT AIR DAM, WHICH GAVE 22.6 KG (50 LB) OF DOWNFORCE AT HIGHWAY SPEEDS

SPECIFICATIONS

MODEL 1973 Pontiac Firebird
Trans Am

PRODUCTION 4,802

BODY STYLE Two-door, four-seater
fastback.

CONSTRUCTION Steel unitary body.

ENGINE 455cid V8.

POWER OUTPUT 250–300 bhp.

TRANSMISSION Four-speed manual
or three-speed Turbo Hydra-Matic
automatic.

SUSPENSION *Front:* coil springs;
Rear: leaf springs with live axle.

BRAKES Front discs, rear drums.

MAXIMUM SPEED 212 km/h
(132 mph)

0–60 MPH (0–96 KM/H) 5.4 sec

A.F.C. 6 km/l (17 mpg)

DASHBOARD
Second-edition
Trans Ams had a
standard engine-
turned dash insert,
Rally gauges, bucket
seats, and a Formula
steering wheel. The tacho
was calibrated to a very
optimistic 8,000 rpm.

STANDARD EQUIPMENT INCLUDED
POWER STEERING, FRONT DISCS,
SAFE-T-TRACK DIFFERENTIAL,
AND DUAL EXHAUSTS

THE TRANS AM'S SPEEDO WAS
ONE OF DETROIT'S WILDEST,
MAXING AT AN UNTRUTHFUL
160 MPH (257 KM/H)

DECORATIVE DECAL
The "screaming chicken"
graphics gracing the bonnet
were new for 1973. Created
by stylist John Schinella, they
were a modern rendition of
the American Indian phoenix
symbol. Along with the rear-
facing "shaker" bonnet scoop,
the Trans Am now looked as
distinctive as it drove.

NAME IN DISPUTE
The Trans Am name was
"borrowed" from the Sports
Car Club of America, and
the SCCA threatened to sue unless
Pontiac paid a royalty of $5 per car.

ALTHOUGH BASED ON
CHEVY'S F-BODY CAMARO,
FIREBIRDS LOOKED AND
HANDLED MUCH BETTER

HONEYCOMB WHEELS, COLOURED
SILVER, WERE A $36 OPTION

EVOLUTION OF THE PONTIAC FIREBIRD TRANS AM

DETROIT'S OLDEST WARRIOR, the Firebird is the only muscle car that's been in the brochures for 30 years. Based on the Camaro's F-body, the Firebird debuted in 1967, but the wild Trans Am didn't appear until '69. Surprisingly, there was little fanfare until the hot 1970 restyle. Steep insurance rates and a national shift away from performance iron didn't help sales, but in 1973, the year of the "screaming chicken" bonnet decal and Super Duty V8, Trans Ams left showrooms like heat-seeking missiles. Nearly killed off by GM, the T/A soldiered on into the emasculated '80s and '90s – the only affordable brute-performance car to survive recession, legislative lunacy, and every gas crisis going.

A '77 TRANS AM SETS THE PACE IN THE MOODY 1978 THRILLER *THE DRIVER*

1968

THE FIREBIRD MAY HAVE shared the Camaro's sheet metal, but mechanically they were miles apart. With five different mills, from 230 to 400cid, the Firebird was a classic example of the pony car building-block philosophy: come up with a horny-looking machine and then hand the customer a colossal option list.

KEY FEATURES
• Introduced mid-1967
• Specially-designed grille, tail-lights, and pleated seats
• Convertible available
• Firebird 400 has 325 bhp four-barrel powerhouse
• 82,560 sold in inaugural year

1971

THE SECOND-EDITION Trans Am had sexy curves oozing understated power. Quietly introduced in March 1969, the first Trans Am was sleek, sensual, and modern, and suited to only one body style – a quasi-fastback, which meant that the convertible was a thing of the past. The standard power unit was a potent 345 bhp Ram-Air III.

KEY DEVELOPMENTS
• Body package has rear spoiler, front-wing air extractors, and rear-facing bonnet scoop
• New front bumper grille moulded out of Endura rubber
• Softened spring rates
• Convertible deleted

1973 PONTIAC
Trans Am

REAR BUMPER
1973 was the "Year of the Bumper" because of Federal guidelines that rear bumpers should withstand low-speed impacts unscathed.

FLARED WHEEL ARCHES MADE THE TRANS AM LOOK EVEN TOUGHER

FOR 1973 THE FASTBACK BODYSHELL WAS GIVEN A FULL-WIDTH REAR-DECK SPOILER

BODY BY FISHER
Pontiac wanted customers to believe that Trans Am bodies were hand-built by an old-time carriage-maker.

DUAL EXHAUSTS WITH CHROME EXTENSIONS WERE STANDARD

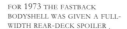

DLR 3055 D
MASSACHUSETTS

1974

FOR 1974 THE TRANS AM looked even better. Styling changes included a shovel-nosed front, lower rear wing line, new grille inserts, and horizontal slotted tail-lights. Standard equipment was lavish, with Rally gauges, power steering, dual exhausts, and Rally II wheels. Factory price was $4,446, and 1974 model production was 10,255.

KEY DEVELOPMENTS
- Full-width rear-deck-lid spoiler
- Special heavy-duty suspension
- Last year of Super Duty 455 without catalytic converter
  - Only 212 cars fitted with SD 455 and manual box

1987

THE MID-80S TRANS AM was smaller, lighter, more practical, and closer to its Camaro cousin. This year Trans Ams could have the Corvette 350cid V8, pushing out up to 225 horses, but only with automatic. Rally-tuned suspension improved the handling of V8 Birds dramatically. But even so, this was hardly the Trans Am's finest year.

KEY DEVELOPMENTS
- Four-cylinder Firebirds depart
- Nearly all engine choices shared with Camaro
- Optional 305cid V8 couldn't outrun a Toyota Supra
- V6 version returns 7 km/l (20 mpg)

1991

AFTER A FRONT-END facelift, the Trans Am looked a bit cluttered and gawky. In 1990 port injection went into the 305cid V8, making it marginally quicker, and in mid-1991 a convertible joined the coupe. Driver's-side airbags were now standard on all Firebirds, and dealers could install a new street-legal performance package to boost power output by up to 50 bhp.

KEY DEVELOPMENTS
- 350cid V8 returns 6 km/l (17 mpg)
- Even lower nose treatment
- Trans Am graphics appear on bottom of door
- Wide honeycomb wheels

1996

THE FOURTH-GENERATION car was a radical departure from the Eighties, with a partly composite plastic construction. Its swooping lines and raked screen echoed the Banshee concept car. Even the Europeans showed interest and, compared to sanitized Japanese sports coupes, the Firebird is still a disarming confection of American brawn.

KEY DEVELOPMENTS
- Available with V6 or V8
- Construction and safety features conform to EEC export regulations
- Handsome five-spoke alloy wheels
- Rear tea-tray spoiler
- Deep cow-catcher nose

GRAPHIC APPEAL
The bonnet graphic actually helped sales and gave the Trans Am a unique identity.

SUPER DUTY V8 WAS AVAILABLE ONLY ON TRANS AMS AND FIREBIRD FORMULAS

EARLY SEVENTIES MODELS
From '71 to '73 the Trans Am rolled on in almost identical external guise. Underneath that vibrating scoop, power output of the 455 HO dropped to 250 bhp from the Super Duty's initial 310 horses.

DUAL BODY-COLOURED MIRRORS WERE STANDARD, WITH REMOTE CONTROL ON DRIVER'S SIDE

NEW FRONT VALANCE PANEL WITH SMALL AIR DAM APPEARED IN 1973

PONTIAC

DLR 3055 D
MASSACHUSETTS

TRANS AM

1975 AMC
Pacer

THE PACER'S BODY WAS ALMOST AS WIDE
AS IT WAS LONG

THE 1973 FUEL CRISIS HIT America's psyche harder than the Russians beating them to space in the Fifties. Cheap and unrestricted personal transport had been a way of life, and then suddenly America faced the horrifying prospect of paying more than forty cents a gallon. Overnight, shares in motor manufacturers became as popular as Richard Nixon.

Detroit's first response was to kill the muscle car dead. The second was to revive the "compact" and invent the "sub-compact". AMC's 1975 Pacer, "the first wide small car", had the passenger compartment of a sedan, the nose of a European commuter shuttle, and no back end at all. Ironically, it wasn't even that economical, but America didn't notice because she was on a guilt trip, buying nearly 100,000 of the things in '75 alone.

PLANS DISRUPTED
Originally, AMC envisaged the Pacer to be fitted with a rotary engine that General Motors had been developing. When this was abandoned, the Pacer had to be redesigned to accommodate sixes instead.

GLASS
The Pacer had the largest glass area of any contemporary American sedan, making the $425 All Season air-conditioning option almost obligatory. Outward vision, though, was superb.

BUMPERS
Originally slated to use urethane bumpers, production Pacers were fitted with steel to save money.

WINDSCREEN
The aerodynamic windscreen aided fuel economy and reduced interior noise.

BONNET
The sloping bonnet made for excellent driver visibility.

1977 AMC GREMLIN
The Gremlin was AMC's first entry into the sub-compact market in 1970. Front-end, bonnet, and doors came from the compact Hornet. Total tooling costs were only $5 million and an amazing 700,000 were sold.

STEERING
The Pacer's rack-and-pinion steering was one of the first available on a US car.

STYLING
Motor Trend *magazine called the Pacer's styling "the most innovative of all US small cars". Credit went to Richard Teague, who also penned the '84 Jeep Cherokee.*

INTERIOR
Inside was stock Detroit, with sporty front bucket seats and cheesy polyurethane dash. But all that glass made it very hot.

1975 AMC PACER

In the mid-Seventies, the Pacer was sold as the last word; "the face of the car of the 21st century" bragged the ads. Happily, they were wrong. Pundits of the time called it a "football on wheels" and a "big frog". Surprisingly, the Pacer was never a cheap car. Add a few interior options and air-conditioning and you could easily be presenting the dealer with a cheque for $5,000.

INTERIOR SPACE

The Pacer had more headroom and legroom than the contemporary Chevelle or Torino, and felt spacious.

SPECIFICATIONS

MODEL 1975 AMC Pacer
PRODUCTION 72,158
BODY STYLE Three-door saloon.
CONSTRUCTION Steel unitary body.
ENGINE 232cid, 258cid sixes.
POWER OUTPUT 90–95 bhp.
TRANSMISSION Three-speed manual with optional overdrive, optional three-speed Torque-Command automatic.
SUSPENSION *Front:* coil springs; *Rear:* semi-elliptic leaf springs.
BRAKES Front discs, rear drums.
MAXIMUM SPEED 169 km/h (105 mph)
0–60 MPH (0–96 KM/H) 14 sec
A.F.C. 6.4–8.5 km/l (18–24 mpg)

1976 CADILLAC
Eldorado

THE LAST CONVERTIBLE ROLLED
OFF THE LINE ON 21 APRIL 1976

BY 1976, CADILLACS HAD become so swollen that they ploughed through corners, averaged 4.6 km/l (13 mpg), and were as quick off the line as an M24 tank. Despite a massive 500cid V8, output of the '76 Eldo was a lowly 190 brake, with a glacial top speed of just 175 km/h (109 mph). Something had to change and Cadillac's response had been the '75 Seville.

But the '76 Eldo marked the end of an era for another reason – it was the last American convertible. Cadillac were the final automobile manufacturer to delete the rag-top from their model line-up and, when they made the announcement that the convertible was to be phased out at the end of '76, the market fought to buy up the last 200. People even tried to jump the queue by claiming they were distantly related to Cadillac's founder. One 72-year-old man in Nebraska bought six. A grand American institution had quietly passed away.

FUNKY MIRROR
The heavy chrome adjustable door mirror was electrically operated and incorporated a thermometer that displayed the outside temperature.

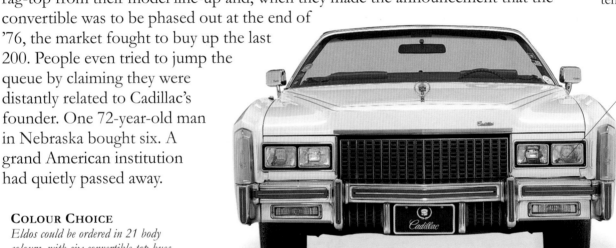

HEADLIGHTS
Twilight Sentinel option automatically turned the headlights on and off according to outside light conditions.

COLOUR CHOICE
Eldos could be ordered in 21 body colours, with six convertible-top hues.

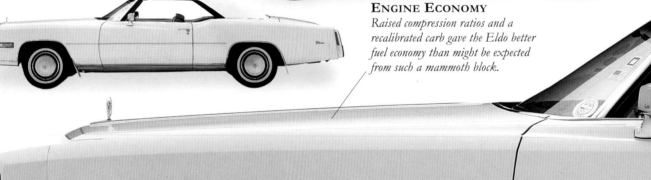

ENGINE ECONOMY
Raised compression ratios and a recalibrated carb gave the Eldo better fuel economy than might be expected from such a mammoth block.

INTERIOR
Technically advanced options were always Cadillac's forte. The Eldo was available with airbag, Dual Comfort front seats with fold-down armrests, and six-way power seat.

INTERIOR WOOD WAS CALLED "DISTRESSED PECAN GRAIN"

ALL ELDOS HAD A CATALYTIC CONVERTOR AS STANDARD

FAMILY ARMS
The Cadillac shield harks back to 1650 and the original French Cadillac family. French model names were used in '66 with the Calais and DeVille ranges.

ENGINE
Already strangled by emission pipery, the need to maximize every gallon meant that the big 500bhp V8 was embarrassingly lethargic. Even lower ratio rear axles were used to boost mileage. Hydro-Boost power brakes were needed to stop the 2,337 kg (5,153 lb) colossus.

SPECIFICATIONS
MODEL 1976 Cadillac Eldorado Convertible
PRODUCTION 14,000
BODY STYLE Two-door, six-seater convertible.
CONSTRUCTION Steel body and chassis.
ENGINE 500cid V8.
POWER OUTPUT 190 bhp.
TRANSMISSION Three-speed Hydra-Matic Turbo automatic.
SUSPENSION Front and rear independent coil springs with automatic level control.
BRAKES Four-wheel discs.
MAXIMUM SPEED 175 km/h (109 mph)
0–60 MPH (0–96 KM/H) 15.1 sec
A.F.C. 4.6 km/l (13 mpg)

1976 CADILLAC ELDORADO CONVERTIBLE
Big and slab-sided, the '76 Eldo used a front-wheel drive arrangement that had first been used on the '67 Eldorado and is still used today. The '76 Convertible had big vital statistics, measuring 5.7 m (225 in) long, 2 m (80 in) wide, and costing $10,354. Even so, such was the demand for these last convertibles that some changed hands for as much as $20,000. The last 200 off the production line were all-white, with white wheel covers.

FITTINGS
Interiors could be specified in Merlin Plaid, lush velour, Mansion Knit, or 11 types of Sierra Grain leather.

SAFETY RUBBER
These strips at the front and rear of the car were rubber crumple zones, designed to absorb impact in the event of a crash. Cadillac had problems matching the rubber with the colour on the rest of the car.

BRAKES
Eldorados had standard four-wheel discs with transistorized rear control.

PRESERVE WHAT'S LEFT!

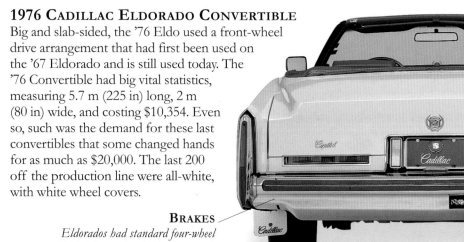

1978 CADILLAC
Seville

BY THE EARLY SEVENTIES, the corpulent Cadillac could average only 4 km/l (12 mpg). The energy crisis of '74 made the now-obese marque a soft target, and suddenly high-profile establishment figures were hastily trading in their "Standard of the World" gas-guzzlers for BMWs and Mercedes. A celebrated cartoon of the day showed a Caddy owner, hand over his eyes, pointing a revolver at his doomed Eldorado.

The Cadillac Seville debuted in 1975. Marketed to compete with Mercedes and Jaguars, it was deliberately European in size, ride, handling, and economy. There was precious little ornamentation, and it was half a bonnet shorter than other Cads. The press called it "the best Caddy for 26 years", even if it did have to suffer indignities like a diesel engine option and fuel-economy computer. A compromise car it may have been, but the downsized Cad sold strongly from day one, and helped Cadillac weather the worst recession since 1958. For a small car, the Seville was a portent of big things to come.

— AMERICA'S ENERGY CRISIS —

IN MARCH 1974, AS A REPRISAL for those who had supported Israel during the Middle East war, the Organization of Petroleum Exporting Countries (OPEC) announced an oil embargo. With America soon in the grip of soaring fuel prices and frustrating queues at petrol stations, President Nixon made a televised address, warning that the nation faced the worst energy crisis since World War II. The battle raged on under the Carter administration, which called for dramatic energy cuts to avert a "national catastrophe". In reaction to calls for fuel economy, GM were the first to introduce a line of diesel cars, claiming a 40 per cent mileage advantage over petrol-powered autos. As OPEC oil prices continued to rise, even luxury marques like Cadillac had to bow to America's new energy-conscious outlook.

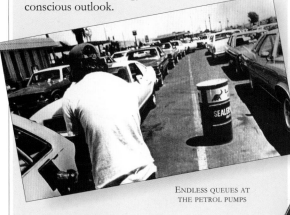

ENDLESS QUEUES AT
THE PETROL PUMPS

ENGINE
The '75 Seville's standard 350cid Oldsmobile-sourced V8 engine had electronic fuel injection, and was mounted on a steel subframe secured to the body with Isoflex damping cushions to reduce harshness and noise vibration. In 1978 came the addition of a 350cid diesel V8, which made history as the first Cadillac oil-burner.

INTERIOR
Interior trim was standard Dover cloth in seven colours, or optional Sierra Grain leather in 10 shades. A novel trip-computer option offered 11 digital displays indicating details such as fuel, inside and outside temperature, engine speed, and estimated arrival time. Standard equipment included tilt steering wheel, a fuel-monitoring system, power seats, and controlled-cycle wipers.

BODY FINISH
Bodies used Zincrometal to resist rust, and were finished with a generous seven coats of paint.

BATTERY
The Seville used an innovative Delco "Freedom" battery that never needed topping up.

SEVILLE SCRIPT
Other names were considered, such as Sierra, Medici, Minuet, Canterbury, Debonair, Camelot, Councillor, and Renaissance, but Seville was chosen, reinforcing the Cadillac bloodline.

SPECIFICATIONS

MODEL 1978 Cadillac Seville
PRODUCTION 56,985
BODY STYLE Four-door sedan.
CONSTRUCTION Steel unitary body.
ENGINE 350cid V8.
POWER OUTPUT 170 bhp.
TRANSMISSION Three-speed Turbo Hydra-Matic automatic.
SUSPENSION *Front:* coil springs; *Rear:* leaf springs with self-levelling ride.
BRAKES Front vented discs, rear drums.
MAXIMUM SPEED 185 km/h (115 mph)
0–60 MPH (0–96 KM/H) 11.5 sec
A.F.C. 5.5 km/l (15.5 mpg)

1978 CADILLAC SEVILLE

In 1970, Cadillac sent a questionnaire to Mercedes owners, asking them what they thought of the idea of a small Cad. Launch price of the Seville was $13,700, $6,000 less than a comparable Merc, and sales of the new car rightly worried Mercedes. From May '75 to April '76, no fewer than 44,475 Sevilles were delivered, compared with 45,353 Mercedes.

REFINED REAR VIEW
The restrained rump is a far cry from the excess of full-sized Cads, with a gently tapering rear deck, simple rear lamp and bumper treatment, hidden exhausts, and no rear overhang. Motor Trend called the Seville "delicate, bold, and pure".

RIDING IN STYLE
The Seville's plush interior reflects the tastes of 1,700 luxury-car owners who, in 1973, were invited to judge the prototype. Inside, there was a seat-belt warning that chimed rather than buzzed, since the device was meant to remind politely rather than order. Not content with such refinements, one oil sheikh cut and lengthened six Sevilles to accommodate desks, bars, and a sunroof.

FRONT ASPECT
The Seville's front end is unmistakably Cadillac, with cross-hatch grille and classic bonnet crest mascot. The computer-designed body derived from the Chevy Nova.

Future Classics

Having hit hard times, the US auto industry in the Nineties had no choice but to allow designers to build the cars of their dreams. Now there's nothing to eclipse the resurgent American car.

1987 CHEVROLET CAMARO IROC-Z CONVERTIBLE

THE WINDS OF CHANGE are howling through the corridors of Motor City. After the troughs of the '70s and '80s, the '90s mark the rebirth of the American car. Proof of Detroit innovation can be found in the latest Corvette, Camaro, Mustang, Viper, and Prowler – truly distinctive cars that promise the most exhilarating ride since the magic carpet.

Big is back, and so is horsepower. The last-of-the-line Chevy Impala SS seems a splendid reincarnation of the tyre-smoking '60s screamer of the same name. And the Dodge Ram V10 is the King Kong of pickups. With the Viper's outrageous motor upfront, this was built for one purpose alone – having serious fun.

Enjoyment is back on the market-place menu, enhanced by technology. Engines like Cadillac's 32-valve Northstar and Chrysler's 500cid V10 are epic power plants and among the best in the industry, while GM's fine electric EV1 is an instant classic and a half-billion-dollar technical *tour de force*. Motown is proving that the glory years could return, with talent to take on the best in Europe – and win.

In 10 years, auto buffs will be misty-eyed over the current Mustang and Corvette. Already the Prowler and the Viper are being feted as works of art, and the Cadillac STS is every bit as refined as a Jaguar sedan. Only the threat of the dreary "sports utility vehicle" could halt this remarkable renaissance. So come on, Detroit, keep giving us reasons to leave those stodgy imports alone.

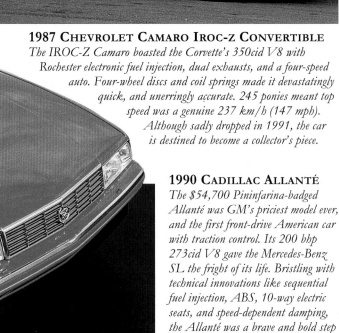

1987 CHEVROLET CAMARO IROC-Z CONVERTIBLE
The IROC-Z Camaro boasted the Corvette's 350cid V8 with Rochester electronic fuel injection, dual exhausts, and a four-speed auto. Four-wheel discs and coil springs made it devastatingly quick, and unerringly accurate. 245 ponies meant top speed was a genuine 237 km/h (147 mph). Although sadly dropped in 1991, the car is destined to become a collector's piece.

1990 CADILLAC ALLANTÉ
The $54,700 Pininfarina-badged Allanté was GM's priciest model ever, and the first front-drive American car with traction control. Its 200 bhp 273cid V8 gave the Mercedes-Benz SL the fright of its life. Bristling with technical innovations like sequential fuel injection, ABS, 10-way electric seats, and speed-dependent damping, the Allanté was a brave and bold step for Cadillac into the Nineties.

1992 DODGE VIPER R/T

No other car packs the sheer wallop of the Viper. A 450 bhp V10, top speed of 290 km/h (180 mph), and jackhammer acceleration make this a four-wheeled riot. Coming showroom-fresh from a mass-production car maker, the Viper makes no sense at all. Which is why it's so mischievously marvellous.

1993 FORD MUSTANG COBRA

The late-model Mustang may not look like an emergent classic, but it's always offered a large helping of serious heave. Not for nothing did all those Highway Patrol guys choose the 5-litre as a high-speed pursuit machine. That high-output 302 V8 could crack the standing quarter in 14 seconds dead and hit 60 (96 km/h) in 6.5. That's quick.

1995 BUICK RIVIERA COUPE

GM stylist Bill Porter fielded his glam, all-new Riviera in 1994. A svelte two-door five-seater, the new Riv is more than worthy of the hallowed name that's always been reserved for a very special kind of Buick. The current model, with its sloping roof line and tapering flanks, proves that Detroit has always been able to sculpt in steel.

1997 DODGE COPPERHEAD CONCEPT CAR

A Viper of a different colour, the Dodge Copperhead Concept Car is a '90s Austin-Healey. Keen to trade on their street-rod heritage, Chrysler have joined in the worldwide sports-car renaissance with a bang. With coil springs, a high-output 220 bhp aluminium V6, and five-speed manual, it's anything but just a pretty face. In an engagingly humorous touch, the tyres have been given a snakeskin tread.

1997 PLYMOUTH PROWLER

Chrysler's wild child, the Prowler looks drop-dead gorgeous, and makes a noise like God clearing his throat. And, believe it or not, this is a production car you can buy straight off the showroom floor. Beautifully detailed, gloriously impractical, it's a complete and utter wow, and proof that once again Chrysler are pushing auto styling over the edge and back again.

INDEX

1958 EDSEL CORSAIR CONVERTIBLE

1957 FORD FAIRLANE TOWN SEDAN

1959 FORD FAIRLANE 500
GALAXIE CLUB VICTORIA

1964 OLDSMOBILE
F-85 DELUXE

1956 BUICK ROADMASTER

1957 MERCURY TURNPIKE CRUISER

ACKNOWLEDGMENTS

DORLING KINDERSLEY WOULD LIKE TO THANK THE FOLLOWING:

Fay Singer for design assistance; Ashley Straw and Al Deane, photographic assistants; Cricket, studio assistant; Jenny Glanville and Kirstie Ashton Bell at Plough Studios; Cobra Studios, Manchester; Dave King (US photographer); Ken McMahon at Pelican Graphics; Richmond Denton for the jacket design; Terry Clarke; Barry Cunlisse of the AAC (NW); Michael Farrington; Andy Greenfield of the Classic Corvette Club (UK); Peter Grist of the Chrysler Corp. Club (UK); William (Bill) Greenwood of the Cadillac Owners Club of Great Britain; Rockin' Roy Hunt; Geoff Mitchell; Mr DeVoe Moore, Tallahasee Car Museum, Tallahasee, Florida; Colin Nolson; Tony Paton; Tony Powell at Powell Performance Cars; David and Christine Smith; Dave and Rita Sword of the AAC; Marc Tulpin (Belgian representative of the AAC); *Classic American* magazine; Geoff Browne at *Classic Car Weekly*; Pooks motor bookshop and Cars and Stripes for original advertising material and brochures; Philip Blythe for supplying number plates; and Julie Rimington for compiling the index.

DORLING KINDERSLEY WOULD LIKE TO THANK THE FOLLOWING FOR ALLOWING THEIR CARS TO BE PHOTOGRAPHED:

Page 22 Peter Barber-Lomax; p. 26 Mr. DeVoe Moore, Tallahassee Car Museum, Tallahassee, Florida; p. 30 The Rt. Hon. Greg Knight; p. 34 Liam Kavanagh; p. 38 Tony Paton; p. 44 Colin Nolson; p. 46 Nando Rossi; p. 48 John Skelton; p. 50 Alfie Orkin; p. 54 Mike and Margaret Collins; p. 56 Tallahassee Car Museum; p. 60 Dream Cars; p. 62 Dream Cars; p. 64 Steve Rogers; p. 66 Dream Cars; p. 70 Mike and Margaret Collins; p. 72 Phil Townend; p. 74 Geoff Mitchell; p. 76 Geoff Cook; p. 78 Gavin and Robert Garrow; p. 80 John Gardner; p. 82 Peter Morey; p. 84 Bob and Kath Silver; p. 86 Garry Darby, American '50s Car Hire; p. 88 David Gough; p. 92 Charles Booth; p. 94 Rockin' Roy Hunt – '50s aficionado; p. 96 Steve Friend; p. 98 Rockin' Roy Hunt – '50s aficionado; p. 104 Mark Surman; p. 106 Alex Greatwood; p. 110 David Stone; p. 112 M. Fenwick; p. 114 Teddy Turner Collection; p. 118 Dream Cars; p. 120 Tony Powell of Powell Performance Cars; p. 122 Michael Farrington; p. 126 A & M Motors; p. 128 Maurice Harvey; p. 132 Geoff Mitchell; p. 134 Max and Beverly Floyd; p. 136 Colin Nolson; p. 138 Benjamin Pollard of the Classic Corvette Club UK; p. 140 courtesy of Peter Rutt; p. 142 Roy Hamilton; p. 146 Barrie Cunliffe; p. 150 Neil Crozier; p. 152 Lee Birmingham (dedicated to Bob Richards of Newport Pagnell); p. 154 Rick and Rachel Bufton; p. 160 Alex Gunn; p. 162 Alan Tansley; p. 164 Tony Powell; p. 168 Tallahassee Car Museum; p. 170 Cared for and cruised in by Mark Phillips; p. 172 Mike Webb; p. 174 Ian Hebditch and Jane Shepherd; p. 176 Roger Wait; p. 180 Valerie Pratt; p. 182 Tim Buller; p. 184 William (Bill) Greenwood (COC of GB).

PHOTOGRAPHIC CREDITS
l=left, r=right, t=top, c=centre, a=above, b=below.
All photography by Matthew Ward except:
Andy Crawford: pp. 150–51
Dave King (London, UK): p. 13
Dave King (New York, US): pp. 26–29, 56–59, 168–69

THE PUBLISHER WOULD LIKE TO THANK THE FOLLOWING FOR THEIR KIND PERMISSION TO REPRODUCE THE PHOTOGRAPHS:
The Advertising Archives: 9c, 94tr; **Archive Photos:** 29tl, 41br, 42bl, Reuters/Buick 167tr; **Neill Bruce:** 21tr, 102bl, 167tcr, Midland Motor Museum, Bridgnoth 53tl; The Peter Roberts Collection c/o Neill Bruce 24cl, 25tr, 33tr, 37tcl, 53tcr, 69tcl, 124tcl, tcr, 125tl, tcr, 145tr, 166tc, 167tl, tcl, 186cr, 187tr; **Chrysler Jeep Imports UK:** 187cr, b; The image is reproduced with kind permission from **The Coca-Cola Company:** 12cl; **Bruce Coleman Collection:** 154cl; "Sunbeam Mixmaster" Mixer, c.1955 United States, chrome-plated metal, plastic, glass, Cooper-Hewitt, National Design Museum, Smithsonian Institution/Art Resource, NY: Museum Purchase through the Decorative Arts Association Acquisition Fund 1993-150-1: photo by Dave King 76tr; **Corbis-Bettmann:** 17tl, 20bl, 22cr, 40cr, 41cb, 122tr, 148tcr, tr, cra, 180bl; **Corbis-Bettmann/UPI:** 10tr, 11b, 12bl, 14bl, 17tr, 18tr, 25tl, tcr, 28tl, 29tr, 41tl, 42tr, 53cl, 57c, 66cr, 101bl, br, 103tr, 117tcr, 120c, 136bl, 142cr, 148tcl, 156bc, 157bc, 159tr; Supplied by **Ford Motor Company Limited:** 125tr, 145tcl; ©**1978 GM Corp.:** 36tc, 37tr, 69tr; **The Ronald Grant Archives:** *The Driver* ©Twentieth Century Fox/EMI Films Presentation 178cla, *The Getaway* ©Warner Brothers 157tl, *Tucker: The Man and His Dream* ©Lucasfilm Ltd. 26tr, *Vanishing Point* ©Twentieth Century Fox/Cupid Productions 150cr; **Hulton Getty:** 11cr, 40bc, 100cr, 156cr; Courtesy of **The Kobal Collection:** 21tl, 60tr, 62tr, *Bullitt* ©Warner Brothers 150tr, *Christine* © Columbia 96tr, *Starsky and Hutch* 158bl; **Ludvigsen Library:** 53tcl, 58tr, tl, 59tr, 68tc, 108tc, 109tcl, cr, 117tcl, tr, 130tr, 131tr, 138tr, 144tcl, 145tl, tcr, 149tl, tcl, tcr, 159bl, 176c, 179tr, 186tl, 187cl, tl; **NASA:** 103tl; **National Motor Museum, Beaulieu:** 24tc, tr, 25tcl, 41cr, 48c, 52tcr, tr, 104cl, 116tr, 134tr, 158tr, 166tl, 172tr, 178tr, N Wright 21br, 33tcr, 43br, 52tl, 56tr, 69tl, 103br, 108tr, 109tl, tcr, 116tl, tc, 117tl, 124tr, 125tcl, 131cr, 136ca, 144tcr, tr, 149tr, 156cb, 157tr, 167cl, 178tc, 179tl, tcr, 186bl; **Peter Newark's American Pictures:** 16bl, br, 20cr, 24tl, 25cr, 32tcr, 36tl, 90tr, 117cl, 130cl; **Popperfoto:** 184cra; **Pictorial Press, London:** 64tr; **Quadrant:** 28tr, 53tr, 138cl; Autocar 14tr, 15t; Auto Images 11tr; Simon Everet 36tr; Mr Sol Feinstein 68tr; Phil Talbot 37tl, tcr, 43tr, 115tc, 166tr, Trans-UN 179tcl; *Rex Features:* 41bl, 100bl, Jay Hirsch 18bl; SIPA *Saturday Night Fever* ©Paramount 159tl; **Phil Talbot Car Photography:** 102cr.

1960 FORD SUNLINER

NOTE
Every effort has been made to trace the copyright holders. Dorling Kindersley apologizes for any unintentional omissions and would be pleased, in such cases, to add an acknowledgment in future editions.